William J. Robertson

Public School History of England and Canada

William J. Robertson

Public School History of England and Canada

ISBN/EAN: 9783337192594

Printed in Europe, USA, Canada, Australia, Japan

Cover: Foto ©Paul-Georg Meister /pixelio.de

More available books at **www.hansebooks.com**

EXPLANATORY.

This little book is intended to lead up to the High School History, just as the High School History leads up to Green's Short History of the English People. The language has been made as simple as possible, especially in the earlier portion of the work, so that no needless obstacle may be placed in the path of the young child's progress.

The author is largely indebted to Miss Buckley, and Gardiner, Green, Freeman, and Justin McCarthy for facts and suggestions. Nevertheless, he has very freely departed from any or all of these authors, where, in his opinion, circumstances demanded a different line of treatment.

The Canadian portion of this work is the same as that in the High School History; the only change being the omission of the indented notes.

ST. CATHARINES,
August 30th, 1892.

PUBLIC SCHOOL.
HISTORY OF ENGLAND.

CHAPTER I.

BRITAIN BEFORE ENGLAND.

1. **Early Britain.**—The land we call England is that part of the Island of Great Britain south of the River Tweed, with the exception of a small area on the western side, known as Wales. England covers about 50,000 square miles, and Wales a little over 7,000. Yet a great many people live in this little space, and a great many more have left its shores and settled all over the globe. The inhabitants are called English: but this was not always the case, for long before there were any English in England, the land was inhabited by at least three different races of men.

A great many years ago, when the surface of the country was very different from what it is now, and lions, tigers, elephants, and elks roamed over its plains and through its forests, a rude people, with little knowledge of tools and weapons, occupied the country. Then came another race with better weapons and some knowledge of cooking, and the care of domestic animals. Both races, however, made their weapons of stone, and for this reason are called the men of the "Old and New Stone Age." These things we know by the remains found in mounds or *barrows* of earth, and in caves and river-beds. Then came another race, evidently from the East, near Persia, that had some skill in working metals, such as bronze and iron. These people we call "Celts," and they were the inhabitants found in Britain when written history first tells anything about the island.

About 600 B.C. the Phœnicians, a trading people from the Mediterranean Sea, visited the country in quest of tin; then, a hundred years later, came the Greeks from Massilia or Marseilles, in France. It was about this time that the name "Britannia" was given to the island of Great Britain.

2. Roman Conquest.—At last, in the year 55 B.C., a great Roman general, Julius Caesar, came across the Channel from France (then called Gaul), with an army, and defeated the Britons who had gathered on the coast to keep him from landing. He soon returned to Gaul, but came back the next year, and once more defeated the Britons. Again he left the island—this time to return no more.

When Caesar visited Britain he found the people on the southern coast fairly civilized. They had war-chariots, and fought with spears, axes and pikes. They wore ornaments of gold and silver, and clad themselves in mantles and tunics of cloth such as were worn by the people on the opposite coast of Gaul. In fact, these Britons along the southern coast kept up a trade with their neighbors, the Gauls, who were at this time much more civilized than the people of Britain living inland. The latter were a very savage and rude people, dwelling in wretched huts, or in caves in the earth. They dressed in skins of beasts, their food being milk and meat, and further north, roots, leaves, and nuts. The more savage wore no clothing, but stained their bodies and limbs somewhat in the same fashion as the North American Indians do. Their religion was Druidism, and the oak was their sacred tree, under which they worshipped and offered up sacrifices. These sacrifices were often human beings, who were burnt in large cages of wicker work at the command of the Druids, or priests, who had great influence over the people and made their laws.

The Romans, who were to play an important part in the history of Britain, came from Italy and had for their chief city, Rome. They were a very stern and hard people, and at the time when Caesar visited Britain, had conquered nearly all the known world. But they made good laws and forced the people they subdued to obey them.

After Caesar left Britain, the Romans made no further efforts to conquer it until 43, A.D., when their Emperor Claudius came with an army, and after much fighting took possession of the south of the island. The British chief, Caractacus, fought bravely against settled down in families and tribes in their place. The new-comers did not like walled towns and cities—but preferred to live in open villages and till the soil, either destroying the towns of the Britons or allowing them to fall into ruins.

2. Social and Political Condition of the English.—The English, as these tribes came to be called, were not a nation as we understand the word; but were a number of free and independent tribes that under their chiefs had come over to Britain to conquer and plunder. After the Britons were expelled, they settled down from their roving sea-life in separate village communities, and began to till the soil. There were three kinds of people in these communities. First of all, we have the *Eorl*, a man of higher birth and greater wealth than the rest. Then came the *Ceorl* or churl, a freeman of lower birth, who nevertheless had his own house and tilled his own piece of land. Last of all we have the *slaves*, either Britons or men who had sold or lost their freedom, and who might be sold out of the country by their masters. Only freemen were allowed to take part in the village *moot* or meeting, where all questions in dispute were settled. A man found guilty by his fellows of a crime usually could escape by paying a fine. He could prove his innocence by getting his neighbours to swear he was an honest man. This was called "*compurgation.*" Otherwise he had to undergo the "ordeal," which consisted in walking blindfold with bare feet over hot ploughshares, or in dipping the hand into boiling hot water. If unhurt after this "ordeal" he was declared innocent.

The villages were some distance from each other; but when any important matter of peace or war had to be considered, men from several villages met in what was called the "Folkmoot," or meeting of the tribe. Here they chose their aldermen from the Eorls, to lead them to battle, or to speak and act for them in the great meeting of the wise men of the tribes known as the "Witangemot." After a time the Witangemot began to choose one man from the aldermen to lead—and he was the "king." He was always elected, and could not appoint his successor; but the custom was to choose the king from the same family on account of its supposed descent from Woden, their god of war.

3. The English become Christians.—When the Angles, Saxons, and Jutes came to England they were heathens, and believed in gods, water-spirits, and wood-demons. Their chief god was Woden, who rewarded them after death for their bravery and for the number of their enemies they killed. Heaven was to them a place where they could fight and carouse, for these German tribes were very fond of eating and drinking. From the names of their gods we get our names for the days of the week, such as Wednesday or Wodensday, from the god Woden.

It took some time to get the English to accept Christianity, for being a steadfast race they clung to their own customs and religion. At last, as the story goes, some English slaves were taken to Rome to be sold, and Bishop Gregory the Great, Bishop of Rome, when a young man, seeing how fair and beautiful they were, asked whence they came, and was told they were Angles. "Not Angles," said he, "but Angels," and when he became bishop he sent, in 596, a missionary named Augustine, with forty monks to convert the English. Augustine landed in Kent, and his first convert was Ethelbert, King of Kent, whose wife was a Christian from France. Afterwards, many of Ethelbert's people were baptized as Christians, and Augustine became the first Archbishop of Canterbury. From Kent the Roman missionaries carried the new religion to Northumbria, where King Edwin ruled. Edwin called his Witan together and, after listening to the missionaries, they also accepted Christianity.

But other Christian missionaries had been busy in the north of England before Augustine came to the country. These came from the small rocky island of Iona, on the west coast of Scotland, where a mission station had been planted by Columba, an Irish monk. For the Irish had become Christians under the teaching of St. Patrick more than a hundred years before, and Irish missionaries made their way to the north and middle of England and did much to introduce Christianity among the fierce and heathen English. After a time, in 664, the Irish missionaries and those from Rome having disputed about some trifling matters relating to church services, the King of Northumbria decided in favour of the latter, and the work went on under bishops in sympathy with the Roman usages. The effect of their teaching was soon seen, for the rude and restless English settled down to steady work, began to learn trades, and to build up small towns around the monasteries which now sprang up in the land. The English also lost much of their fierceness and love of plunder and fighting, and began to love learning as taught them by the monks.

4. Supremacy of Wessex. For a long time after the English came they remained divided under their several kings. In the north there was a powerful kingdom called Northumbria, in the inland another called Mercia, while in the south and west we find another called Wessex. Indeed at one time there were seven of these little kingdoms, known as the "Heptarchy;" but their boundaries were continually changing through the wars waged by one against the other. When one king became stronger than the others he held a kind of supremacy over them, and was known as the "Bretwalda." At first the King of Northumbria was "Bretwalda," then the King of Mercia, and finally in 827, Egbert, King of Wessex, got the supremacy and was Bretwalda from the south to the Firth of Forth. He was also king of all the English south of the Thames. In these days, a king was not called King of *England*, but King of the *English*. So, for over 200 years the kings of Wessex held the chief power over the English people.

CHAPTER III.

STRUGGLE BETWEEN THE ENGLISH AND THE DANES.

1. The coming of the Danes.—But peace did not come to the English when Egbert became king, for new enemies appeared. These were the Danes, a people of the same blood as the English, but living in Denmark and Norway. They were called Northmen or Norsemen, and unlike the English, had remained heathens. They were as fierce and warlike as the English had been before Christianity changed their habits and softened their manners. They came in great numbers in their boats, and landing on the coasts of England, Scotland, Ireland, and France, plundered the inhabitants, carrying off prisoners, and burning the homes of the defenceless people. They specially delighted in robbing and burning monasteries, partly because they were the homes of the priests of the Christian religion, and partly because much wealth was gathered there. Besides the monks could not offer much opposition to them. Egbert and his son and grandsons did their utmost to drive back these robbers. At times the English were successful and defeated the enemy, but they gradually lost ground until a great part of England was subdued by the Danes. Northumbria, Mercia, and East Anglia were thus taken by them, and then they turned their arms against Wessex. Here four grandsons of Egbert reigned in succession and strove to keep back the Danes. The last of these kings was Alfred, who began to reign in 871. He was chosen king over his brother's son, who was a mere lad, because the English wanted a brave leader at this perilous time, and Alfred had shown his courage in many a fierce fight with the invaders.

2. **Alfred the Great.**—Few kings have been such good rulers as Alfred, and few have had so many difficulties to overcome. When quite a little lad at his mother's knee he was fond of reading and learning, although books at that time were very scarce. He was sent to Rome when four years old, and there learned much which helped him greatly after he became king. He was troubled all his life with a painful disease, and at the very outset of his reign had to do battle against the ravaging Danes. But he bore himself bravely and manfully at all times, although for the first seven years of his reign he met with nothing but defeat in his struggle against the enemy. In 878, so great was his distress, he had to fly in disguise to the marshes and woods of Somersetshire. There, it is said, while hiding in a swineherd's hut, he allowed the good wife's cakes to burn, so intent was he on thinking out a plan by means of which he could save his country. At last he gathered his scattered followers together in Athelney, an island in Somersetshire, and inspiring them with his own hope and courage, attacked and defeated the Danish leader, Guthrum, at Edington. He then made him sign a treaty, called the Treaty of Wedmore, whereby the Danes kept that part of England north of a line from London to Chester, while Alfred kept all south of that line. By this treaty the Danes held Northumbria, East Anglia, and part of Mercia, and this land became known as the Danelagh. Many of the Danes became Christians, and Alfred's supremacy over the Danelagh was recognized. This treaty gave the land peace for many years, and

Alfred now tried to improve the condition of his people, and to give them good laws.

3. Alfred's Government.—Among other good things that Alfred did, he collected the old laws of the English and added others from the Ten Commandments and the laws of Moses, and these he put in force. He built monasteries and schools and sought to fill them with pupils under wise and learned teachers. He translated books, which were then written in Latin, into English, and so may be said to be the Father of English literature.

Not content with trying to educate his people, he took great care that they should be taught to defend themselves against the Danes. He divided his men into two bodies, one to go out to fight against the Danes, if needful, and the other to guard the homes of the people. He also built ships to keep the Danes away from the shore, and thus began the English navy. His time was always fully occupied, one portion being given to sleep, another to prayer, and a third to work. Thus it was that Alfred, although often ill and troubled by wars and invasions, did more for his people and his kingdom than most kings who have ruled in England.

4. Alfred's successors.—Alfred died in 901, and was succeeded by his son Edward (the Elder). Edward, his sons Athelstan, Edmund, Edred, and his grandson Edwy, gradually but surely won back the Danelagh from the Danes, until in 959, an English king once more ruled over all England, and both English and Danes became subjects of Edgar the Peaceable, Edwy's brother. By this time the Danes and the English were much alike. They were of the same hardy race, and though their languages differed somewhat, they easily learned to talk with one another. The Danes had become Christians while in England, and had lost much of their rudeness and love of fighting and plundering. We, to-day, can tell where they lived by the names of towns they founded, these nearly always ending in "by." Thus Grimsby, Derby, and Kirkby, are places of Danish origin, while towns whose names end in "ham" or "ton" are English towns.

5. Dunstan.—Edgar did not really rule England, that was the work of a great man in his reign, Archbishop Dunstan. It was Dunstan's task to make the English and Danes live peaceably together, and this he did by allowing the Danes to keep their own laws and customs. Like Alfred the Great, he loved learning, and sought to educate the people. He brought in from abroad good teachers, and encouraged the monks to write books and lead pure lives and be diligent in teaching and caring for the people. Under Dunstan commerce revived, for fleets guarded the English shores against the attacks of the Northmen, and enabled traders from France and Germany to visit England. Men of the same trade began to unite in societies or *guilds* to look after their own interests, while the householders of each *burgh* or borough claimed the right to manage their own affairs.

6. **Social changes.**—A great change had by this time come over the English people since they first came to England. The king had now become much more powerful by reason of the increase in the number of his personal followers or thegns. These thegns got land from the king and became a kind of nobility, and did not recognize any authority except that of the king. Again, many of the ceorls had given up their freedom during the troublous times of the Danes. Not able to defend themselves they became the "men" of rich and powerful nobles, and had to work for them in return for protection. These "villeins" (from "villanus" a husbandman), although no longer free, were not badly treated. They had houses and land of their own; and for food had barley-bread, fish, vegetables, fruit, and buttermilk. Nevertheless they could no longer take part in the village meeting, nor move from place to place without their masters' permission.

The lower order of freemen, the ancestors of our yeomanry, lived comfortably on their own homesteads. They had an abundance of good food and clothing and were a sturdy, manly class, with a strong love of freedom and independence. It is from this class, living chiefly in the North of England, that so many brave men have come, who on many battlefields have saved England from her enemies, both at home and abroad.

The nobles having less to do than the ceorls, lived idle and often riotous lives. Their slaves and villeins did all their work, and provided for all their wants. When not engaged in fighting, they passed their time in hawking, hunting, racing, wrestling, and other rough out-door sports. In their halls the ladies spun or embroidered, and amused themselves with travelling gleemen who sang and played ballads to while away the tedious hours. It was from the nobles and bishops that the Witangemot was chosen, which had great power in choosing the king, in making laws and treaties, and governing the people. In olden times every freeman had a right to a voice in making the laws; but now this was impossible, and it fell to the king and his Witan to do all the governing.

7. Danish Conquest.—This was the state of the English people in Dunstan's time. Dunstan did not remain the king's minister long after Edgar died, for a quarrel having arisen in the church about the right of the clergy to marry, Dunstan, who favored an unmarried clergy, retired to Canterbury, and a few years later died.

The next king after Edgar was another Edward, and then came Ethelred, rightly called the Unready or "Uncounselled," because he would not take good advice. In Edgar's time the Danes from Denmark and Norway were kept off, but now, Ethelred being a weak king, they landed in great numbers, and once more the land was plundered and the murdered. Ethelred tried to buy them off, but this only brought them back in greater numbers. Then Ethelred married Emma of Normandy, hoping that her people would help him against the Danes. At last he had a great many of them treacherously murdered on St. Brice's Day, 13th November, 1002. But this only made matters worse, for among the slain was the sister of the Danish king, Swegen or Sweyn. To revenge his sister, Swegen came over with a large army, and Ethelred fled to Normandy. Sweyn died, but his son Cnut, a still more terrible enemy, continued the war. When Ethelred died in 1016, his son Edmund Ironsides fought so bravely and well that Cnut agreed to divide England with him. Edmund, however, died, and then Cnut became king of all the country.

8. Danish Rule.—Cnut, although cruel in his earlier days, ruled justly and mildly after he became king. He governed by the English laws, and tried to stop the trade in slaves that went on between Bristol and Ireland. English and Danes alike obeyed him, and for eighteen years the troubled land had peace. His reign came to an end in 1036.

Cnut had married Emma of Normandy, Ethelred's widow, and

by her had two sons, Harold and Harthacnut, who in turn succeeded him. They were wild, vicious, and brutal young men. Fortunately their reigns were soon over, Harthacnut, the last to rule, dying in 1042. The English then sent over to France for Edward, the son of Ethelred and Emma, and once more an English king ruled in England.

CHAPTER IV.

THE NORMAN CONQUEST

1. The Normans.—Edward, surnamed the Confessor on account of his being placed in the Calendar of Saints, was not wholly an English king, for his mother, Emma, was a Norman ; and Edward himself had been brought up among the Normans, and in tastes and feelings was more Norman than English. We must explain who these Normans were, that now began to interfere in English affairs.

When England, in the time of Alfred, was troubled with the Northmen landing on her shores, France, too, was suffering from their ravages. Large boat-loads of these pirates sailed up the River Seine, and one band seized Rouen. The French king, being feeble and cowardly, gave a large tract of land along the Seine to Rollo, or Rolf, a famous chief of the Northmen, on condition that Rollo should become a Christian and settle quietly down. The land thus wrested from the French was called Normandy, and was ruled by Rollo and his descendants. After the Normans had been in France a while they became much more polished and civilized by being brought into contact with the French, who were a lively, quick-witted people with refined tastes for music, art, and architecture. Thus it came to pass that the Norsemen in France had a different language and were much more civilized than their kinsmen in England. It was among these people that Edward had been brought up, while his mother Emma was living in England as the wife of

Cnut. Edward, too, it is said, was a fast friend of his cousin William, the young Duke of Normandy, and it was quite natural that when Edward became king of England he should favour the Normans who followed him into England. To these he gave high offices, much to the displeasure of the English; and, when William of Normandy later on visited him in England, Edward is said to have promised him the Crown.

2. Godwin.—Among others who were angry with the king for favouring foreigners was Godwin, Earl of Wessex, whose sister Edith, Edward had married. Godwin was a very powerful noble, and during Edward's reign really did most of the ruling, for Edward spent his time in religious duties, and looking after the building of a great abbey called Westminster, on the banks of the Thames. Shortly after Edward's reign began, Godwin and the king became unfriendly towards each other on account of the influence of Edward's Norman favourites in the land. It happened that a quarrel arose between the people of Dover and some Normans in which several Normans were killed, and because Godwin would not punish his own countrymen without a fair trial, Godwin and his sons had to leave England for Flanders. While he was away the Normans did much as they pleased, and there was so much discontent in England that Edward had to permit Godwin to return. The Normans saw that their influence was at an end, and most of them went back to Normandy. Godwin now was the chief man in England, and when he died a few years later, his son Harold succeeded to his power, and ruled well for Edward, who cared little for aught save his religious duties.

3. Harold.—Edward had no children, and the English people had begun to look to Harold as their future king. William of Normandy expected to be made king, but Edward invited over, from Hungary, Edward, the son of Edmund Ironsides, to succeed him. This man, however, died, and left a young son, Edgar, known afterwards as the Atheling. Harold and William were now the rival claimants for the throne. A story is told that once Harold was shipwrecked on the coast of Normandy, and falling into William's hands was forced to take a solemn oath that he would help William to become king of England. To make the oath still more solemn, William, it is said, secretly placed sacred relics under the altar. However, when Edward was dying in 1066, he named Harold to succeed him, and the Witan gladly chose him to be their king.

4. **Norwegian Invasion.**—Harold was scarcely crowned before he had to do battle for his kingdom. Among his enemies was his own brother Tostig, who, having been exiled some time before, had gone to Norway. He now came back with the Norwegian King Hardrada, and sailing up the Humber landed with a large army in Yorkshire. Harold was watching the southern coast for the army of William of Normandy, who had gathered a large force of desperate men from different parts of Europe to invade and plunder England. William had sought and obtained the blessing of the Pope on his enterprise, because Harold had broken his solemn oath. As William did not immediately arrive, Harold marched to meet the Norwegian king. A great battle was fought at Stamford Bridge, in Yorkshire, in which Tostig and Hardrada were both killed, and the Norwegian army defeated.

5. **Battle of Hastings.**—Hardly, however, had Harold's army recovered from the effects of this battle when a messenger came to tell him that William had landed at Pevensey in Sussex. At once Harold hastened to meet this new invader, gathering, as he marched, the men of the south to his side to defend the country He found the Normans encamped at Hastings, and at once began preparations for battle. In this Harold was not wise, for his men were worn out and tired with travel, while the Normans were fresh and strong. Harold was advised to lay the country waste, and starve William out; but this he would not do. On the 14th October, 1066, near a hill called Senlac, a little distance from Hastings, a famous battle began. It was to decide whether England was to be governed by the English or by the Normans. Both armies were brave and stubborn, but they fought very differently. The English fought, like their forefathers, on foot, closely ranked together, and defended by a breastwork of shields and palisades. Their weapons were javelins and two-handed axes. The Norman knights were used to fighting on horseback, man and horse being clad in mail. Besides, the Normans brought into battle archers whose arrows did deadly work. The English were posted on the face of the hill, and so long as they refused to stir the Normans could not break their ranks.

The Normans in vain strove to break through the firm wall of English shields, and at one time so sturdy and fierce was the resistance of Harold's men that the Normans began to give way, and a cry arose that William was slain. But William snatched off his helmet to show his followers that he was unhurt, and then making his warriors pretend to flee, led the English to pursue them. Then, an opening being made among the English shields, the horsemen turned, rode in and cut the English to pieces. Nevertheless, the battle lasted for many hours, for a chosen band of Harold's men gathered round their king, and kept the Normans at bay. Then William ordered his archers to shoot their arrows upwards so that coming down they would strike the English on the head. One of these arrows pierced Harold's eye, and he fell. His men fought stubbornly over his body, seeking to save their king, until they were cut down. At last Harold was slain by four Norman knights, and the battle was won by William. Harold's body was given to his mother by the victor to be buried in its royal robes under a heap of stones near the battlefield.

With Harold ended the English kings, for William marched to London, and the Witan not being able to offer him any opposition chose him king. He did not claim the crown as a conqueror, but as the rightful heir of Edward the Confessor. As we shall see in the next chapter, it took William several years to get all England to accept him as king.

CHAPTER V.

THE EARLY NORMANS.

1. William I., or the Conqueror.—William, the son of Robert, Duke of Normandy, and Arlotta, a tanner's daughter, was crowned King of England on Christmas Day. He was a tall, strong man, who loved fighting and hunting. To those who stood in his way and opposed him, he was harsh and cruel; but in the main he loved order and just government. He made many good laws for the English, although in some instances he acted very sternly and tyrannically. But he would not allow any one else to oppress the people, and his strong hand kept his Norman followers under control.

2. **Feudal System**—The men who helped William to gain the Battle of Hastings did so in the hope of gaining rich estates and fine homes in England. They fought for gain, and now that William had become king they looked to him to give them their reward. This William found he would have to do, as the English in the North and West were not fully conquered, and without the aid of his knights he could not keep his hold on the land. On the plea that all those who had fought under Harold were traitors, he took their lands and divided them among his Norman friends. Whenever a rising took place against his rule, he would crush it out with great cruelty, and then would keep the estates of the unfortunate rebels, or give them away to his friends. In this way most of the land of the English passed to the king and his greedy followers. But William did not give these lands for nothing. He made each landowner take an oath that whenever called upon he would aid the king with men and money, and under no circumstances would rebel against him. To prevent these Norman barons from becoming too powerful, he gave them their lands in different counties, so that they could not unite against him, or have too many followers in one place. These barons in turn gave out a portion of their estates to their followers, who also had to give aid to their "lord" when called upon. But William was afraid that his barons might get their men to fight against the king, as often happened in France and Germany, and so made each landowner take an oath to obey the king first, under pain of forfeiting his estates. This was all very different from the English system, by which each freeman held his own land. Now all the land was held from the king, directly or indirectly, and the "vassal" had to kneel bareheaded before him and place his hands in the king's hands, and then swear to give faithful service. He then got from the king his "fief" or "feudum," which was to belong to him and his heirs for ever. This mode of holding land is called the "Feudal System." It was slightly known in England before William became king, for the English kings had been wont to

give lands in somewhat the same fashion to their thanes or immediate followers.

3. Risings Against the Normans.—It took William more than three years to become master of all England. Shortly after his coronation he had to return to Normandy, and while he was absent the English in the West and North, aided by the Scots and Danes, rose against their oppressors. A massacre of Normans took place at York, and William hastened to take a terrible revenge. York was retaken from the English, and then William, to put a barrier between himself and the Scots, laid desolate the whole country between York and Durham. Everything was destroyed—towns, villages, crops, and cattle—and the poor inhabitants were left to starve, or were driven into Scotland. More than 100,000 innocent people lost their lives, and the land ceased to be cultivated for many years.

The only persons who now held out against William were a few hundred English outlaws under the leadership of Morkere and Hereward-the-Wake. This brave little band of patriots for nearly a year kept William at bay, by taking refuge in the Isle of Ely, where they were protected from attack by streams and fens. But in 1071 William built a causeway across the Fen, and the patriots were either killed, scattered, or forced to make their submission.

4. New Forest and Domesday Book.—There was now a forced peace in the land, and William made many changes, some of which were good, and some very bad. Among many cruel things which William did the worst was the laying waste of 90,000 acres of land in Hampshire to make a forest in which he could keep game and hunt. Much of this land was barren, but some of it was fertile, and the poor people living on it were driven out. William loved the "high deer," and any man found killing his game was sentenced to have his eyes put out. To William a deer was more valuable than a man.

Another change of a different kind was the surveying of all England to find out how much land was cultivated, and how much forest, bog, and fen. In this way William was able to tell what taxes each person should pay. All these facts were written in a book called Domesday Book, because it was the book by which the Doom or final decision of the judges was given. It is from this book we get most of our knowledge of the condition of England at this time. It was prepared in 1086.

5. Chief Effects of the Norman Conquest.—Besides the New Forest and Domesday Book there were many other important results of bringing the Normans into England. William ruled with a strong hand, and by allowing complaints to be made before the King's Court he kept his barons from oppressing the English. Sheriffs were appointed to look after the royal revenue from the shires where the laws of the English were allowed. He kept the Church under control, but allowed the clergy to have their own courts. Strong castles were built all over the land to keep the English in check. One of these arose on the banks of the Thames, and is called the Tower of London. But most important of all were the changes made in the social habits and customs of the English. The Normans were a courtly, refined people, with a love of music, art, learning, and architecture, while the English were coarse in their habits and tastes, and cared for little except eating, drinking, and brawling. At first the Normans and English did not intermingle, for the Normans despised the English as a rude and conquered people. After a time the two people came closer together, and then the good results of the Conquest were seen. The English became more refined, with higher and better tastes; and the Normans gained much from the English, who were a sturdy, honest, freedom-loving people. The language of the nation, too, was affected. For though it remained English many Norman-French words were added, especially words that tell of the social life and habits of the conquerors. With the Normans came also an increased commerce with the rest of Europe, the knowledge of many trades, and skill in many arts.

6. Death of William I.—William's reign was a troubled one. When not putting down revolts in England, he was busy looking after his interests in Normandy, where the French king sought to injure him. Then his son Robert made war against him, and nearly killed him in battle. At last, in 1087, while attacking a town in France called Nantes, his horse stumbled and hurt him so severely that he died shortly afterwards at Rouen. He was succeeded by his second son, William Rufus.

7. Character of William Rufus.—The Conquerer left three sons, Robert, the eldest, William, and Henry. To Robert he left Normandy and Maine, but he named William to succeed him in England, because he knew that Robert was too weak and good-natured to keep his unruly barons in check. William Rufus, or the Red King, was as able and fierce as his father, but not so just and wise as a ruler. His one good quality was that he would not allow his barons to rob and oppress the English, that power he kept for himself. For that reason the English came to his aid against his brother Robert, whose cause the Norman barons supported. Robert landed with an army at Pevensey, near where the Battle of Hastings was fought, and William called upon the English to assist him. With their aid he defeated Robert and drove him out of the country.

8. Anselm and the King.—Among the great men who lived at this time was Lanfranc, the Archbishop of Canterbury. He was a wise and good man, and in the Conqueror's time had been Rufus' tutor. So long as Lanfranc lived, Rufus governed fairly well, but when he died Rufus began to rob and oppress his people. To get money he kept high offices in the Church, such as bishoprics and abbacies, vacant. The incomes from these offices would then go into the king's treasury. When Lanfranc died the king did not appoint his successor until after many years. Perhaps he would not have appointed any had he not become very ill. He then repented of his sins and forced the learned and gentle Anselm to become Archbishop. Anselm was very unwilling to take the crozier or crook of office, for he knew that the king, as soon as he was better, would forget to carry out the promises made when sick. And so it happened. No sooner had the king recovered than he began again his evil ways, and Anselm, having tried in vain to control him, was glad to leave the country. The king now had no one to restrain him, and from this time to the end of his reign, in every possible way, he robbed and plundered his subjects. One of his instruments in this work was Ralph Flambard, his *Justiciar*, or chief of the justices, who taxed the people heavily and unjustly.

9. The Crusades.—During this reign the Crusades began. Peter the Hermit, encouraged by the Pope, went through Europe preaching against the Turks, because they ill-treated Christian pilgrims who visited the Holy Sepulchre in Jerusalem. A multitude of people, sewing a colored cross (*crux*) on their arms, went forth from Europe to fight against the Turks. With them went Robert, William's brother, having, however, first pledged his duchy to William for a sum of money with which to go on the expedition. This was in 1096. So while Robert was absent William governed both England and Normandy, and took English men and money into France to help him in his wars.

10. Death of Rufus, 1100 A.D.—The people groaned under their heavy burdens and the famine which now came ; but the end was near. One day Rufus was hunting in the New Forest, and after a time being missed by his attendants they sought for him, only to find him dead, with an arrow in his breast. Some thought that he had been shot accidentally by Walter Tyrrell, while others, with perhaps good reason, believed that one of the many oppressed by the cruel forest laws had seized the opportunity to take the wicked king's life. Rufus died " in his sins," and his body was not given a religious burial. His brother Henry at once hastened to Winchester and seized the royal treasure, fearing Robert's return from the Crusades. So Henry became king, Robert being absent in the Holy Land.

11. Henry 1.—Henry, the youngest son of the Conqueror, was a quiet thoughtful man, with so much learning for his time, that he was called "Beauclerc," or "Fine Scholar." Nevertheless he kept a firm hand on his barons, and as he knew that his throne depended on the good-will of the English, he gave them a "charter," and restored the laws of Edward the Confessor. He relieved the people from many of their unjust burdens, and, to please the English still more, married Edith, the daughter of Malcolm of Scotland, and grand-daughter of Edmund Ironsides. All these things Henry did because he knew that when Robert returned from the Crusades he would claim the throne and would be supported by most of the barons. After a time Robert came home, and as expected, the barons rose in his favour. Peace, however, was made between the brothers, Robert receiving a pension from Henry.

But Robert governed his duchy of Normandy so badly, that Henry went over with an army, and defeating him at the battle of Tenchebrai (A.D. 1106), took him prisoner. Robert remained in prison the rest of his life, while Henry ruled over both England and Normandy.

12. Henry's Good Government.—Normans and English were now coming nearer together, and the union was made still closer by Henry's good laws. Bishop Roger, his Justiciar, or chief judge, helped Henry to bring the revenues of the kingdom into order. The people got back their shire-moots, and the sheriffs every year went to the King's Court to pay in the rents and taxes to the royal treasury. The money was paid out on a chequered cloth, and the room where this took place became known as the "Court of Exchequer." The King's justices, too, went from place to place each year to settle disputes, and to see no wrong was done.

In this reign many towns and cities bought from the king charters giving them the right to manage their own affairs. The Normans were accustomed to settle their disputes by "trial by battle," which was a great public duel, whereas the English used the "ordeal." The citizens of the towns were now not required to use the "trial by battle," and their trade was freed from tolls. The good laws and good order in the land brought in people from abroad. Among others were the Flemings, who introduced the art of weaving wool.

13. Henry and the Church.—Henry, like William Rufus, had a dispute with Anselm, who had returned to England. It was about the right of electing bishops. Rufus had kept the bishoprics vacant, and to prevent this Anselm wanted to have the bishops elected by the clergy. Henry, on the other hand, wished Anselm to do "homage" for the land of his See, or Archbishopric, and this Anselm at first refused to do, as it seemed to give Henry too much power in spiritual matters. Finally the matter was settled by Henry agreeing to the election of bishops by the clergy of the cathedrals, and by the bishops doing homage to the king for their lands.

14. Death of Henry, 1135 A.D.—The last days of Henry were very sad. His only son William was drowned while attempting to cross from Normandy to England. He then wished his daughter

Matilda, the wife of the Count of Anjou, to succeed him; but this did not please the barons, who disliked the thought of being ruled by a woman. Henry, however, made his barons swear to support Matilda and her baby son. Soon after this Henry died, and the land was once more thrown into confusion by the disputes and wars of rivals for the throne.

15. **Civil War.**—Although the barons had sworn to support Matilda, yet the most of them chose Stephen, the son of Adela, the Conqueror's daughter, to be their king. They did not care to have a woman rule over them, and they knew that Stephen was weak and good-natured, and could not hinder them from having their own way. So Stephen came to England and was crowned king in Matilda's absence. But Matilda's uncle, David of Scotland, with the help of some of the barons, made war against Stephen in her behalf, and fought and lost the famous "Battle of the Standard" at Cowton Moor, in Yorkshire. This battle took place in 1138, and its name arose from the fact that the English had as their standard a ship's mast hung with sacred banners. This was, however, only one of many battles fought between the barons who supported Stephen and those who supported Matilda. At one time Matilda was victorious and Stephen was a prisoner; and then it was Stephen who was victorious and Matilda a prisoner. In 1147 Matilda, discouraged, left England for a time.

16. **Misery of the People.**—In no reign did the people suffer so much from the wickedness and cruelty of their rulers as in the reign of Stephen. The struggle between Stephen and Matilda left the barons to do much as they liked. They built strong castles, coined money, and made war against one another. Their castles were nothing but robbers' dens whence the barons came forth to plunder, slay, and burn. "They burnt houses and sacked towns. If they suspected any one of concealing his wealth, they carried him off to their castle, and there they tortured him to make him confess where his money was. They hanged men up by the feet and smoked them with foul smoke. Some were hanged up by their thumbs, others by their heads, and burning things were hung on to their feet." The people cried to Heaven for help, but for years no help came. "Men said openly that Christ and His saints slept."

17. Death of Stephen, A.D. 1154.—At last, after nineteen years of suffering, relief came. Stephen's son died, and Henry, Matilda's son, landed with an army in England to fight his own battles. Theobald, the Archbishop of Canterbury, now used his influence with Stephen to put an end to this wretched strife. Stephen saw that he must, sooner or later, yield, now that he had no son to succeed him, and agreed that Henry should have the throne after his death. Not long after Stephen died, and Henry became king, peace was once more restored, and as we shall see, with peace and a strong ruler, the miseries of Stephen's reign came to an end.

CHAPTER VI.

THE CROWN, THE CHURCH, AND THE BARONS.

1. Henry II.—Henry was only twenty-one years of age when he came to the throne; but he was already a statesman and an able ruler. He was a stout, strong man, with red hair and grey eyes; and was so restless and active that he could scarcely find time to eat his meals. He loved order and good government, although his temper which was fiery and passionate, sometimes made him cruel and unjust. He ruled over England, Normandy, and Maine, his grandfather's possessions; and, besides, had Anjou and Touraine from his father, Geoffrey, Count of Anjou; Brittany, through Constance, wife of his brother Geoffrey; and Poitou, Aquitaine, and Gascony by his wife Eleanor, a woman who had been divorced from Louis VII., King of France. Thus Henry ruled over more French territory than the king of France himself. Henry was the first of the Plantagenets, a line of kings whose name arose from the fact that Geoffrey of Anjou, Henry's father, had worn a sprig of broom, *planta genista*, as his device during the crusades. Another name for the same line of kings is the *Angevin*, because they had for their family possession, Anjou.

2. Henry's Reforms.—One of the first things Henry did was to make the barons pull down their castles, so that they could no longer use them as strongholds in which to carry their plunder and

torture their victims. His grandfather, Henry I., had made a beginning in sending out judges on circuit, and Henry II. followed and extended his plan. Judges now made their circuits more regularly, and it was arranged that in each shire there should be four knights, and in each neighbourhood twelve men, who should place before the judges all cases of evil-doing, and should swear to the guilt of the accused, or to the facts about any property in dispute. This was the beginning of the Grand Jury of to-day. The "ordeal" was still in use; but it was abolished forty years later. As the Grand Jury, in many cases, did not know all the facts, the custom was introduced of calling on twelve men, who had the necessary information, to state what they knew about the matters in dispute. This body of twelve was called the "Petty Jury." Its decision as to the guilt or innocence of the accused was called the "*verdict*," which means "*truly said*." So we see that at the outset our juries not only heard the evidence but also acted as witnesses. It was not till many years had passed that the jury ceased to do aught except hear the evidence and give the decision.

Henry also lessened the power of the barons by allowing them to pay money to the king instead of giving military service. By this means, and by allowing the small landowners, or yeomanry, to keep arms and defend themselves, he did much to put a stop to such outrages as took place in the reign of Stephen.

3. Henry and the Church.—Henry's love of order and good government led him to try to make the clergy submit to be judged by the ordinary courts of the land. At this time nearly all the men of any education were clerks or clergy, or in some way connected with the church. William I. had granted the clergy their own courts; and when a clerk committed a serious crime he could not be put to death, for the church courts had no power to inflict such a punishment. So it came to pass that a great many crimes like theft and murder were not duly punished, and wicked men escaped very easily, if they in any way belonged to the clergy. Henry tried to change this, and to have but one kind of law for all classes of his subjects.

4. Becket.—As you may think, the clergy were very much against such a step, and Henry thought if Thomas Becket were made Archbishop of Canterbury, his help would enable him to carry out this reform. Becket had been Henry's bosom friend and his chancellor, or man of business. He was gay, reckless, and extravagant while Henry's chancellor, and Henry thought that if he made him Archbishop he would use his influence with the clergy in favour of Henry's plans. When, however, Becket became Archbishop he changed his habits entirely, and instead of supporting Henry, he upheld the cause of the clergy. Henry was very angry at Becket's conduct, and when Becket refused to be bound by his own signature to the "Constitutions of Clarendon," drawn up in 1164, and making the desired changes, Henry drove him out of the country by the insults and indignities he put upon him.

5. **Becket's Murder.**—While Becket was absent, Henry persuaded the Archbishop of York to crown his son Henry. This was a new cause for quarrel, for no sooner had Becket returned to England, than he suspended the Archbishop of York for crowning the king's son. Then Henry, who was a man of very violent temper, exclaimed, "Will no one rid me of this turbulent priest!" Four knights, who were only too well pleased to have such an excuse, left France, where Henry was, crossed over to England, and murdered Becket in his own cathedral at Canterbury. Henry was very sorry for what his foolish passion had brought about, and immediately sent a messenger to the Pope to say that the murder was committed without his consent. Later on, to satisfy the people who thought a great crime and sin had been committed by murdering a bishop in a church, Henry did penance at Becket's tomb, allowing himself to be scourged on his bare back by the monks.

6. **Conquest of Ireland, 1172.**—Henry was glad to have an excuse, after Becket's murder, to leave England, and a good one was found in the state of Ireland. This island was inhabited by people of the same race as the Britons, and like England had been troubled with attacks from the Danes, who managed to get a footing on the eastern coast. The Irish people could not wholly drive them out, although they fought many battles with them. These wars had a bad effect on the Irish, for instead of remaining at peace, the Irish chieftains fought against one another with so much ferocity that the civilization and learning that had existed in Ireland before the time of the Danes began to die out. To save the land from disorder and misrule, the Pope gave Henry permission

to conquer Ireland. The opportunity was given when an Irish king, Dermot of Leinster, came over to England to get help against one of his enemies. Henry allowed Richard de Clare, or "Strongbow," to go and to take along with him a small army of Norman adventurers. Strongbow soon defeated Dermot's foes, and marrying Dermot's daughter, settled down as his heir. He conquered so much territory in Leinster that Henry thought it wise to cross over and get him to acknowledge the king as his "lord." This Strongbow did, and Henry received homage from some of the Irish chiefs about Dublin, as well as from Strongbow. This was only the beginning of the conquest of Ireland, for Ireland was not wholly subdued until more than four centuries after.

7. **Death of Henry, 1189.**—Henry's life was full of trouble. He had trouble with the barons, with the Church, with his wife Eleanor, and with his sons. His wife, who was not kindly treated, stirred up strife and caused his sons to rebel against him. The kings of France and Scotland sought to take advantage of Henry's difficulties to wrest territory from him. But Henry was more than a match for all his enemies. He defeated his sons, took the king of Scotland prisoner, and put Eleanor in confinement during the rest of his life. Two of Henry's sons died, and the remaining two, Richard and John, joined the king of France in an attack on their father's possessions in Touraine. When Henry was shown a list of those trying to injure him, and saw therein the name of his favorite son, John, he cried, "Shame, shame, on a conquered king," and, heart-broken, two days after, died.

8. **Richard I., The Lion-Hearted.**—Richard, Henry's elder surviving son, succeeded his father. He can scarcely be called a king of England, for during the ten years he held the throne he was not one year in the country. It is doubtful if he understood the English language, or could speak the English tongue. The only use he had for the English people was to supply him with money for his foreign wars and for his crusading adventures. He was a very strong, brave man, and while abroad in the armies of the crusaders performed many remarkable acts of daring and courage. The English had but little reason to love him as a ruler, yet they were proud of his strength, valour, and fame as a warrior. Nevertheless, in some ways, his neglect of his kingly duties,

and his greed for his subjects' money, did good. To get money he sold to many towns and cities the right to govern themselves. In this reign London got its first Lord Mayor, Henry Fitz-Alwyn, A.D. 1191. He also sold offices and honors belonging to the Crown and the Church, and would have sold London could he have found a buyer.

Almost at the beginning of his reign he went to the Holy Land to war against the Turks and to take Jerusalem. He left his mother and William Longchamp to govern in his absence. When Longchamp was put aside by the barons in 1191, Richard's brother John sought to rule in his place but was not permitted. Richard, meanwhile, was doing great deeds of valour in the Holy Land, but did not succeed in taking Jerusalem, although once in sight of it. He had for rivals in the crusading armies, Philip of France, and the Duke of Austria, the latter of whom, it is said, he grossly insulted. It happened that Richard, returning from the crusades, fell into the hands of his old-time enemy, and by him was sent a prisoner to the German Emperor. The Emperor would not release him until he had paid a ransom of £100,000, and this large sum (for money was worth a great deal more then than now) the English people had to raise to free their king. John had tried to persuade the Emperor to keep Richard a prisoner, and for this and other acts of treachery Richard, on his return, took away John's castles and lands. Richard now spent a few months in England, collecting all the money he could get to make war against his enemy, Philip of France, and then went to Normandy. He never came back, for while besieging the Castle of Chaluz, an archer took deliberate aim and shot him. Before he died he forgave his slayer, but Richard's followers were more revengeful, and put the poor archer to a very painful death. Thus came to a violent end Richard, Cœur-de-Leon, the hero of many a romantic tale.

9. **John, surnamed Sansterre or Lackland.**—John, Richard's brother, now came to the throne of England. He is the one king of England about whom no good can be said. Although able, handsome and, when he wished, pleasant and agreeable, he was cruel, licentious, and teacherous. He was chosen king of England over his brother Geoffrey's son, Arthur, a lad twelve years of age; but his claims to his father's French possessions were disputed.

Arthur was the rightful Count of Anjou, and Anjou and Brittany held by him. In the war that followed Arthur was taken prisoner, and no more was heard of him. The rumour spread, and was generally believed, that he was murdered by his uncle; some say, with John's own hands. Philip of France, as John's feudal lord, callèd upon him to answer the charge of murdering his nephew; and as John paid no attention to the summons, Philip made war upon him and took from him all his possessions north of the Loire. John had now only his mother's lands, Gascony and part of Aquitaine. In this way the kings of England lost Normandy, Maine and Anjou. Now that most of their French possessions were gone, the kings of England paid more attention to the wants and wishes of the English people. English men and English money were not, henceforth, so liable to be taken abroad to be used in their king's foreign quarrels.

10. **John quarrels with the Pope.**—Not content with murdering his nephew, John must needs plunder and torture his own subjects. No class of his people was free from his insults and outrages. He kept in his pay a large number of foreigners, who fought his battles and helped him to put at defiance his barons. The Church, too, felt his heavy hand, for clergy and laity alike were victims of his greed and brutality. When Hubert, the Archbishop of Canterbury died, some of the monks of Canterbury secretly chose his successor. John, when it came to his ears, was greatly enraged and had another one chosen. The matter came before Pope Innocent III. and he put both choices aside, and induced the monks to elect Stephen Langton, a man of great learning and worth, at that time living at Rome. But John would not allow Langton to come to England. Then in 1208 the Pope placed the land under an "Interdict," that is he forbade the Clergy to marry the people in the Church, or to bury their dead. For four years the churches were closed, and their dead were buried in ditches and fields. But John cared for none of those things. He took his revenge by robbing and murdering the clergy, using for this purpose his hired foreign troops. One outrage followed another until the Pope called upon Philip of France to invade England and take the throne from John. This Philip proceeded to do; but John, at last greatly alarmed, placed his crown and kingdom at the

Pope's feet, promising to be his vassal and pay him a sum of money yearly in token of his supremacy. By this act John put himself under the Pope's protection and Philip had to withdraw. John now felt free to give full vent to all his wicked passions, and the barons were powerless to stop his outrages. Fortunately for them and for England, Langton the new Archbishop, was a true patriot, and determined to do all he could to free the people from John's oppressive rule. The nation now was becoming more united; English and Norman met at the Universities as equals, and in many other ways the old distinctions between the two peoples were fading away. It was well that this was so, for now all classes had to unite against a cruel and tyrannical king.

11. Magna Charta, A.D. 1215.—Langton now became the leader of the barons. He brought forth the charter containing the laws of Henry I., and urged the barons to demand that John should agree to be bound by them. John delayed his consent, hoping to collect his foreign troops, and then crush his opponents. But the barons were much in earnest, and hearing of John's treachery, took up arms, and forced John, who was quite unprepared for a war, to sign the Great Charter, or "Magna Charta." This famous charter was signed at Runnymede on the Thames, on the 15th June, 1215. Most of its provisions were old, and had been in other charters, such as that of Henry I. But the Great Charter is important because it was wrung from an unwilling king, and because it states very clearly and positively the rights of the people. It contains a great many clauses, of which the principal are: *first*, that the king could levy no taxes without the consent of the bishops and the barons; *second*, that no man could be imprisoned, dispossessed of his land, or otherwise punished, without a fair trial by his peers or equals. Its two great principles are the right of the people to control their own taxation, and the right to be free from the king's arbitrary arrest and punishment. It also maintained the freedom of the English Church, and the right of towns and cities to the management of their own affairs.

12. Death of John, 1216.—The Barons were so anxious to have the Charter carried out, that they appointed twenty-five of their own number to watch the king, and if he refused to do as he had promised, they were authorized to seize the king's castles. But John did not intend to keep his word, and putting off the barons with excuses, he managed to get his paid troops together, and then began a civil war. The barons were not able to cope with him, and called upon Louis, the son of the French king, to come to their aid with an army, and to be their king. Louis landed with a large force, and it looked as if England was once more to be ruled by French kings. Fortunately, John, sorely vexed at losing his baggage, jewels, and crown while crossing the Wash, took ill and died. His son, Henry, a lad nine years old, was chosen by the barons to succeed him.

CHAPTER VII.

DE MONTFORT'S PARLIAMENT.

1. **Henry III., A.D. 1216.**—Henry III. was chosen king by a few of the barons, although only a child. There was, however, no choice, except between him and the French Prince Louis, then in England with an army. The barons preferred Henry, fearing that Louis would give their lands to his French followers; and Louis, finding that the barons had deserted him, returned to France with his army. As Henry was too young to rule unaided, the governing power was given into the hands of William Marshall, Earl of Pembroke. The Great Charter was again agreed to, but the clause providing for the people's consent to their own taxation was left out.

The Earl of Pembroke died in 1219, and then Peter des Roches, Hubert de Burgh, and Archbishop Langton governed for Henry. In 1227 Henry began to govern for himself, although he kept advisers, and this, some say, marks the beginning of the English "Privy Council."

2. **State of the Country.**—We must now see how the country and people had prospered since the Norman Conquest. In the time of William I. and his son Rufus, the people suffered at the hands of their kings, through heavy and unjust taxes. Matters were better in the reign of Henry I., although taxes were still very heavy, but better laws were put in force. The reign of Stephen was full of

misery and wretchedness; but it was followed by the wise and firm rule of Henry II. Henry's sons, Richard and John, governed badly, and the people had to endure heavy taxation and civil war. Highwaymen, like Robin Hood and his companions, infested the woods and roads, robbing and sometimes murdering travellers. Wealthy men, especially abbotts and monks, were the chief victims, for Robin Hood often took money from the rich and gave it to the poor. He thought the rich Normans and monks were oppressing the poor English, so he took this way to make things more equal.

As a rule the harvests were good and food was plentiful. Even laborers had oaten and wheaten bread, barley beer, herrings, and cheese. The yeomanry wove their own clothing, and made their own tools in the winter months. They practised wrestling, archery, and other manly games and sports, and for a more serious pastime attended their manor and other courts, where their local affairs were looked after. In the towns, trade increased, although the king too frequently levied heavy tolls. Fairs were held annually, and at these the people met, bargained, and indulged in games and sports, such as archery, which was encouraged by law. As the king took tolls on all goods sold, he was sometimes tempted, when in want of money, to call a fair when it was not really needed. After Stephen Langton died in 1228, the Pope filled English bishoprics and other good positions in the church with Italian priests. He also sent to England for money to carry on his wars in Italy and elsewhere. The Black Friars and White Friars, men who had made a vow to live a life of poverty, came to England, and went around barefooted and poorly clad, teaching the people. One of these Friars, Roger Bacon, was a great thinker and discoverer in science.

3. Simon de Montfort.—When Henry began to govern alone, it was soon seen how weak he was and how unfitted to rule. Like many other weak men, without intending it, he succeeded in doing a great deal of harm. He was much like Edward the Confessor, fond of architecture and church building, and easily ruled by favourites. Like Edward he brought into the country a host of foreigners who got from his hands the best gifts, lands, houses, offices, and English heiresses. First, he had a swarm of his mother's relations from Poitou; and then, after his marriage with Eleanor of Provence, another swarm from his wife's native land.

Henry was very extravagant, and to get money had to call together his barons and bishops. These assemblies came to be called Parliaments, from the French *Parler*, to speak. The demands for money came so often, that the barons lost patience, especially as most of the money went to foreigners. At last, Simon de Montfort, although the son of foreign parents and married to the king's sister, determined to check the evils of Henry's weak rule. De Montfort was a man of great ability and moral worth, and was known in his time as Sir Simon the Righteous. A good reason for action was given when it was found that Henry had foolishly squandered a large sum of money in a war in Sicily, for the sole benefit of the Pope. In 1258, Parliament was called at Oxford to raise money to pay the Pope, and the barons came to the meeting armed, and prepared to force the king to accept advisers who would reform the Government. By the "Provisions of Oxford," Henry had to accept a council to advise him; to give back the castles taken from Englishmen; and to hold three Parliaments a year. The king's son, Edward, agreed to these "Provisions," and De Montfort was among the first to give up his castles.

4. **De Montfort's Parliament.**—But no real improvement was made in the government of the country. Some of the barons were satisfied to get back the castles, and to have the foreign favourites driven out of England, whilst others were jealous of the power and influence of Earl Simon. So in a little while matters were no better than before the "Provisions" were passed, and Henry had recovered nearly all his lost authority. At last, civil war broke out, and Earl Simon, supported by fifteen thousand Londoners, defeated the king at the Battle of Lewes, (A.D. 1264), and took him prisoner. Shortly afterwards, Prince Edward, who played a gallant part in the battle, surrendered himself to the Earl.

De Montfort now ruled for over a year, and in that year made a very important change. Until this time, no one had been summoned by the king to grant money in parliament except the barons, bishops, and great landowners. The people of the towns and cities, and the smaller landowners, were taxed without having any representatives in parliament. In fact, all that parliaments were called for was to get grants of money from the people. Now, however, Earl Simon called a parliament, and among others summoned two knights from each shire or county, and two citizens from each borough or town. This was the beginning of our modern Parliament, in which there are representatives of all classes of the people. But in Earl Simon's time, and for many years after, bishops, barons, knights, and burgesses, all sat in the same room and voted together; whereas now, they sit in two rooms, or chambers, and vote separately.

5. **Death of De Montfort, A.D. 1265.**—Not long did Earl Simon hold the reins of power. Simon's sons gave offence, and the barons were jealous of him. Prince Edward, who saw how things were tending, managed to escape from his keepers, and rallying his own and his father's friends around him, was soon at the head of a large force. Simon was not prepared for an attack, and had to take refuge with the Welsh prince Llewellyn. Edward defeated Simon's son at Kenilworth, and then marching with young Simon's banners in front of his army, he was able to come very close upon the Earl before he was aware of the danger. From a church tower at Evesham, in Worcestershire, Simon saw the enemy approaching. "Commend your souls to God," he said to his small force of undisciplined Welsh, "for our bodies are the prince's." In the battle that followed, Sir Simon the Righteous was slain, and his body sadly mutilated. In another year the civil war was over, and then the peace of Kenilworth gave back to the barons their estates, and restored order in the land. Henry III. died in 1272, after a long reign, in which much harm, and some little good was done. He will be remembered by Westminster Abbey, the rebuilding of which he began, and by the fact that in his reign was the first English parliament.

CHAPTER VIII.

STRUGGLE WITH WALES AND SCOTLAND.

1. **Edward I.**—After the death of Earl Simon and the defeat of the barons, Prince Edward went to the Crusades, and did not return until nearly two years after his father's death. Edward was

one of our best kings. He was a tall and powerful man, a great warrior and statesman—one who loved his people, although sometimes harsh and unjust. He had been a good son, and was an affectionate husband and father. In his reign many wise and good laws were made. From Earl Simon he had learned much, and now when he was made king he put Simon's teachings in force. He began at once to stop the abuses carried on by the barons, who drove the farmers' cattle away without paying for them, and took money from the people unjustly. He had silver halfpennies and farthings made into coins. Before his time the silver penny was made with a deep cut in the shape of a cross, and when a halfpenny or farthing was needed the coin was broken into two or four pieces.

2. **Conquest of Wales.**—Edward was fond of war, for he was a good general, and loved to do daring deeds and win fame. So we find that he had been king but a short time before he determined to conquer the northern part of Wales. The Britons had by this time lost nearly all the land they held after the English conquest, and now only North Wales remained to them The kings of England claimed that the Welsh kings should do homage to them, and sometimes they did. But Llewellyn, the Welsh prince of Edward's reign, refused to do homage, and Edward marched into Wales with an army to force him to submit. Llewellyn after a sharp struggle agreed to recognize Edward as his feudal lord. But after four years of submission, the brave and high-spirited prince once more sought to gain his independence. Edward again marched against him, and took a number of Swiss soldiers accustomed to fighting in a hilly country to contend against and pursue Llewellyn in his mountain strongholds. How it would have ended we know not, but Llewellyn was killed in a skirmish and then Wales was conquered. To please the Welsh, Edward gave them his son Edward as their prince. From that time, the eldest son of the sovereign has been called the Prince of Wales.

3. **Reform in the Laws.**—For nothing is Edward's reign more noted than for its wise laws. The land laws were improved, and a measure was passed to prevent too much land being held by the church or by religious bodies, who gave no feudal service for it. The law courts were now changed. The office of Justiciar was abolished, and instead of one court we have now three : the *King's Bench*, the

Court of Common Pleas, and the *Court of the Exchequer*. Lastly, as the Chancellor heard cases for the king, his court after a time became known as the *Court of Chancery*. But a subject could appeal from any of these courts to the king himself, and by him have his wrongs righted.

4. Expulsion of the Jews.—Edward, however, was not always just to his subjects. One cruel thing he did. In England there were many Jews, the first of whom came over in the time of the Conqueror. They were a peaceable, industrious, and money-making people, but they were very unpopular. This was due, partly to their religion and race, and partly to the dislike of their practice of lending money, and charging high rates of interest thereon. Needy nobles were often glad to borrow from the Jews, and as the latter knew that they were disliked and the debts due to them would not be paid, if payment could be avoided, they charged heavy interest in return for the risk they ran. In these days, it must be remembered, taking interest, or usury, was looked upon as wrong and sinful by many people. The Jews were also accused of clipping coins and other dishonest practices. Edward knew how unpopular these persecuted people were, and, although it was for his own interest to protect them, he banished them from the land. He allowed them to take away their wealth, and England was much poorer in consequence of this cruel deed. From this time until the rule of Oliver Cromwell, nearly four hundred years later, Jews were not allowed to live in England.

5. First full Parliament.—Edward acted more wisely when, following the example of Simon de Montfort, he called a true English Parliament in 1295. Like Simon, he summoned two knights from each shire, and two burgesses (citizens of a town) from each borough, as well as the nobles, bishops, and higher clergy. The nobles and bishops were summoned by name, and the knights and burgesses by the sheriff's writ or command. Edward thought that when all had to pay taxes, it was only right that all should have a voice in granting these taxes; or, as he said, "what concerned all should be approved by all." The elections by which knights and burgesses were sent to Parliament were very different from ours of to-day. Every time Parliament met there was a new election. The people that sent the member had to pay his expenses; and for that reason, and also because it was known that Parliaments were called only to get money grants, both members and people had but little love for them.

6. **War with Scotland.**—From these reforms and changes which concerned England alone, we must now turn away to Edward's dealings with Scotland. In 1286, Alexander III., king of Scotland, fell over a precipice and was killed His grand-child, Margaret, daughter of the king of Norway, was his nearest heir. This little maid was going to Scotland to be made queen, when she died, and the throne was left vacant. There were many claimants among the late king's relations, those having the best claim being John Balliol and Robert Bruce. The Scotch lords could not agree upon a king, and asked Edward to decide. The English kings always claimed to have the supremacy over the Scotch kings; but this claim was not always allowed. Before Edward would consent to decide who should be king, he called the Scotch Parliament together at Norham, near the border, and made them promise that whoever should be chosen, should give him homage as the feudal lord of Scotland. He then decided in favor of Balliol, who did homage to Edward, and became king of Scotland. Edward was an exacting lord, and wished to have cases, which had been tried before Scotch courts, taken to English courts for final settlement, and this demand the Scotch resented. Very soon Balliol found his position very unpleasant, and taking advantage of a war going on in France between Edward and the French king, threw off Edward's yoke, crossed the border, and ravaged Cumberland.

Edward was now very angry, and marching north with a large force, stormed Berwick, and massacred its inhabitants. He then seized Edinburgh, Stirling, Perth, and Montrose. At Montrose, he took Balliol prisoner, and then appointed an English Council to govern in his stead. To humble the Scotch still more he carried off to England the crown jewels, and the "sacred stone," on which the Scotch kings were wont to be crowned at Scone. This stone, it was said, was the very stone on which Jacob had rested his head at Bethel, when he saw the angels ascending and descending the ladder from heaven. The stone was put into the seat of the royal chair at Westminster Abbey, and on it kings and queens have been crowned to this day. Wherever this stone went, according to a

Scotch prophecy, there would a Scotch king reign; and, so it happened in England, about three hundred years after.

For a time the Scotch submitted to Edward's rule; and then William Wallace, a brave knight, gathered a few faithful and true men together and defeated the English at Lanark, Scone, and other points. His forces having greatly increased, he met the English army at Stirling Bridge, and there won a famous victory. Once more the Scots were free, and Balliol was king, although a prisoner in England.

While these events were taking place in Scotland, Edward was in Flanders, helping the Flemings against the French king. He had troubles on every side: from Ireland, Wales, France, and Scotland; and he was much in need of money. He asked for a large sum from the clergy, but at first they would not give it, until he refused them justice and protection. He laid heavy taxes on his people, and in other ways ruled harshly and unjustly, until Parliament complained and resisted, and then Edward acknowledged he was wrong, and promised he would never more levy money without the consent of Parliament, and that he would always right the grievances of his people before a fresh grant of money was made. This new charter was given in 1297, and is very important.

The next year, having heard what the Scots were doing, he marched north, and defeated Wallace at Falkirk (1298), although the Scots fought bravely against overwhelming numbers. Wallace escaped for the time, but in 1305 was betrayed by his servant into the hands of the English, and was hanged on Tower Hill, in London.

It was not till near the end of Edward's reign that the Scotch again seriously attempted to recover their lost independence. Then Robert Bruce, the grandson of Balliol's rival, escaped from the English court, and going to Scotland, met and killed in a church at Dumfries, his rival and enemy Comyn. Soon Bruce had a band of desperate Scotch nobles around him, and a little later he was crowned at Scone. When Edward, now aged and ill, heard of this new revolt, he hastened to chastise Bruce and the Scotch. Swearing to have his revenge on Comyn's murderer, he travelled slowly northwards. When near the border he sent an army ahead which drove Bruce back to the Grampian Hills. He was busy taking vengeance on Bruce's supporters when death seized him, at Burgh-on-Sands, A.D., 1307. He was succeeded by his eldest son, Edward Caernarvon, Prince of Wales.

7. **Edward II.**—The new king had few of his father's great qualities. He was an idle, frivolous youth, fond of gaiety and low companions. He was brave enough when roused; that, however, seldom happened. His father had left him three commands: to subdue Scotland, to send his heart to the Holy Land, and never to bring back Gaveston, a banished and profligate favourite. Not one of these did he carry out. He left the Scotch war to take care of itself, and so Bruce won back nearly all he had lost to Edward I. He buried his father at Westminster, and he recalled Gaveston. Gaveston soon got Edward into trouble by his insolence and wastefulness. He was twice banished, but Edward brought him back. Then Parliament put the government into the hands of a number of bishops and peers, called "Ordainers," who tried to control the King. Once more Gaveston was exiled and recalled, and then the barons took the law into their own hands and beheaded him.

8. **Battle of Bannockburn, June 24, 1314.**—Bruce in the meantime had been winning town after town from the English, until near all Scotland was in his hands, save Stirling Castle, which was closely pressed. To save this fortress Edward went into Scotland with an army of 100,000 men. He met Bruce with his army of 30,000 Scots at a little stream or *burn* called the Bannock, near Stirling Castle. The battle was fought on June 24th, 1314, and was to determine whether Scotland was to be free or not. Everything seemed in favour of the English, with their large army of brave knights and archers. Bruce, however, had dug pits in the space between his army and the English, and in them had placed sharp stakes, the whole being covered over with turf. The Bannock flowed between the armies and on each side of it was a low boggy piece of land in which horses sank. Bruce knew he had most to fear from the English horsemen, and made his spearmen in the front rank kneel to meet their charge. When the English knights charged the Scots, after the English bowmen had thinned their ranks, their horses plunged into the concealed pits, and floundered in the bogs, and so became an easy prey to the Scotch archers and spearmen.

The English sought a way around this bog and the pits to attack the Scotch; but at the moment when the Scotch cause was in the greatest danger, a number of camp-followers came over the hills on the Scotch flank, waving their garments and giving utterance to shrill cries. In their confusion the English thought this was a new Scotch army coming to the rescue, and panic-stricken they turned and fled. The battle was won, and Scotland was free.

9. Death of Edward II.—Edward escaped from the battle-field and returned to England, but it had been better for him had he been killed then and there. The rest of his reign is a tale of intrigue, misgovernment, and misery. There was famine in the land, and many died. The king took new favourites, and this led to new quarrels with the nobles. The only good thing to be told is that owing to these quarrels Edward gave the Commons a share in making the laws, as well as a share in paying the taxes. So serious did these quarrels become that Edward's queen, Isabella, turned against him, and went to France, where she carried on a shameful intrigue with Lord Mortimer. In 1326 she came back with a small army, and, being joined by the barons, took the king prisoner, put his favourites to death, and made him agree to give up his crown to his son Edward, a lad of fifteen years of age. Then he was removed from prison to prison and finally to Berkeley Castle, where he was barbarously murdered A.D. 1327.

CHAPTER IX.

THE HUNDRED YEARS' WAR—THE PEASANTS' REVOLT.

1. **Edward III.**—For four years young Edward was a king in name only, the power being in the hands of his mother and her favourite, Lord Mortimer. Edward was early married to Philippa of Hainault, a noble and brave woman. In 1330, seeing how Mortimer abused his position, he had him seized and put to death. He then began to rule for himself.

Edward III. like his grandfather, Edward I., was fond of war, and tried to bring Scotland under the control of England ; but in this he did not succeed, although for a time he placed the son of Balliol on the Scotch throne. His invasion of Scotland led to trouble with Philip VI. of France, who was an ally of the Scotch. Philip attacked Gascony which belonged to Edward, and Edward made this attack, and the French interference with the Flemings, an excuse for beginning a war with France, which lasted on and off nearly one hundred years. The English were very anxious that nothing should stand in the way of their wool trade with Flanders. This trade was a great source of wealth to many English farmers who kept large flocks of sheep and sold their wool to the Flemish manufacturers.

2. Beginning of Hundred Years' War.—Not content with fighting the battles of the Flemings, Edward claimed the crown of France. He said his mother, Isabella, had a better claim to the throne than Philip VI., as she belonged to an elder branch of the French royal family. This claim was worthless, for by French law no person could succeed to the throne through a woman. Edward knew this but he was anxious to win fame and gain territory in France. The English nobles and knights, who were fond of military displays and feats of arms, encouraged Edward in his claims, as it gave them a chance to win renown. It was a sad war for the French peasants and labourers, whose fields and homes were destroyed and burned without mercy by the gay lords and knights. It was also a bad thing for England whose men and money were wasted on a war that could never bring any good to her people.

3. First Campaign.—The war began in 1338, and the first campaign ended in 1347. In 1340, the English won a famous naval victory at Sluys, off the Flemish coast, when thirty thousand French were lost. In 1346, a still more important battle was fought at Crecy, in the north of France. Several things make this battle noteworthy. At it Edward, Prince of Wales (called the Black Prince, on account of the colour of his armour), by his daring and skill, won his knightly spurs—although only a lad of sixteen years of age. At it, too, the English archers proved that they were more than a match for mounted knights clad in heavy armour. Gunpowder is said to have been first used in this battle. Next came the siege of Calais which lasted nearly a year. When the town was taken in 1347, Edward was so angry at the resistance the inhabitants made that he would have hanged six of the chief citizens who offered themselves with halters around their neck, as a sacrifice for the people, had not Queen Philippa begged their lives, and Edward, to please her, spared them. The French inhabitants were, however, turned out of the city, and English people put in their place, so that the city remained English until retaken by the French in 1558.

4. **Second Campaign.**—The war began again in 1355. Philip was dead, and John II. was King of France. The Black Prince now led the English, and once more the English archers showed their skill and prowess by defeating a large army, composed of the flower of French chivalry, at the battle of Poitiers in 1356. The English had but 12,000 men to the French 60,000 ; but the Black Prince drew up his men at the end of a narrow lane among the vineyards, and posted his archers so that they could shoot down the French as they came on. Sad havoc was made in the ranks of the knight who fell from their horses, and, cumbered with their armour, could offer but little resistance. King John was taken prisoner and carried to London where he died. To nobles and knights mercy and courtesy were shown ; to the poor peasants there came nothing but the ravages and cruelties of a rude soldiery. At last the peace of Bretigny was made in 1360, and Edward gave up his claim to the French crown, keeping, however, Aquitaine, Poitou, Gascony, and Calais.

5. **Third Campaign.**—What was gained in the second campaign was lost in the third. The Black Prince foolishly plunged into a war in Spain, and the French king, Charles V., took advantage of it to recover his lost territory. Charles would not come to open battle, but harassed the English in every possible way. The Black Prince was ill, and this made him irritable and cruel, so that people turned from him. Finally, he had to return to England, and then the English gradually lost ground until all Edward's gains were gone except Calais, Bordeaux, and Bayonne. So ended Edward's attempt to win a French kingdom.

6. **Rise of the People.**—There were, however, some good results of this foolish and costly war. The barons and knights spent a great

deal of money abroad, and much of this money was obtained by leasing their lands for long terms of years. The rent paid was called *feorm:* hence the name of *farm* given to the land thus leased. They also allowed their villeins or serfs to buy their freedom. The king himself raised money by selling to his serfs their freedom.

In this reign an important change took place in the industries of the country. Edward brought over weavers from Flanders, who taught the people to weave their own wool into cloth, instead of sending it abroad to be woven by others and then brought back again to be worn. Trade grew with Normandy, Flanders, and Gascony, in fish and timber, wool and wine, and salt, respectively. Gold coins also came into use, the first being used in 1344. Parliament now began to meet in two separate chambers; the knights and burgesses in one, and the bishops and barons in the other.

7. Statute of Labourers.—In 1348, a great calamity came upon England. This was a dreadful plague, known as the "Black Death," which swept over Europe from the East, and which, it is estimated, destroyed one-half the population of England. The people died so fast that it was difficult for the living to bury the dead. One effect of the plague was that there were not enough people left to till the soil and harvest the crops. Labourers were now in great demand, and, naturally, they asked for higher wages. But the owners of the land made the laws, and they passed the "Statute of Labourers," by which wages were not to be increased. The labourers tried to escape from places where wages were low to where they were high, so it was enacted that a labourer should not leave his own parish. If he did, he was liable to be branded with the letter F *(fugitive)* on his forehead. If a labourer was found unemployed, any land owner could make him work for him. These unjust laws made the people very unhappy and discontented.

8. Chaucer, Langland, and Wiclif.—We see this by the writings of a great poet, Geoffrey Chaucer, who lived at this time. Also in the poem, *The Vision of Piers' Plowman*, by Langland, who wrote for the people, we find this discontent voiced in very plain and bitter words. At this time, too, lived John Wiclif a great religious reformer. Wiclif was a learned clergyman who seeing how the priests neglected their duties wrote against their greed and hypocrisy. He translated the Bible into English, and sent out "poor priests" to teach the people. His followers were accused of making the people discontented with their condition by pointing out how harshly they were treated.

9. **Statute of Kilkenny—1367.**—Besides the "Statute of Labourers," many other important measures were passed in this reign. It was enacted that the Pope should not give livings in England to foreigners; that the people should not take questions of law to foreign courts for a decision; and that the English language instead of the French should be used in the courts of law.

Ireland, which was only partly conquered, was treated cruelly and unjustly. In 1367, the Statute of Kilkenny was passed. Its purpose was to prevent the English in Ireland from becoming Irish in language, dress, and customs, and from intermarrying with the Irish. In those days a price was set on an Irishman's head, just as if he were a wolf or a bear. But these laws had very little effect, for most of the descendants of the English that went to Ireland adopted the Irish ways and customs.

10. **Last Days of Edward III.**—As Edward grew old, his mind gave way, and he passed under the influence of bad advisers and unworthy favourites. Queen Phillipa was dead, and a bold wicked woman, Alice Perrers, gained great control over him. The Black Prince was dying, and this left the chief power in the hands of Edward's third son, John of Gaunt, or Ghent, Duke of Lancaster. His government was not a good one; so, in 1376, Parliament met, and the Commons for the first time *impeached* the king's ministers; that is, had them tried before the House of Lords, who acted as judges. The ministers were removed and Alice Perrers was driven away from the poor old king, but they soon came back again. The Black Prince, who would have governed well had he lived, died in 1376. He left a young son, Richard, a lad of ten years of age, as heir to his grandfather's throne. In 1377, Parliament under the guidance of John of Gaunt, put a poll-tax on the people, that is, a tax of so much a head on every person in the land, over a certain age. Shortly afterwards Edward died (1377) and left his grandson Richard to succeed him.

11. **Richard II.**—Richard, the son of the Black Prince, came to

the throne when eleven years of age. A council was appointed to help him to rule; and although not on the council, the king's uncle, John of Gaunt, had great influence. The oppressive poll-tax was again placed on the people, and was made so heavy that great discontent spread among them. Wiclif's followers, the "Lollards," went through the country and helped to make the labourers, villeins, and smaller farmers, more and more restless.

12. Peasant Revolt, 1381.—When a people are in a dissatisfied mood it takes but little to make them do acts of violence. So when a tax collector insulted the daughter of a tiler, her father killed the ruffian. This was a signal for a general rising in Yorkshire, Kent, Essex, and other counties. Wat Tyler headed the men of Kent, and John Ball, one of Wiclif's priests, preached to the angry multitude at Blackheath, asking them the question:

'When Adam delved, and Eve span,
Who then was the gentleman?"

Under Jack Straw, a thatcher, came the men of Essex, armed with scythes, clubs, and other rude weapons. The mob moved on to London, opened the doors of the prison, and burnt and destroyed many buildings. No one among the nobles and ministers seemed to know how to treat these misguided people. The king alone, although a mere lad of sixteen years, kept cool and undismayed. He rode out to meet one body of the rioters, and asked them what they wanted. They asked to be freed from the hated poll-tax, to have the market dues taken off, to be allowed to pay rent instead of working for their lords, and to have the villeins set free. When the king promised to do these things, the people, glad at heart, went home. But while Richard was treating with these men, another body broke into the Tower and murdered the Archbishop of Canterbury and the Treasurer; while a third body remained under Tyler in London. Richard went out to Tyler's men and sought to quiet them. Tyler placed his hand on the rein of the king's horse, and Walworth, Mayor of London, struck him and killed him. The mob would have killed the king and Walworth had not Richard cried out: "I am your Captain, follow me." The king then led the way, and the crowd followed him quietly outside London. He gave the people written promises to remedy their wrongs, and then they went home. But these promises were never carried out, for the nobles and land owners collected their men, and went through the country putting many to death. Richard's charters, Parliament said, were no good, and the cruel laws against the poor labourers and villeins were once more put in force. It looked as if nothing had been gained by this rising; nevertheless, shortly after this time the laws were made less severe, and the villeins gradually were given their freedom.

13. **Power of Parliament.**—The first half of Richard's reign was full of the intrigues of the king's uncles, of whom there were five living, and of the nobles and bishops who made up the king's council. John of Gaunt for awhile had the most influence; but after the Peasant Revolt which showed the people's dislike of him, he withdrew to Spain for a time. Then another uncle, the Duke of Gloucester, was the chief man. Parliament had much power and could refuse to grant money until grievances were redressed; but it had no power to appoint the king's advisers. Besides, Parliament was much under the control of great nobles, and was often moved by a spirit of faction. In 1387, a Council of Eleven was appointed to look after the king's affairs, and this made Richard very angry. He was not yet strong enough to throw off the yoke of his uncles and rule alone, and had to look on and see some of his dearest friends put to death by his council. He, however, bided his time.

14. **Richard's Rule.**—Not long after this, in 1389, Richard suddenly announced that he himself would rule in the future, and his council, taken by surprise, gave the reins into his hands. For eight years he ruled well, and many good laws were passed. In 1393, it was enacted that all persons bringing bulls or sentences of excommunication from the Pope into England should lose their property. Richard also visited Ireland, and did something to bring order and good government into that unhappy country.

Well had it been for Richard if he had thus continued to rule wisely. But, in 1397, he began to take his revenge on his uncles and their friends for their treatment of him years before. Gloucester was sent to Calais and was there murdered, while others were either put to death or imprisoned. Now that the chief men were removed, Richard made Parliament do as he wished, and for a time he was an absolute king. He was very fond of dress and show, and wasted the public money by his foolish extravagance. Some good things he did, but they were done by his own will, and without the people's consent. For that reason they began to hate him.

15. Richard's Fall, 1399.—But the end was near. Among those who had been spared by Richard was his cousin, Henry Bolingbroke, the son of John of Gaunt. Bolingbroke quarrelled with the Duke of Norfolk, and Richard, instead of allowing them to settle the quarrel by a public combat or trial by battle, banished them both ; Norfolk for life, and Bolingbroke for six years. The next year old John of Gaunt died, and Richard seized his estates, which rightfully belonged to his son Henry. Then Richard, fearing no harm, went to Ireland. While he was absent, Bolingbroke landed in Yorkshire to recover his father's estates. He was soon joined by great nobles like the Percies of Northumberland, and when, a little later, Richard returned, he found his kingdom was gone from him. Deserted by the people, Richard fell into the hands of Henry and had to resign his crown. The next day Henry was chosen king by Parliament. Of Richard's end we know nothing with certainty, but his body was shown to the people a year later, and it is supposed he was murdered in one of the prisons by order of Henry.

CHAPTER XI

THE HOUSE OF LANCASTER.

1. Henry IV.—Henry, son of John of Gaunt, was the first king of the House of Lancaster, so-called from the duchy of Lancaster which he held through his father. Henry's title to the crown was a parliamentary one, for the Earl of March, a grandson of the Duke of Clarence, Edward III.'s second son, had a better claim by birth. Parliament, however, still claimed the right to say who should rule, although it was fast becoming the custom for the eldest son to succeed his father on the throne.

The early years of Henry's reign were full of plots and rebellions. The great nobles, who made Henry king, were not very obedient, and if Henry displeased them, they took up arms against him. First there was a plot to restore Richard, and then Owen Glendower rebelled in Wales. While Henry IV. with the aid of his brave son Henry, Prince of Wales, was trying to subdue Glendower, the two Percies (the Duke of Northumberland and his fiery son, Harry Hotspur), angered because the king had not treated them well in the matter of some prisoners, taken from the Scotch, joined the Scots and Glendower against him. A great battle was fought at Shrewsbury, in 1403, in which the king defeated his enemies, and Harry Hotspur was killed. Two years later, Northumberland was killed in battle. Glendower, too, was subdued by the Prince of Wales, and peace once more came to England.

2. **Important Measures.**—Henry knew that he could not depend on his nobles, and therefore tried to keep on good terms with his parliaments, and with the church. This led to some very important measures being passed. So much money had been spent on the French wars, that the people were now unwilling to give large grants, and Parliament took advantage of the weakness of the king's hold on the throne, to make him do much as they wished. They also forced the House of Lords to give them the sole right to make grants of money to the crown.

This was a step in advance. Not so, however, were the cruel laws against heresy passed to please the church and the great landowners. The church feared the teaching of the Lollards, and the landowners blamed them for stirring up the peasants and villeins to revolt. Both church and landowners were afraid of the people rising and taking away their property. So, in 1401, a law was passed that any one continuing a heretic after due warning should be burnt alive. In February of that year, William Sawtre, a rector of Norfolk, was taken to the stake, and there gave up his life for his belief.

3. **Henry IV.**—Henry's reign was a short one. He died in 1413, and was succeeded by his eldest son, Henry, Prince of Wales. He had other sons, all able men, the ablest being John, Duke of Bedford.

Henry V. was but twenty-five when he came to the throne, and had already earned the reputation of a great general. He is also said to have been notorious for his wild and reckless doings. Once, we are told, he was sent to prison by Judge Gascoigne, because he behaved insolently to the judge in court. Whatever faults he may have had as a prince, we know that he was on the whole a good king, and much loved by his people. He was too fond of war, and he persecuted the Lollards; these were his chief faults. But he was exceedingly brave, true to his word, and put the good of his people foremost in all his acts.

One very important change he permitted Parliament to make. Henceforth the petitions of the Commons to the king were not to be altered by him before he gave his assent to them. After a petition or *bill* had received the king's assent, it became a *statute* or law.

4. State of the People.—There was but one feeble plot against Henry, so strong was he in the good-will of his people. The nation had recovered somewhat from the Black Death, which again visited it in 1407. Serfs and labourers were gradually gaining their freedom, and the yeoman could now pay rent for his farm instead of giving labour to his lord. That the condition of the labouring class had greatly improved is shown by the laws against extravagance in dress. Trade with other countries was extending, and this led to an increase in shipbuilding. The coal trade of Newcastle was growing, and many merchants were becoming rich.

Against this bright side of the picture we must place the restlessness among the people, the blame of which the Church and the nobles put upon the Lollards. The result was that Henry put in force the laws against heresy, and, among others, Sir John Oldcastle, a leading Lollard, was hanged in chains and burnt.

5. The French War Renewed.—To keep his nobles quiet, and to call away the attention of the people from their grievances, Henry renewed the war with France. There was no good reason for attacking France; but Henry loved war, and his nobles loved plunder. The King of France was insane, and his unhappy country was torn by strife among the great French nobles. The opportunity to recover the lost territory was too good to be neglected, so Henry revived Edward III's claim to the French crown.

In August, 1415, Henry landed in Normandy and laid siege to

Harfleur. It was a terrible siege, and the English lost many men through sickness in the army. Having taken Harfleur, Henry marched toward Calais, and in Oct. 1415, on the plains of Agincourt, with nine thousand men he defeated sixty thousand Frenchmen. It was the battle of Crecy over again; the English archers overthrowing with dreadful slaughter the French knights and nobles. More than one hundred princes and nobles were slain, and eleven thousand men were left dead or dying on the field.

Henry's army was strong enough to win a victory, but not strong enough to conquer and hold the country. So Henry returned to England, and after two years spent in preparation, once more invaded France. He now conquered Normandy, and took Rouen after a siege of six months, in which many women and children died through starvation. Everything at this time favored Henry's designs. The Duke of Burgundy, a French prince who ruled over a large territory, was treacherously murdered by some friends of Charles VI., the French king; and his followers and subjects, in revenge, joined Henry. It was not possible for the French to hold out any longer, and by the Treaty of Troyes, in 1420, Henry married Catharine, the daughter of Charles, and was appointed Regent of France. On the death of Charles, Henry was to become king.

Henry now returned to England full of honors, and his people were proud of his victories. But he did not live long to enjoy his conquests, for in 1422, at the early age of thirty-four, he died, leaving a young son, Henry, only ten months old, to succeed him.

6. Henry VI.—John, Duke of Bedford, was left as guardian of his baby nephew, and was also appointed Regent of France and Protector of England. He was a brave man, and an able general and ruler. He did his work well, and continued his brother's conquests in France. The Duke of Gloucester, Bedford's brother, was left to rule in England, while Bedford was fighting in France. Gloucester quarrelled at home with his uncle Beaufort, the chancellor, and abroad with the Duke of Burgundy, England's best and strongest ally. Bedford, with much difficulty, managed to keep for a time Burgundy on England's side, but after Bedford's death, in 1433, he returned to his allegiance to the French king.

7. Jeanne Darc.—We must now tell the story of the romantic rescue of France through the efforts of a poor village girl. All France, north of the Loire, was in the hands of the English, and Bedford was closely besieging Orleans. The French people were nearly hopeless, and it seemed but a matter of a few days when Orleans must yield, and with its surrender all hope of saving France from complete conquest would vanish. In a little village in Lorraine lived a young girl of eighteen, Jeanne Darc, the daughter of a labourer. She was very ignorant, and knowing little of courts and camps, but pure and pious. She saw the misery of the land and was filled with a great pity for her country. In visions, she seemed to be told to go to Charles, the son of the French king, and to offer to crown him at Rheims. Her parents and friends tried to prevent her from going; but her "voices" left her no choice. Guided by a knight, she made her way to the French camp, and told Charles her mission. It was his last hope and he gave her her way. Clad in white armour, and mounted astride of her horse like a man, with the French banner waving over her, she led the rude French soldiery to the relief of Orleans, now on the point of surrendering. The effect was magical. Once more hope burned in the hearts of the French; and the English soldiers looked on in surprise and awe while Jeanne led her troops through their ranks, and entered Orleans. Soon the siege was raised. The English thought her a witch, who put fear in the hearts of their soldiers; while the French hailed her as a messenger from God come to deliver them from their enemies. Jeanne led her soldiers from victory to victory, until her mission was accomplished, and Charles was crowned at Rheims. Then she asked permission to go home; her "voices" had left her, and her work was done. But Charles would not let her go; he feared his soldiers would not fight well under any other leader. Some of the French generals were jealous of her, and at the siege of Compiégne, in 1430, let her fall into the hands of the English. Charles made no effort to save her, and she was taken to Rouen, where she was tried for witchcraft. Condemned in 1431 to be burnt alive, her courage and faith never forsook her. Her last word at the stake, while the flames raged fiercely around her, was "Jesus." Her name yet lives green in the memory of the French people.

8. End of Hundred Years' War.—The war lasted some time

after Jeanne's death, but the English steadily lost ground. Bedford died, and Burgundy went over to the side of Charles VII. Year after year saw new conquests by the French until, in 1453, the war came to an end, and of all Henry V's possessions in France nothing remained to the English but Calais.

9. Weak Rule of Henry VI.—Henry was a feeble king; kind, merciful, and generous; but so weak in intellect that he was wholly unfitted to rule. In the early years of his reign England was distracted by the quarrels of his uncles, of whom Gloucester was the most mischievous and troublesome. Parliament, too, had not so much power as in the days of the Plantagenets, and the right to vote for members was now taken away from many people. Unseemly quarrels often broke out in Parliament; so much so that the members of one Parliament brought cudgels up their sleeves. Later on, when Henry began to rule for himself, he was much influenced by his wife, Margaret of Anjou, a strong-minded woman, who loved power and brought her foreign friends with her. The people cared little who ruled so long as their money was not wasted. This, however, Henry's friends did, and the heavy taxes caused a rebellion.

10. Jack Cade's Rebellion, 1450.—The men of Kent, always among the first to resist, led by Jack Cade, and aided by the men of Surrey and Sussex, came down in large numbers to London, and demanded that their grievances should be righted. We hear nothing of serfdom, or of wages, in their complaints, and this shows what a change for the better had taken place since the days of Wat Tyler. Cade's followers asked for free elections, for a change in the king's advisers, and that the king's foreign favourites should be sent out of England. The rising was soon at an end, and Jack Cade was killed shortly afterwards.

11. Wars of the Roses.—People began now to look to Richard, Duke of York, to right the affairs of the country. Richard was descended on his mother's side from Lionel, Duke of Clarence, second son of Edward III., and on his father's side from Edward, Duke of York, fourth son of the same king. He thus had as good a claim to the crown as Henry VI. When Henry, in 1454, became insane, Richard was made Protector. Henry, however, partially recovered, and then he drove the Duke away from his court. This was too much for York to endure, and he took up arms, claiming the crown as his by right of birth. Then followed a dreadful struggle, which lasted for many years. It is known in history as the Wars of the Roses, because the Lancastrians wore a *red* rose, while the Yorkists chose a *white* rose. Battle followed battle, sometimes one side being victorous, and sometimes the other. Margaret had to do battle for the rights of her son and husband, for Henry was often insane and always feeble and helpless. In 1454, at St. Albans, the queen's party was defeated by York; and he was again victorious, in 1460, at Northampton. But at a great battle at Wakefield, in December 1460, the Duke of York was killed, and Margaret, in mockery of his claims, had his head, decked with a paper crown, placed on the walls of York city. Then Edward, son of the Duke of York, took up his father's cause. At Mortimer's Cross, in 1461, he defeated the Earl of Pembroke, and marching down to London, was made king. In the same year the rival forces once more met, this time on Towton Field. In this bloody battle 20,000 Lancastrians, and nearly as many Yorkists, were killed, but victory rested with **Edward IV.** Henry and Margaret found a refuge in Scotland, and for a time Edward reigned undisturbed.

CHAPTER XI.

THE HOUSE OF YORK.

1. The Wars of the Roses, Continued.—The Wars of the Roses were not yet over. For ten years more the wretched struggle went on. In 1463, Margaret, aided by the French and the Scotch, sought to recover the throne for her husband and son, but was defeated at Hedgely Moor and Hexham. Then, in despair, she fled with her son to Flanders, and Henry VI. fell into the hands of Edward IV., who treated him kindly. Perhaps this would have ended the war had not Edward displeased his most powerful supporter, the Earl of Warwick, by marrying Elizabeth Woodville, the beautiful widow of Sir John Grey. Warwick wished

Edward to marry a French princess, or a daughter of his own. He was angry, also, because Edward began to give good positions to his wife's relations. On the other hand, Warwick's daughter married the Duke of Clarence, Edward's brother, and this displeased Edward.

About this time a rising took place against Edward, which led to the battle of Edgecote (1469), in which many Yorkists were killed. Edward blamed Warwick and proclaimed him a traitor. Warwick thought it wise to leave the country, and he went to France where he met Margaret. Then an agreement was entered into that Margaret's son, Edward, should marry Warwick's daughter, Anne, and that Warwick should aid in placing Henry VI. once more on the throne.

Warwick and Margaret now returned to England, and Edward IV., finding himself unable to withstand them, fled to Flanders. Henry VI. was taken out of the Tower and once more became king. For six months he reigned supported by Warwick the "Kingmaker," then Edward got help from his brother-in-law the Duke of Burgundy, and came back to recover his crown. He met Warwick at Barnet, and defeated and killed him. Then Margaret rallied her friends for the final struggle. At Tewkesbury, in Gloucestershire, she was totally defeated, and her son, Edward, was stabbed on the battlefield by Richard, Duke of Gloucester, Edward IV's. brother. This battle was fought in 1471, and two weeks later the old king, Henry, died in the Tower, murdered it is thought by the command of Edward IV.

2. **The New Monarchy.**—And now England for a time had peace, and order was restored in the land. Edward was a handsome man, a good general, and a strong ruler; but he was selfish, cruel, and licentious. His base passions brought shame to many an English household. He loved power, and the people were so well pleased to have a strong government which could keep order, that they let him do much as he liked. Most of the nobles had been killed in the Wars of the Roses, for the war was carried on almost entirely by rival nobles and their personal followers or retainers. The farmers, tradesmen, and merchants had taken no part in the struggle, and went on their way as usual. Nevertheless, the almost constant fighting did much harm to the industries of the

country, and so all classes were glad to have peace restored. This Edward knew, and took advantage of it to demand money from merchants and rich people. This money was at first willingly paid as a "benevolence" or gift, but when the demands became frequent the people began to complain. They, however, could do nothing, as they were without leaders now that most of the nobles were killed, and Edward called his Parliament together only once in eight years. By means of "benevolences" and a pension from France in consideration of not invading that country, together with an income granted early in his reign, Edward could do without parliaments, and so rule absolutely. This way of ruling was a new thing in England, and it continued through several reigns. To distinguish it from the rule of the Plantagenets and the House of Lancaster it is known as the "New Monarchy."

3. Caxton.—Edward's love of power and his fear of treason led him to do many cruel things. He had his brother Clarence impeached and put to death. Clarence was fond of Malmsey wine, and Edward, in mockery of his taste, had him drowned in a butt of his favorite beverage.

It is pleasant to turn away from these quarrels between the King and his nobles, to Edward's encouragement of William Caxton, the first English printer. Caxton was a native of Kent, who had gone to Flanders in his youth, where he learned the art of printing. In 1476 he came back to England with the first printing press, and opened a little shop near Westminster, where he advertised that he would do printing "right chepe." Edward, Gloucester, and many nobles patronized him. He printed service books for the clergy, and histories of chivalry for the knights. The first book printed (1477) was the *Dictes and Sayings of the Philosophers*. He not only printed books but translated them from foreign languages. Books before his time were very dear and little read, for new copies had all to be written out by hand. Henceforth many could afford to buy books, and this helped to spread education among the people.

4. **Edward V.**—Edward IV., worn out by his vices, died in 1483, and at once a struggle for power began between the queen and her friends on the one hand, and Richard, Duke of Gloucester, and his followers on the other. Richard said that Edward, Prince of Wales, and Richard, Duke of York, the sons of Edward, were not

legitimate, because their father had been betrothed to another woman before he married their mother, Elizabeth Woodville. But before he put forward his own claim he seized young Edward, and after a short time placed him in the palace in the Tower. Richard was appointed Protector, and the queen and her second son took refuge in the sanctuary at Westminster. Richard forced the queen to give up the Duke of York, and he was placed in the Tower with his brother. Then Richard suddenly turned on his former friend, Lord Hastings, and charging him in the Council with plotting against him, called in his men, who hurried Hastings out and beheaded him on a log of timber near at hand. A few days later Richard caused himself to be proclaimed King, on the ground that Edward V. and his brother were illegitimate.

5. **Richard III.**—Richard began his reign with the execution of Earl Rivers and Sir Richard Grey, uncle and half-brother of Edward V. This he followed up with the murder of his nephews in the Tower. It was said that he caused them to be smothered, while sleeping, with pillows. Richard III. was a brave man, a great warrior, and in some respects a good king. His enemies described him as deformed and repulsive, and called him the "Hunchback." His deformity consisted in one shoulder being somewhat higher than the other, and in one arm being partially shrunken. He had a thoughtful, delicate countenance, with good manners and tastes. If one half the stories told about him are true, he must have been very cruel. We must, however, remember that these tales are told by the enemies of his family.

Richard tried to rule well, passing a law against "benevolences," protecting commerce, and summoning parliaments. Nevertheless he was hated for his murder of his nephews, and his own peace of mind had departed with the cruel deed. Soon plots began to be formed against him, and the Duke of Buckingham, for taking part in one of them, was beheaded. Richard continued to rule till 1485, when Henry Tudor, Duke of Richmond, a descendant of John of Gaunt, on his mother's side, and Owen Tudor, a Welsh gentleman on his father's side, landed at Milford Haven in Pembrokeshire, and claimed the crown. His title was a very weak one, but the Lancastrians joined him, and so did the Welsh, also many of Richard's most powerful subjects. Richard hastened to meet him, and the opposing armies met on Bosworth Field When the battle began, Lord Stanley and Earl Percy deserted Richard, who, brave to the last, rushed into the thickest of the fight, eager to exchange blows with his rival. He was soon stricken down, and died on the field. His crown was found in a hawthorn bush, and placed by Stanley on Henry's head.

With the Battle of Bosworth Field, in 1485, ended the Wars of the Roses. With it, too, began the famous line of kings and queens known as the House of Tudor. Henry VII., soon after his coronation, married Elizabeth, daughter of Edward IV., and although the marriage was not a happy one, it united in the reigning family the claims of both the Lancastrians and Yorkists, and so helped to bring peace to the distracted nation.

6. **End of Mediæval History.**—With the reign of Henry VII., we pass into modern history. A great change now began to come over the people of Europe. Their knowledge of the earth was greatly increased by the discovery of America by Columbus, and by the many voyages to the new world that followed. Navigators made their way to India by sailing round the Cape of Good Hope. The knowledge of other planets was now extended by great scientific discoveries; and men's minds were aroused by the study of Greek literature, the "New Learning," brought to Italy from Constantinople by exiles from that city. The printing press was doing its work in making books cheap and thus spreading knowledge. But with all these changes for the better there was also the growth of the power of kingship. Nearly all the nobles had been killed in the Wars of the Roses, and the middle and lower classes had not yet learned to fight their own political battles. Gunpowder had come into use, and as the king had nearly all the cannon, he could batter down the strong walls of the castles of the nobles, and so keep them in subjection. So for several reigns we shall find that there was very little control over the king.

CHAPTER XII.

HOUSE OF TUDOR.—THE REFORMATION.

1. **Henry VII.**—The first king of the House of Tudor was a cautious, intelligent man, with little love for anything or anybody but himself. In France he had studied the methods of foreign kings in ruling without parliaments, and when he became king of England he tried to get as much power as he could. He saw that the best way to do this was to lessen the power and influence of the few nobles left after the Wars of the Roses, and to gather as much money as possible, so that he could do without parliaments. To break down the power of the nobles, he had a law passed against *liveries* and *maintenance*; that is, a law forbidding nobles to keep more than a certain number of men in *livery* or *uniform* He knew that these men would, if occasion arose, take up arms against the king in the interests of their lords. The law was strictly put in force; and Henry went so far as to have his friend, the Earl of Oxford, fined £10,000, because when Henry visited him, Oxford, to do the King honor when he left his castle, drew up in line a large number of men in livery. Henry had a court formed of some of the leading men in his Privy Council, to punish powerful offenders for breaches of the law. The ordinary courts did not dare to put the law in force against great nobles, who with their retainers, overawed judges and juries. This new court was called the "Court of the Star Chamber," because it met in a room whose ceiling had star-like decorations. For a time it did good service in punishing men for such offences as maintenance, forgery, and breach of the peace. It however, became a very tyrannical body, and took away from the ordinary courts many of their rightful duties.

Henry also revived Edward IV.'s practice of raising money by "benevolences" or forced gifts. Cardinal Morton was the chief instrument he used for this purpose. If a man made a great show of wealth, the Cardinal told him he certainly must be able to give a rich gift to the king. On the other hand, if he lived in a poor house, and kept few servants, he was told that since he lived so frugally he must be hoarding money, and therefore was well able

HOUSE OF TUDOR.— THE REFORMATION. 61

to grant the king a goodly sum. This artifice was known as "Morton's fork," for if a man escaped one tine of the fork, he would certainly be caught on the other. Henry also took advantage of the confusion due to the civil wars, and of the defects in titles of property, to seize the estates of landowners, or else make them pay heavily to keep them. By such means and by forcing the French king to pay him a large sum to withdraw his troops from Boulogne, Henry gathered so much wealth that when he died he left nearly £2,000,000 in his treasury.

2. Lambert Simnel and Perkin Warbeck.—Although Henry had married Elizabeth of York in the hope of satisfying the Yorkists, there were still many who were dissatisfied with his rule. Henry had taken the precaution to put in the Tower the Earl of Warwick, the son of the Duke of Clarence, Edward IV's brother. This, however, did not prevent an impostor, Lambert Simnel, from coming forward as the Earl of Warwick, and claiming the throne. He found many Yorkists ready to support him, but in a battle at Stoke, Simnel was defeated, and being taken prisoner was made a scullion in the King's kitchen.

A more serious rebellion arose when Perkin Warbeck, a native of Tournay, claimed the crown as Richard, Duke of York, second son of Edward IV. The Yorkists said this boy had escaped when his brother Edward V. was murdered in the Tower. A great many believed that Warbeck was the Duke of York. The kings of France and Scotland acknowledged his claim; the latter, James IV., going so far as to give him in marriage his cousin, the beautiful Catharine Gordon, the "White Rose of Scotland." James, also, helped him to invade England in 1496; but the invasion failed, and Perkin went to Ireland. Thence he made another attempt to get a footing in England, this time in Cornwall. His courage, however, failed as Henry's army approached, and he tried to escape. He was taken prisoner, put in the Tower, and a few years later, with Warwick, was executed.

3. Foreign Alliances.—Henry saw that the kings of France, Aragon, and other nations had much power over their subjects, and he sought to secure their support by making alliances with them. His elder daughter, Margaret, he gave in marriage to James IV. of Scotland, to keep that country from molesting his northern frontier.

Then to secure the friendship of Ferdinand, the crafty king of Aragon, he arranged that his elder son, Arthur, should marry Katharine, Ferdinand's daughter. Arthur died a few months after the marriage, and then, Henry and Ferdinand, not to lose the benefit of the alliance, got the Pope's consent to Katharine marrying Henry, Arthur's brother, a lad six years younger than his bride.

4. Other Important Events of Henry VII's reign:—In this reign an important law affecting Ireland was passed. This was Poyning's Act (1497) which said that English laws should have force in Ireland, and that the Irish Parliament should not make any new law without the consent of the King's Council. We must remember that only a small portion of Ireland along the Eastern coast, called the "Pale," was much under the control of the English at this time. The greater portion of Ireland was still unconquered, and was ruled by Irish chieftains.

In this reign, too, Columbus discovered America (1492); and the Cabots, John and Sebastian, sailed from Bristol and discovered Newfoundland and Labrador. About the same time Vasco de Gama, a Portuguese, made the first voyage to India from Europe around the Cape of Good Hope.

Not less important than these discoveries was the learning brought to Italy, and thence to England, by the Greeks who fled from Constantinople when that city was taken by the Turks in 1453. English students went to Italy to study Greek literature, and returning introduced the study of Greek into the great English Universities, Oxford and Cambridge. The New Testament was now read in Greek, whereas formerly it was read in Latin only. Among the great scholars of this time who loved this "New Learning" were Colet, Erasmus, and Sir Thomas More.

5. Henry VIII.—Henry VII. died in 1509, and was succeeded by his only surviving son, Henry, a young man of eighteen years of age. Besides Henry there were two daughters, Margaret, married to James IV. of Scotland, and Mary, who married, first, Louis XII., the aged king of France, and after his death, the Duke of Suffolk. The descendants of these princesses were to play an important part in English history.

Henry VIII. was a handsome youth, fond of pleasure and out-door sports, and frank and hearty in his manner. He was well-educated and an excellent musician; but withal, vain, self-willed, and extravagant. His selfishness grew with his years until all the good qualities of his youth were lost. Nevertheless, outside of his own court, the people loved him and "Bluff King Hal" was to the very last popular in England. Henry's first acts as king were for the good of the country. He encouraged ship-building, established dock-yards, and punished the miserable instruments of his father's exactions.

6. **Foreign Wars.**—Henry loved display and flattery, and he longed to play a great part in European politics. At that time France and Spain were the most powerful nations in Europe, and a keen rivalry existed between them. Henry was anxious to hold the balance of power, and much of his reign is taken up with the intrigues of the French and Spanish kings to win his favour. Almost at the beginning of the reign, he joined Spain and Germany in a war to defend the Pope against France. He accomplished nothing, however, beyond wasting the treasure his father had so carefully stored up for him.

A more successful war was carried on against Scotland, whose king, James IV., to help his ally, the King of France, attacked England in 1513. He was met at Flodden Field by the Earl of Surrey, and, with many of his nobles and knights, killed. This was not the only war with Scotland in this reign, for in 1542, James V. the nephew of Henry, attacked England; but like his father, he met with a disastrous defeat.

7. **Wolsey.**—During many years Henry was much guided by Thomas Wolsey. Wolsey had risen step by step by humoring the king and falling in with his pleasures till he became Chancellor, or chief law officer, Archbishop of York, papal legate, and a Cardinal of the Church. He was a man of great ability and shrewdness, strongly attached to Henry, and desirous of making him all-powerful; but at the same time vain, proud, and fond of money and show. Wolsey was a friend of the "New Learning" and showed his interest in education by founding a college at Oxford. He, however, tried to rule without parliaments, and to fill the king's treasury by fines and forced loans. Wolsey himself grew

rich and built great palaces, Whitehall and Hampton Court, with money given by the king.

In his dealings with the courts of Spain and France, Wolsey sought to gratify his own ambition. At this time Charles V., Emperor of Germany and King of Spain, was the strongest ruler in Europe. He was the nephew of Henry's queen, Katharine, and Wolsey hoped through his influence to become Pope. For this reason, he for a time kept Henry on the side of Charles in his contests with Francis I. of France, for the chief power in Europe. Wolsey, however, was not appointed Pope, and then he encouraged Henry to make friends with Francis against Charles. This displeased the English people, for Charles was the ruler of Flanders, and they did not want their trade with that country injured.

58. Fall of Wolsey.—In the meantime, Henry, who had been married eighteen years, grew tired of Katharine and wanted to marry Anne Boleyn, a young and beautiful maid of honour at the court. Henry pretended to think he had done wrong in marrying his brother's widow, and found in this an explanation why all his children had died in infancy except the Princess Mary. He now asked the Pope to grant him a divorce from Katharine, and expected his request would be granted, as he had written in defence of the Roman Catholic religion against the German reformer, Luther, and had received from the Pope the title, "Defender of the Faith," a title still borne by the monarchs of England. The Pope sent Cardinal Campeggio to England to inquire into the matter, and he tried to persuade Katharine to go into a nunnery. This Katharine would not do, but stood firm for her own rights and those of her child. Wolsey and Campeggio heard Katharine's plea for justice and mercy, but came to no decision. The case was left in the hands of the Pope, who called upon Henry to go to Rome, and there have the case decided. Henry knew what the decision would be and he refused to go to Rome. Wolsey was known to favour a marriage between the King and a French princess, and Anne Boleyn found no difficulty in persuading Henry that the reason why the divorce was not granted was his hostility. Seeing Henry's change of feeling, Wolsey made haste to win his favour by giving him his palaces and by retiring to York. Sir Thomas More now became Chancellor. But Wolsey's enemies were active, and induced Henry to have him arrested for high treason, because he had broken a law made in the reign of Edward III. and Richard II., against bringing any foreign authority into the realm. This Wolsey had done by acting as papal legate, and by holding a court for the Pope in England. Broken-hearted at the loss of the King's favour, Wolsey began his journey to London. When he reached Leicester he was so ill that he had to take shelter in the Abbey there. "Had I served my God as diligently as I have served the King," he said to the lieutenant of the Tower, "He would not have given me over in my gray hairs." His sickness was unto death, and the man who had served the king so faithfully, and loved him so truly, only escaped the penalty of treason by dying Nov. 30th, 1530.

9. **Act of Supremacy.**—Henry found a new and able minister in Thomas Cromwell, one of Wolsey's retainers. He advised the King to make himself Head of the Church, and then procure a divorce from his own courts. At first Henry did not like to act on this advice, but when he found that it was the only way by which he could marry Anne Boleyn, he determined to carry out Cromwell's suggestion. Parliament was called in 1529, and because it was willing to do the king's bidding it lasted for seven years. During its existence many important laws were passed, mostly at the command of Cromwell and Henry.

Henry's first step in throwing off the Pope's authority over the English Church was to force the clergy to acknowledge him "Head of the Church," by threatening them with the loss of their goods and lives for having recognized the authority of Wolsey as papal legate. The clergy agreed to this with the limitation, "so far as the laws of Christ permit." Then Parliament passed three laws, one of which forbade the clergy from sending "first fruits" to Rome; a second, forbade the taking of appeals to Rome; and the third, called the "Act of Supremacy," made Henry "Head of the Church." The latter Act was passed in 1534.

Before this, however, in 1533, Cranmer, who had been made Archbishop of Canterbury, granted in the council of bishops the coveted divorce, and Henry immediately married Anne Boleyn. In the same year Anne's daughter, Elizabeth, was born. Parliament, to please Henry, declared the Princess Mary illegitimate, and settled the succession on Anne's children.

10. Cromwell's Rule.—Cromwell and Cranmer were now Henry's chief advisers. Cromwell was a stern man, and had been employed by Wolsey to suppress some of the smaller monasteries on account of the evil lives of their inmates. Now that he was the king's minister he bent all his energies to make him an absolute ruler in both Church and State. Parliament was forced to pass the most infamous laws. One of these forbade people accused of treason the right to be heard in their own defence. Cromwell himself was the first to suffer under this wicked law. He also employed spies to let him know what the people were doing and saying; and by telling the king tales of plots against his life, made him cruel and unjust. None were too good, or too high in rank, to escape Cromwell's vengeance, if he thought by taking their lives the king's power would be increased. He had an Act passed by which any man might be called upon to take an oath that he believed the divorce was right and valid. Among those who were asked to take the oath was Sir Thomas More, the king's Chancellor, and at one time the king's trusted favourite. More was a great and pure-minded man, perhaps the greatest in his day, and had written a book called "Utopia" in which he advocated many reforms, for which the labouring men of England had to wait centuries. Now when asked to swear that he believed that the divorce was right and to accept the Supremacy he refused. He was sent to the Tower, and later on, with Bishop Fisher, was beheaded. He died as he had lived, bravely and cheerfully.

11. State of the People.—These were sad days for the poor of England, and for those who could not make their consciences bend to the king's tyranny. Much land had gone out of cultivation, as landowners had found it more profitable to raise sheep than to till the soil. Landowners, too, were enclosing the *common land*, and thus taking away from the poor one means of making a livelihood. The retainers of the nobles were now cast adrift, and, with other men out of work, took to robbing and plundering. As the punishment for theft and robbery was death, many criminals, to escape detection, murdered their victims.

The minds of the people were unsettled by the religious changes going on in Europe. Martin Luther, a German priest, had begun to write and preach against some of the practices and doctrines of the Roman Catholic Church. He soon had many followers in Germany. The movement spread rapidly, and the *Protestants* (as they were called in 1529) became numerous in Switzerland, Germany, Scotland, France, and other countries. In England they were few in number, until Henry broke away from the Pope; after that many began to follow Luther's teachings. Henry himself did not believe all that Luther taught: he still clung to many of the beliefs of the Roman Catholic Church. With the help of Cranmer and others he drew up the ten Articles of Belief for the English Church which were accepted by the Convocation of the clergy. He also allowed the Bible to be translated into English and read in the churches. Both Cromwell and Cranmer were prepared to go much further than Henry in making religious changes. The monasteries had much wealth, and some of the monks in the smaller ones were ignorant and licentious. Cromwell and the King made this an excuse for destroying many of the monasteries, and for seizing their lands and money. Henry gave away much of this spoil to his nobles and favourites: the rest he put in his own treasury. One effect of this spoliation was that now there were no places where the poor could be fed and sheltered, or nursed when sick. Another was the arousing of a strong feeling of discontent in the north and west, where the adherents of the Roman Catholic faith were very numerous. A rebellion, known as "The Pilgrimage of Grace," broke out to restore the old religion and to get rid of Cromwell. Henry promised to remove their grievances, and the rebellion came to an end; but after the rebels had gone home, troops were sent among them, and their leaders were put to death.

12. **Death of Cromwell.**—Meanwhile, a sad fate had befallen Anne Boleyn. The crown she so eagerly coveted was not long in her possession. Gay, frivolous, fond of pleasure and admiration, her levity excited Henry's jealousy. At last, in 1536, he accused her of unfaithfulness, and had her executed. The next day, Henry married Jane Seymour, a young lady at court. It was now the turn of Princess Elizabeth, the daughter of Anne Boleyn, to be declared illegitimate by Parliament.

Jane Seymour died in 1537, leaving an infant son, Edward. She had been a Protestant, and her brother, the Earl of Hertford, was also a Protestant. He soon became the leader of the *Protestant* party at court, while the Duke of Norfolk and his son, Earl Surrey, were at the head of the *Roman Catholic* party. Cromwell, to strengthen the Protestant cause, made a match between Henry and the Princess Anne of Cleves, a German Protestant. In this way he hoped to bring the Protestant States of Germany into a closer alliance with England. Anne was very awkward and homely, and Henry, as soon as he saw her, took a strong dislike to her. In a few months he had put her away by a divorce, and had made Cromwell feel the fierceness of his disappointment and anger. Cromwell had so many enemies in the King's council, that he knew his fate was sealed when the King deserted him. Charged with treason, he flung his cap on the ground, exclaiming, "This, then, is the guerdon for the services I have done." He was at once attainted, and without being given a chance of making a defence, was hurried to the block.

13. Last Days of Henry.—Twice more was Henry married. His fifth wife was a beautiful girl, Catharine Howard, niece of the Duke of Norfolk. In a little while she was shown to have been unchaste before her marriage, and, like Anne Boleyn, she was beheaded. Then he married Katharine Parr, a widow, who by her tact managed to outlive him.

Meantime, a great change had come over Henry since his accession. The joyous, frank, handsome young king, had become cold, selfish, suspicious, and cruel. His very form had changed; he was now coarse, unwieldy, and disfigured by a grossness that was repulsive and disgusting. His temper was so uncertain, and he changed his views so often, that his subjects seldom knew what they were expected to do or believe. When the Duke of Norfolk was in his favor, laws were passed against Protestants; and when Cromwell and Cranmer guided him, laws were passed against Roman Catholics. So we find in this reign men and women executed, some because they did not believe Henry's Protestant opinions, others because they were opposed to the Roman Catholic creed, part of which Henry retained in his laws. Towards the close of his reign the Earl of Hertford, Jane Seymour's brother, had great influence, and he induced the king to put Norfolk's son, the accomplished Surrey, to death. Norfolk himself was sent to the Tower and would have lost his head, had not Henry, to the **great relief** of his court, died in 1547.

Parliament had given Henry great power, and among other things allowed him to name in his will who should succeed him. He seemed to have repented of his unjust treatment of the Princesses Mary and Elizabeth, for while leaving the crown to his son Edward, he named Mary as Edward's successor in case he died without heirs; while Elizabeth in turn was to follow Mary. In case all of Henry's children died without heirs, then the descendants of Henry's younger sister Mary were to succeed. Thus we see that the Scotch descendants of Margaret, the elder sister, were left out of the line of succession.

CHAPTER XIII.

RELIGIOUS STRUGGLES.

1. **Edward VI.**—Edward was a delicate boy of ten years of age when his father left him the crown. He was unusually bright and clever, and had been carefully educated. His mother and his mother's family were Protestants, and Edward himself had been trained under Protestant tutors; so it is not surprising that he was a very strong believer in the Protestant religion. He is said to have been self-willed, like his father, although he seems to have been also very conscientious.

Henry had left a Council of Regency to assist Edward in governing, the chief members of which were the king's uncle, Edward Seymour, Duke of Somerset, and Cranmer, Archbishop of Canterbury. Somerset soon persuaded Edward to make him Protector, and this gave him great power. Somerset was a well-meaning man, who pitied the sad condition of the people; but at the same time was too anxious to force the Protestant religion on the nation, and too much in haste to grow rich at the public expense.

Almost the first thing done in this reign was to make changes in the form of worship, and as far as possible in the belief of the people. Images were removed from the churches, mass was abolished, and the Church Service read in English, instead of in Latin. The fierce laws of Henry IV. and V. against the Lollards were repealed, so also were the laws of Henry VIII. against Protestants. Priests were allowed to marry, churches were despoiled of their lands to satisfy the greed of the nobles, and Acts of Uniformity were passed to force everybody to accept the new form of worship. Most important of all was the drawing up of the "Book of Common Prayer," (much of which was a translation from the older Latin services) which stated how the people were to worship. Articles of Religion were also set forth to guide the teaching of the clergy. With a few slight changes the doctrines and ritual of the English Church of to-day are the same as those prescribed in the days of Cranmer and Edward VI.

2. **Popular Discontent.**—These changes were made before the people were prepared to receive them. In London and some of the large towns there were many Protestants; but, in the country districts, while many did not wish to have the Pope interfere in the affairs of England, the people wished the Church services and other parts of religion to remain unchanged. So Somerset and Cranmer in their zeal made the people dissatisfied, and this discontent was increased by the laws allowing landowners to take the common lands from the poor, and by the want of employment due to changes (already explained) in the method of farming, To these causes must be added the greed for plunder and for Church lands of Somerset and his friends. Somerset began to build a great palace in London, and to make room for it had to pull down churches and houses. The money for this mansion was really taken from the people. Then, we find that in Henry VIII.'s reign the practice was begun of debasing the public coin, that is, more base metal was put into the silver coin than should be there. By this means the poor were cheated out of their earnings, and the public treasury was filled at their expense. All these evils led to risings in different parts of the country, the most serious of which was one under Ket, a tanner, in Norfolk. With 20,000 men, Ket defeated the King's troops, and asked for a removal of the evils from which the people suffered. Somerset felt for the oppressed and did not like to use harsh means against the rebels; and so it fell to Lord Warwick to crush the rebellion by hired troops from Germany. Somerset's weakness and his love of power led to his downfall. Warwick was ambitious, and he induced the Council to force Somerset to resign the Protectorship. But Warwick was afraid that Somerset might recover his lost authority, and

three years later had him charged with treason and executed. The throng that looked on at his death showed their sympathy with the fallen and well meaning Protector by dipping their handkerchiefs in his blood, as that of a martyr.

Warwick now became Protector, and like Somerset he favoured the Protestants. Gardiner and Bonner, two bishops who were opposed to further religious change, were imprisoned, and Ponet and Ridley, two Protestants, were appointed in their places. Roman Catholics were persecuted because they would not attend the new form of public worship, although we do not hear of any being put to death.

3. **Last Days of Edward VI.**—There is, however, one bright spot in the dark picture of this time. A great interest was beginning to be felt in education. In this reign eighteen grammar schools were founded, and the Blue Coat School was started by Edward himself in 1553, for orphans and foundlings.

Edward's reign lasted only six years. Always a delicate lad, his friends saw that as the years passed consumption had seized him, and that his reign would soon be over. Warwick, (now Duke of Northumberland), and Cranmer, dreaded the successsion of Mary, Edward's sister. Mary was so strict a Roman Catholic that she had been kept under watch for some time in Hertfordshire. With Mary on the throne, the Roman Catholic religion would be restored, and Northumberland's power would be gone. To prevent this, Northumberland persuaded Edward to leave the crown to Lady Jane Grey, the granddaughter of Mary, Henry VIII.'s sister. Lady Jane, although only a girl of sixteen, had been married to Guildford Dudley, Northumberland's son, a short time before, and as she was a strong Protestant, Northumberland hoped through her to continue to rule. In July of 1553 Edward died.

4. **Mary.**—Immediately on Edward's death Northumberland and his friends offered the crown to Lady Jane Grey, who accepted it very reluctantly. Steps were taken to seize Mary, but, warned by secret friends, she escaped to the Duke of Norfolk. The people were much displeased at the plot to put Mary aside, and joined her in great numbers. Soon she was strong enough to move on to London, where she received a hearty welcome. So strong was the feeling in her favour, that Northumberland, who had gone to Cambridge, thought it prudent to throw up his cap for her. This

pretence of loyalty deceived no one, and Northumberland was arrested and put to death for treason. Lady Jane Grey and her husband were thrown into prison, there to await Mary's decision. Cranmer who had consented to the plot against Mary was also imprisoned.

Mary was now Queen, with the consent of nearly all her subjects. For many years her life had been a bitter one. Her mother had been divorced and she herself disgraced by Act of Parliament. She had been kept under constant watch during Edward's reign, because it was known that she loved her mother's people, the Spaniards, and her mother's religion. She thus, true to her Spanish nature, came to hate her mother's enemies, and the enemies of her mother's faith. The bitterness due to ill-treatment was aggravated by ill-health, neglect, and a temper naturally harsh. At her accession she was thirty-seven years of age, small of feature and stature, with dark eyes full of fire, and a harsh man-like voice. Like all the Tudors, she was brave and self-willed to a fault.

5. Wyat's Rebellion.—Her first acts were to restore the Roman Catholic religion and form of worship, and throw into prison the Protestant bishops. She released Gardiner and Bonner, and made the first her Chancellor, and the second, Bishop of London. Most of the people were pleased to have the old form of worship restored, but not so anxious to have the Pope's authority over England brought back. However, she induced Parliament to allow Cardinal Pole, her cousin, to go to Westminster where, in the name of the Pope, he pardoned the nation through its representatives in Parliament, for its heresies in the two previous reigns. Parliament was willing to accept the Pope's pardon; but, when a demand was made for a restoration of Church property, the members, many of whom had been enriched out of its spoils, promptly declared they would not give up the Church lands held by them. Mary herself did what she could to restore the property taken from the Church by the Crown.

Mary was anxious to strengthen the Roman Catholic cause in England by the aid of Spain. Partly because she had this end in view, and partly because she loved her cousin Philip, son of Charles V., and now king of Spain, she listened eagerly to a proposal to marry him. When it was rumoured that Mary was going to marry the king of Spain, great alarm was felt by the people. Some were afraid of the Spanish Inquisition, which under Philip was doing terrible work in Flanders, while others were afraid that England, thus brought so close to Spain, would lose her independence, Spain being at that time the greatest nation in the world. Risings took place in many counties, and the men of Kent, under the brave soldier and accomplished scholar, Sir Thomas Wyat, marched down to seize London, and to put Elizabeth, Mary's sister, on the throne. So strong was the feeling in favour of Wyat, that Mary was urged to escape. Instead of that, however, she rode forth and called upon the people of London to rally round their queen, promising not to marry without her Parliament's consent. Her courage aroused her subjects, and when Wyat, worn out with travel and fatigue, reached Temple Bar, London's gate, he found it closed and London guarded by a large force. His followers were scattered, and with many others he was taken prisoner and executed.

Mary now thought it unsafe to allow Lady Jane Grey to live. On the 12th Feb., 1554, Lady Jane sat at her window and saw the bleeding body of her husband brought back from the scaffold, and then calmly went forth to the executioner's block. Elizabeth, it is said, had a narrow escape, her life being spared through the influence of Gardiner and Philip of Spain. She was, however, closely watched all through Mary's reign.

The rebellion being ended and the rebels punished, Mary married Philip. The marriage was not a happy one. Philip remained in England a year hoping to have a son, but was disappointed. He was also annoyed because Parliament under Gardiner's guidance would not allow him to take the title of king, nor would it allow England to take any part in Spanish wars. So Philip left England and did not return till 1557. His coldness grieved Mary and made her still more bitter towards her enemies.

6. **Persecution of the Protestants.**—Mary, in her mistaken zeal for her religion, now began to put to death those who did not believe as she did. Rowland Taylor, an aged and much loved vicar, was sent to the stake amid the tears of his parishioners. Then came in rapid succession, Rogers, a canon ; Hooper, a bishop ; Latimer, the bold, outspoken preacher of righteousness ; and Ridley, a gentle and devout man. Latimer and Ridley were burned at Oxford, tied

back to back to the same stake. "Play the man, Master Ridley," said Latimer, "we shall this day light such a candle in England as by the grace of God shall never be put out." Then came the most noted of all the victims, Cranmer, the Archbishop of Canterbury. Cranmer had taken a leading part in all the changes in religion made in the reigns of Henry VIII. and Edward VI., and he had also been party to the plan to put Lady Jane Grey on the throne. He was now called to answer for his deeds, and to save his life, recanted. Then finding his life was not to be given him, he recanted back again. Taken to the stake at Oxford, he thrust his right hand first into the flames, because that hand had basely signed his recantation. Nearly three hundred people it is said perished in three years for religion's sake, most of the burnings taking place at Smithfield, near London. Bishop Bonner of London got most of the blame; but Mary and Gardiner, Mary most of all, deserve the odium attached to these cruelties.

7. Loss of Calais.—The people were becoming horror-stricken at these burnings, and many fled to Geneva for safety. Mary's health was rapidly failing, and as her disease grew, so did her wrath and bitterness. Her husband visited her in 1557, to get her aid in a war against France, and Mary foolishly consented to join him. England was in no condition to go to war, her treasury was empty, her people discontented, and her army and navy a wreck. What was looked upon then as a great national disaster and disgrace befell the country. Calais, the last possession of England in France, was surrounded by French troops, and Mary, too intent on punishing heretics, failed to send it relief. In 1558 it surrendered, and England lost the last remnant of her conquests in France. Mary, like a true Englishwoman, felt the loss keenly, and in the same year died, worn out by sorrow and disease.

CHAPTER XIV.

THE WISE RULE OF ELIZABETH.

1. **Elizabeth.**—When Mary died, her sister Elizabeth became queen. At this time she was twenty-five years of age, tall and queenly in figure, with fair hair and blue eyes. As a queen she had few faults; as a woman she had many. In her council, surrounded by wise and careful advisers, she weighed everything before acting, and as events proved, seldom made a mistake. The good of her subjects was ever before her, and by her tact, caution, and skill in diplomacy, she kept the country out of war and gave it a chance to become rich and great. She was not content to have England at peace with foreign nations: she also sought to unite the various warring sections of her people and to restore peace and order throughout the nation. How she succeeded events will show. As a woman, she was vain, frivolous, fond of flattery and the attention of handsome courtiers. Frugal, even stingy, in all else, she spent large sums of money on dress and finery, leaving, it is said, three thousand dresses in her wardrobe. Her greatest fault was her habit of using deceit and falsehood to bewilder and overreach her enemies. This she did because, as she said, she was "a weak woman" with many powerful foes at home and abroad. Her education had been well looked after; for, not only was she an excellent horsewoman, dancer, shot, and musician, but she was well read in Greek, Latin, and French, and could converse in Italian and Spanish. She was the friend of the great writers who lived in her day, and at her court they found a hearty welcome.

2. **Elizabeth's early difficulties.**—When Elizabeth began her reign she found her people discontented, her treasury empty, her army and navy weak, and she had powerful enemies in the persons of Philip II. of Spain, and the King of France. To add to her difficulties, Mary, the daughter of James V. of Scotland, and granddaughter of Margaret, Henry VIII's elder sister, claimed the crown of England, on the plea that Elizabeth was illegitimate. Mary was married to the Dauphin of France, and Scotland in her absence was ruled by her mother, Mary of Guise, who acted as Regent. French troops had been brought into Scotland to help

the Regent against the "Lords of the Congregation," or Protestant nobles, who were now becoming very powerful, and were much under the influence of John Knox and Earl Murray, Mary's half-brother.

At this time great struggles were going on in Europe between Roman Catholics and Protestants. Philip II. of Spain was the most powerful ruler in Europe, and he was, with great cruelty, trying to crush out a rebellion in the Low Countries for political and religious freedom. In France a fierce struggle was going on between the Huguenots, or French Protestants, and the French king. So when Elizabeth became queen, the eyes of all Europe were upon her to see whether she would be a Protestant or a Roman Catholic.

At first she would not take the side of either religious party. The Protestants hoped she would be their friend, knowing the religious belief of Anne Boleyn, her mother; while the Roman Catholics were encouraged by her apparent hesitation. Her first task was to free England and herself from the control of Spain. She made peace with France. Philip, who wished to marry her, and the Pope, who tried to get her to espouse his cause, were put off with excuses. At length, when Parliament met, it was ordered that the Prayer-Book of Edward VI, with some slight changes, should be restored to the Churches, and that the clergy should recognize the Royal Supremacy of Elizabeth. Roman Catholics and people of other creeds were not to be molested, provided they attended the service of the English Church. If any refused to attend they were made to pay a heavy fine.

The Bishops for the most part refused to take the oath of supremacy, and were, therefore, removed from their offices and moderate Protestants put in their places. Elizabeth did not like the extreme Protestants, and she chose for her chief adviser in Church affairs Matthew Parker, Archbishop of Canterbury, a man of the same moderate views as her own. In the beginning of her reign, the Roman Catholics were more than half of the population, and Elizabeth had to be very careful, knowing that many of her subjects looked to Mary, Queen of Scots, who was a strong Roman Catholic, as the rightful queen.

3. **Elizabeth and Scotland.**—To offset Mary's influence in

England, Elizabeth aided the Protestant nobles, or "Lords of the Congregation," in Scotland in their struggle with Mary of Guise, who sought to crush out Protestantism. Lord Grey with 8,000 men was sent to help the Scotch against a French force, which the Regent had brought over, and which was now besieged in Leith. While the siege was going on, Mary of Guise died, and the French promised to leave the kingdom. The Scotch Lords also agreed that Elizabeth should be recognized as the queen of England, but Mary, the Scotch queen, would not be bound by this agreement. Shortly after this her husband, Francis II. of France, died, and she returned to rule over her own kingdom. She was warmly welcomed by Protestants and Roman Catholics alike, and her youth, beauty, and winning ways made her a general favourite. Her most powerful subjects and her Parliament were the followers of John Calvin of Geneva, a great Protestant teacher, and Mary did not attempt to force her own religious opinions on her people.

4. **England's Prosperity.**—Elizabeth's enemies abroad, France and Spain, owing to their jealousy of each other, left her at peace until they could settle their own quarrels. In the meantime the nation prospered greatly. Elizabeth's economy filled the public treasury, and the order and good government she gave the nation encouraged the people to make improvements in tilling the soil, and to engage in trade and commerce. Manufactures increased rapidly, and new industries were introduced through the many people that came to England to escape from the wars and religious persecutions in Flanders and France. Cloth-weaving was greatly improved by the Flemings, while later on, through the French, came a greater skill in silk manufactures. Raw gold and silver were brought from America, gold dust and ivory from Africa, and silks and cottons from the East. Increase of trade caused an increase in shipping, and Elizabeth encouraged her subjects to build ships for adventures in the far east, west, and north. Frobisher discovered the straits of Hudson's Bay, Sir Humphrey Gilbert tried to colonize Newfoundland, Hawkins opened up a traffic in slaves with the coast of Africa, and Sir Francis Drake, a famous sea-captain, sailed round the world in a little vessel, bringing home a great treasure, which he obtained by plundering Spanish settlements in America. So great was the increase of wealth among all classes

of the people that many things now considered necessaries, but which then were luxuries, came into general use. Carpets on the floors, abundance of glass in the windows, pillows for the head, chimneys instead of holes in the roof, now became common. Money was spent freely by the gay lords and ladies on fine dresses, jewels, feasts, revels, and pageants. Money was so easily got that it was recklessly spent. Even the poor gained under Elizabeth's rule. An earnest effort was now made to lessen the pauperism that had so long existed. A law was passed making it necessary for each parish to provide for its own poor, and power was given to the parish to levy taxes for that purpose. Work-houses and poor-houses were to be built, where work, food, and shelter could be given to the needy, aged, and helpless. It was not, however, until near the end of Elizabeth's reign that the "Poor Laws" were completed.

5. Religious Discord.—While the country was thus growing in wealth, it unfortunately was not at peace in religious affairs. There were two kinds of people that were not satisfied with the way Elizabeth tried to govern the Church. The Roman Catholics could not take the Oath of Supremacy, and they were forbidden by the Pope to go to the English Church services. On the other hand there was a growing body that thought the English Church was too near the Roman Catholic Church in its form of worship and church government, and that wished to bring the English Church closer to the Churches in Germany and Switzerland. These were the *Puritans*, who wanted, they said, a *purer* form of worship. Elizabeth cared little what people believed so long as they all attended the same Church services. She wished to have one law in the Church for all classes of her subjects, just as there was but one law in the State. So Parliament passed an Act in 1563, that no person could hold an office, or be a member of Parliament, unless he would obey the Queen, and deny that the Pope had any authority in England.

6. Mary, Queen of Scots.—We saw that when Mary returned to Scotland she received a hearty welcome from her people. She was but nineteen at that time, and so beautiful, fascinating, and clever, that few people, even the sternest, could resist her charms. She had not been long in Scotland before she began to plot against Elizabeth for the English throne. Her subjects were ready to aid her; so was Philip of Spain; and so were some of Elizabeth's subjects.

Mary was Elizabeth's heir, and this made Elizabeth's friends anxious. They were afraid that some fanatic would murder Elizabeth to give Mary the crown. So they frequently urged Elizabeth to marry and give them an heir to the throne. She would refuse until sorely pressed by her Parliament, and then would promise to choose a husband. But she never married although she had many lovers and suitors, who, for a time, were encouraged and then quietly rejected. Why she did not marry we do not know. Some think she desired to marry Robert Dudley, Earl of Leicester, who was for many years her favourite. She knew that if she married a Protestant she would displease her Roman Catholic subjects, whereas if she married a Roman Catholic she would anger her Protestant subjects. So she remained a "Virgin Queen" and found in the love and devotion of her people a partial recompense for the lack of husband and children.

The anxiety of Elizabeth's subjects was increased when Mary married, in 1565, Lord Darnley her cousin. Darnley, like Mary, was descended from Margaret, Henry VIII's sister, and his family were Roman Catholics. By this marriage Mary strengthened her claim on the throne of England, and had she now acted with prudence, Elizabeth might have been driven from the throne, or else compelled to recognize Mary as her successor. But Mary, with all her cleverness, could not control her passions, and by giving way to them she lost not only all chance of becoming queen of England, but also caused herself to be driven into exile. She soon tired of her young husband, who was a foolish youth, and wanted to become king, and by his jealousies and follies gave Mary much annoyance. She had an Italian secretary, David Rizzio, with whom she was so intimate that Darnley grew jealous. Aided by a band of rough Scotch lords he broke into Mary's chamber at Holyrood when she was supping with Rizzio. Rizzio was dragged out and stabbed to death, and his body flung down a staircase near Mary's chamber. Mary tried to save him but was held back by Darnley while the murder took place. After a time she pretended to forgive her husband, and three months after the murder, her son, James, was born. Not long after this event, Darnley being ill, Mary had him removed to an old building, Kirk-O'-Field, not far from Holyrood, for quiet and rest. One night when Mary was attending a dance given to her servants in Holyrood, an explosion took place at Kirk-O'-Field, and the next morning Darnley and his page were found dead in an adjoining field. The house had been blown up with gunpowder, and although Darnley and the page had escaped from the house, they had been overtaken and murdered. No one knew whether Mary had planned the deed or not; but the servants of the Earl of Bothwell, a bold, profligate noble, were seen near the scene of the tragedy that evening, and a short time after Mary allowed herself to be carried off by Bothwell to one of his castles and there married to him.

The people of Scotland were horrified at the murder and the marriage, and at once her lords rose against her. She was taken prisoner, and forced to give up her crown to her son. A year later she escaped from Loch Leven Castle, and gathered an army, but she was defeated at Langside, in 1568, by Earl Murray. With difficulty Mary escaped into England when she claimed the protection and aid of Elizabeth.

7. Mary in England.—What to do with Mary was more than Elizabeth could decide. Mary asked to be restored to her throne, and failing that, to be allowed to go to her mother's people in France. The Scotch demanded that she should be sent back to be tried for the murder of her husband. Elizabeth knew that it was unsafe to allow her to go to France, and she was unwilling to hand her over to her Scotch subjects, as that would look like encouraging rebellion. So she kept Mary a prisoner in England refusing either to send her back or bring her to trial. For eighteen years was she thus kept until the numerous plots formed against Elizabeth's life, in the interest of Mary, made it necessary that something should be done. For Mary had not been long in England before the Duke of Norfolk wished to marry her and put her on the throne. This plot was found out in time and Norfolk was warned and sent to the Tower. Then a rebellion broke out in the north, which was put down at the cost of many lives. Then the Pope excommunicated Elizabeth and released her subjects from their allegiance to her. Parliament answered this by making strict laws against the Roman Catholics; and then another plot was formed to murder Elizabeth, to marry Mary to Norfolk, and through the aid of Spain to make

Mary queen. But Elizabeth had vigilant friends in her council, and this plot becoming known Norfolk was executed. So it went on for many years till, in 1587, Anthony Babington entered into a correspondence with Mary to kill Elizabeth, and make Mary queen. The letters passed through the hands of Walsingham, the Secretary of State, and on the evidence he supplied, Mary was tried before a commission of peers and sentenced to death. Elizabeth, for a time, would not consent to sign the death warrant, although urged to do so by Parliament and her ministers. At last she signed it, and the sentence was at once carried out. Mary died protesting her innocence, but the people breathed easier because a great danger was removed.

8. The Spanish Armada.—Meanwhile Elizabeth had been able to keep England out of foreign wars. She was asked to aid the Netherlands against Spain, but refused to do so openly, for many of her subjects did not want to have their trade with the Low Countries stopped. Nevertheless thousands of Englishmen crossed over to the aid of the Netherlanders and fought in their battles against the Spaniards. Among those who left the English shores was Sir Philip Sidney, a brave and noble man, and an accomplished courtier, author, and soldier. He was killed at the Battle of Zutphen. The hatred borne the Spaniards at this time by the English was shown in many ways. There was no open war between England and Spain; nevertheless English ships were fitted out to plunder Spanish settlements in America, and seize their treasure ships returning from the rich mines of the New World. We have already mentioned how Drake returned from his voyage round the world laden with Spanish treasure. When he reached home Elizabeth visited his ship, made him a knight, and did not refuse to accept a large portion of his spoil. So it is not surprising that Philip of Spain was angry, and only waited till his hands were free to attack England. Meanwhile new expeditions were going out against Spanish America, and at last Elizabeth sent an army to the Low Countries to aid the Netherlanders. Philip was also angry because Elizabeth had put to death several priests who came to England from a college at Douay in France to minister to the English Roman Catholics and to persuade them not to attend the English Church services. These priests were accused of preaching disloyalty and stirring the people up to rebellion, and for this many of them were executed, as well as for their religion.

At length Philip's chance came to make the long deferred attack. Mary, Queen of Scots, was dead, and Philip was looked to as the proper person to avenge the wrongs of the Roman Catholics, and to take Elizabeth's place on the throne of England. In 1585 he began his preparations. A great fleet, an "Armada," was to be made ready, and was to take on board 30,000 veteran Spanish troops under the command of the Duke of Parma in the Netherlands. It was then to cross to England, and Philip hoped that when his army landed all the English Roman Catholics would join him. While the "Armada" was getting ready, Drake made a bold attack on Cadiz harbour and burnt many vessels. This he called "singeing the Spanish king's beard." Elizabeth was slow to believe that the attack would be really made, and was loath to give money enough to make her fleet and army effective. What she grudged to do, her subjects did at their own expense. Vessels were fitted out by private gentlemen and sent out to do battle for England's freedom. Lord Howard of Effingham was appointed chief Admiral, but he had by his side the great sea-captains, Drake, Hawkins, and Frobisher, who had fought many a successful battle against Spanish ships. At last, on the 12th July, 1588, the Armada, under the command of the Duke of Medina Sidonia, set sail. It consisted of one hundred and twenty-nine ships of great size, with thousands of soldiers and sailors on board. To oppose it was an English fleet of eighty small vessels, made up of a few of the Queen's ships and a number of privateers. Never was England in greater danger, and never were her people more true to their country and sovereign. Roman Catholics were as eager as Protestants to offer their aid and defend England's shores. The Queen's high courage did not fail her, and her appearance among her soldiers was all that was needed to give them hope and confidence. Beacon lights flamed from the English headlands to give news of the Armada's approach. At last the great crescent of huge ships was seen coming up the Channel, and the small English fleet sailed out to damage it as much as possible. They hung on its rear and flanks to cut off any ship that might be found separated from the main body. At night fire-ships were sent adrift into the Spanish fleet, and in the fear and confusion that followed several Spanish ships were captured and destroyed. The

Spaniards found that their vessels were so large and clumsy that their shot passed over the English ships, which could sail away or around them at pleasure. In despair the Armada began to retreat, pursued by its active and vengeful enemies. To add to their misfortunes a great storm arose which carried the Spanish vessels past Parma's army, and drove them far north. Rounding the Orkneys to return to Spain the vessels were dashed on the rocks, and the shores of the north of Scotland and Ireland were strewn with corpses. Some reached the shore alive only to be murdered by the savage inhabitants of the coast. Of all that great fleet only fifty-three vessels reached Spain. England was saved : the wind and the waves had fought her battles even more effectively than her sailors or soldiers. With the defeat of the Armada passed away the long dread of a great danger, and the nation's joy and relief found expression in the glorious literature that followed.

9. **Elizabethan Literature.**—Not since Chaucer had England a great poet, until Edmund Spenser wrote in this reign the "Faerie Queen." Other great writers followed : Sidney, Raleigh, Bacon, Hooker, and greatest of all, William Shakespeare, who born in 1564 began to write towards the close of this reign his wonderful plays and dramas. To these men, great in an age of great men, Elizabeth was a friend and counsellor. Such an era in literature the nation had not hitherto experienced, and it is doubtful if such another era has since come to the English people. The great events and the daring deeds and thoughts of the time seemed to demand a Spenser and a Shakespeare to give them voice. Nor must we forget the efforts made by Sir Walter Raleigh, at once courtier, author, soldier, and voyager, to colonize Virginia. Though the colony was a failure in his time, he brought back to Europe the potato as well as tobacco, both of which soon came into use. In this reign, too, voyages were undertaken to the northern seas and the East Indies, and Elizabeth gave in 1599 a charter to the East India Company, with the sole right of trading in that fabled land of untold riches.

10. **Ireland under Elizabeth.**—It is sad to turn away from this story of brave deeds and growing prosperity to England's treatment of Ireland. Henry VIII. had tried to make Ireland acknowledge England's laws and accept her religion, and by so doing had

given rise to a great bitterness among the Irish people. Edward VI. tried to force Protestantism on them and failed, as the Irish did not want any change in their religion. Then Mary came and restored the old religion, but began English settlements in two counties. When Elizabeth became queen, she followed her father's policy of making Ireland English. Soon there was a rebellion under Shan O'Neil, which was put down by Sir Henry Sidney in 1567. But the rebellion broke out again under Shan's son, Hugh, Earl of Tyrone, in 1595, when the Spaniards gave their aid. He defeated the English, and Essex, the darling of Elizabeth's old age, was sent against him. Essex made an unwise peace with him, and then returned to England for Elizabeth's approval. She was very angry at his folly and ordered him to keep his house for a time. Essex, in his vain pride, marched to London to seize the queen; but was arrested, tried, and executed. Lord Mountjoy, an able man, was sent in his place to Ireland, and succeeded in suppressing the revolt. In the next reign, as we shall find, large tracts of land were taken from the Irish in the north and given to Scotch and English settlers.

11. Death of Elizabeth.—But the end of this great reign was now near. Elizabeth, after the death of Essex, became despondent. She had lost much of the sympathy of her people, although in memory of her great services they bore with her frailties of temper and disposition to rule arbitrarily. Nevertheless she knew when to yield to her Parliament and people. One of her last and most gracious acts was to abolish "monopolies" on a number of articles of common use. The Parliament had grown in power during these years of peace and prosperity, and it only waited Elizabeth's death to begin again the struggle for its lost rights and privileges.

Elizabeth's end was a sad one. Dejected and wretched, for days she would take no food, nor speak to any one. To the last she refused to name her successor. Asked if James of Scotland, Mary's son, should succeed her, a slight motion of the head was all the sign of approval she gave. On the 24th March, 1603, England's great queen died.

CHAPTER XV.

CROWN AND PARLIAMENT.

1. James I.—Elizabeth was no sooner dead than Cecil, the minister of her old age, sent for James VI. of Scotland, the son of Mary Stuart, Queen of Scots, to be king of England. No one objected, and James came down from Scotland to London and was crowned on the sacred stone of Scone in Westminster. So the old prophecy was fulfilled, and a Scotch king reigned in England under the title of James I.

James was the first of the Stuart line, and, like all his race in England, was obstinate, self-willed, and filled with the notion that he ruled by "Divine Right"; that is, he believed he held the throne from God directly, and not from his Parliament and people. To this belief he added another, viz., that bishops were divinely appointed, and that the kingship was not secure unless the Church was governed by bishops. As he said, "No Bishop, no King." Perhaps he got this idea from the fact that when king in Scotland he had to endure a good many restraints and rebukes from the Presbyterian clergy of that nation. At any rate, as soon as he reached England he cast his lot in with the English Church and left the Presbyterian body to which he had formerly belonged.

James had a few good qualities and a great many bad ones. He was well educated, and had read much on church history and theology. He loved to show his learning, and to that end wrote pamphlets against smoking (which was becoming fashionable) and witchcraft, and in favor of the "Divine Right of Kings." He had a canny Scotch wit and humour, and said many shrewd and pithy things. Nevertheless, he was a foolish king: "the wisest fool in Christendom," as a French statesman called him. He was easily ruled by favourites, and his court was often the scene of drunkenness and low debauchery. James himself was given to gluttony and drunkenness, and as in dress he was slovenly, and in person awkward and ungainly, he made himself contemptible and ridiculous by his actions. The English people had been accustomed to dignified kings and queens, and the change from the queenly Elizabeth to the ricketty James did not tend to make them quietly submit to James' claim to rule "not by the common will but for the common weal.

2. State of the Nation.—At this time, too, the people had become so prosperous under Elizabeth's rule that they had recovered much of the old spirit of freedom which forced the Plantagenets to give Parliament the control of taxation. Elizabeth had felt this in the later years of her reign, and had unwillingly conceded many things to her Parliament. So, when James, with his awkward ways and foreign accent, began to dictate to his Parliament and people how they should be governed, they resented it, and soon made him understand that the English people did not want arbitrary rule.

The nation was in an unsettled condition owing to the different views held by the people on religious questions. The Puritans wanted changes made in the Church services, so as to bring them nearer the form of worship in Scotland and Geneva. They disliked making the sign of the cross in baptism, wearing a surplice, or giving a ring in the marriage service. They, also, were very strict about keeping Sunday, and about indulging in amusements. In questions of state they upheld the liberty of Parliament and the right of the people to make their own laws. Then there was the Church party which wished the Church to remain as Elizabeth had left it, and which was strongly in favour of giving the king a great deal of power. Lastly, there were the Roman Catholics, who wished to restore the Roman Catholic faith. They had been fiercely persecuted in Elizabeth's reign and now looked to James for relief, because his mother had been a strict Roman Catholic. The hope of the Puritans that he would make changes in the Church services to please them, was soon destroyed. James had been so sternly treated by the Scotch Presbyterians that he hated them and their ways; and as the Puritans in many respects were like the Presbyterians, he, at a Conference at Hampton Court, roundly abused them when they asked for changes, and said if they would not conform he would "harry them out of the land." The only good result of this conference was the decision to issue a revised translation of the Bible, which was done in 1611. This is the version still in use.

3. The Puritans begin to Emigrate.—Now that it was seen

that James was wedded to the Church as it stood, many Puritans determined to leave their native land and find a home where they could worship God as they pleased. Among others that left was a small congregation under the leadership of their pastor, John Robinson, and an Elder, William Brewster. It first went to Amsterdam and Leyden and then in 1620 came back to England, whence it took passage in a little vessel called the "Mayflower" for the shores of North America. This little band of 120 souls landed at Plymouth Rock in Massachusetts, and, after suffering great privations for many years, founded a flourishing colony, which was the beginning of the New England States.

4. **Gunpowder Plot.**—If the Puritans were disappointed in James, much more were the Roman Catholics. The relief that they expected did not come; on the other hand, Parliament made the laws more severe against them, and James began to banish their priests, and to fine them for not attending the English Church services. The result was that a few desperate men, headed by one Robert Catesby, formed a plot to blow up Parliament while it was being opened, kill the king and members of Parliament, and then seize one of the younger members of the royal family and place him on the throne. To carry out this plot gunpowder was stored in barrels in a vault or cellar under the House of Lords, and a man named Guy Fawkes was entrusted with the task of setting fire to it at the proper time. Fortunately one of the conspirators did not wish his brother-in-law, who was in Parliament, to be killed, and sent him a warning note not to attend. This led to inquiries being made, and a search taking place the evening before Parliament was to be opened, November 5th, 1605, Guy Fawkes was found concealed in the cellar, and the whole plot was exposed. The conspirators tried to escape, but most of them were seized and put to death. The result of this wicked and foolish plot was that the laws were made still more cruel and oppressive against Roman Catholics.

5. **Crown and Parliament.**—Very soon James began to disagree with his Parliaments." He insisted on his right to collect taxes and place duties on goods without consent of Parliament; and to please his favourites and put money in his treasury, he revived the monopolies which had been given up by Elizabeth. Nearly every

article of common use was made the subject of a "monopoly," and in this way the people had to pay for what they used far more than the things were worth. James' expenses were heavy, for he had to keep an army in Ireland. The people there were discontented and rebellious, because they had been driven out of their holdings in Ulster and their land given to English and Scotch settlers. Besides, James surrounded himself with profligate favourites who wasted his revenue. His first favourite was Robert Carr, a dissolute young Scotchman, who committed a grave crime and in consequence was disgraced. Then came George Villiers, afterwards known as the Duke of Buckingham, who by his beauty and fascinating manners soon became so powerful with James and his son Charles as to be able to influence them to do anything he wished. Villiers was looked upon as an insolent upstart by the great nobles; but he made the proudest and highest in the land seek his favour. All who wished to obtain anything from the king had to win over Buckingham by gifts and presents. In this way, the penniless adventurer, George Villiers, soon became the rich and powerful Buckingham. This man, with his extravagance and insolence, Parliament in vain sought to keep in check. James would not agree to give up his power of imposing taxes, and in 1614 dissolved Parliament because it would not grant him any money until he abandoned his unjust claims.

6. The Spanish Match.—For seven years after this James ruled without a Parliament, and, to keep his extravagant court supplied with money, he did a great many wicked and foolish things. He levied fines, forced loans, and benevolences, and made himself ridiculous by compelling people of small means to take titles or else pay a fine for refusing. He created a new title, that of "baronet," which he sold for £100. Buckingham also used the law courts to fill the treasury, and judges took presents from those who brought cases before them for settlement.

Meanwhile James sought to make friends with Spain, and to this end tried to bring about a match between his son Charles and the daughter of Philip III. This the English people did not want, for they hated the Spaniards and were afraid of having for a queen a Roman Catholic princess. James, however, prided himself on his statecraft and would not listen to the objections of his people. To please the Spanish court he did the most cruel and unjust act of his reign. At this time Sir Walter Raleigh was a prisoner in the Tower on a flimsy charge of treason committed in 1603. Thirteen years was he imprisoned, and, to while away his time, wrote his great work *The History of the World*. Tired of his long confinement, he told James he knew of a gold mine in Guiana, up the river Orinoco, and if he would give him his freedom he would go out and bring the king home a great treasure. James released him, but warned him he must not, at the peril of his life, attack any Spanish settlements. Raleigh set sail, and when he reached the mouth of the Orinoco, he sent an expedition up the river to search for the mine. His men did not find it, but got into a fight with some Spaniards, and Raleigh's son was killed. Raleigh had to return without the expected treasure, and when he reached England he was beheaded, 1618, to please the Spanish king, who complained of Raleigh's attack on one of his settlements.

James was willing to allow others besides Raleigh to suffer, to please Spain. In 1618, a great war broke out in Germany, and lasted thirty years. The Thirty Years' War was due to James' son-in-law, Frederick, the Elector of the Palatinate, accepting the crown of Bohemia, which was claimed by Ferdinand, Emperor of Germany. The war that followed soon became one between Protestants and Roman Catholics, and Spain gave her aid to the Catholic Ferdinand against the Protestant Frederick. Frederick was very unfortunate and lost not only Bohemia, but also his own Electorate on the Rhine. The English people would have gladly gone to war with Spain to restore him to his dominions; but James was so anxious to keep peace with Spain that he refused to give any aid. He thought he could get Spain to restore Frederick to his possessions by a policy of conciliation. Spain, however, would not interfere in his behalf, and it seemed as if the Spanish king was in no hurry to have the marriage take place. Impatient of delay, Charles and Buckingham went in disguise to the Spanish court, hoping that their presence would hasten the match. They had not been there long before Buckingham got into a quarrel, and Charles found that the Infanta did not like him. One excuse after another was made for delay, and although Charles was prepared to promise anything to obtain his end, the marriage was broken off because Spain would not interfere in the interests of Frederick.

6. The Parliament of 1621.—Before this had taken place, James had called his third Parliament to get supplies. Many famous men came up to this Parliament; among others, John Pym, John Hampden, Sir John Eliot, Sir Thomas Wentworth, and Coke and Seldon the famous lawyers. They at once began to complain of the fines, taxes, and monopolies with which the king and Buckingham had been oppressing the people. They also impeached Lord Bacon, the Lord Chancellor, for taking bribes from suitors. Bacon, who was the greatest thinker of his day, had just written a famous book—*The Novum Organum*—on the best way to study science. He acknowledged his guilt, and was fined and driven in disgrace from the bench. Parliament was very much in earnest, and made James give up the monopolies. Besides, it told the king he should break off the proposed match with the Spanish princess and give his aid to Frederick. James thought it impertinent to give him advice on foreign affairs, and when Parliament claimed the right to discuss anything of interest to the people, he tore the protestation out of the Journals of the House and dissolved it. It was about this time (1622) the first weekly newspaper appeared.

7. Close of James' Reign.—Hardly was Parliament dissolved when Charles and Buckingham came back from Spain. They were eager for war and forced James to call another Parliament to get the necessary supplies. A small sum was voted and then Parliament adjourned. Charles had now arranged to marry Henrietta Maria, the daughter of Henry IV. of France, and James was unwilling to call Parliament again because he knew the feeling against the heir to the throne marrying a Roman Catholic. So he did not wait for Parliament to give a larger grant, but sent 12,000 men under Count Mansfield to aid Frederick in the Palatinate. The expedition was a great failure, and most of the men died of disease brought on from want of proper food and clothing. This sad failure hastened the King's end, and he died of ague in 1625, leaving to his son Charles his throne, and a standing quarrel with his Parliament.

CHAPTER XVI.

THE CIVIL WAR.

1. Charles I.—Unlike his father, Charles was dignified and kingly in manner and appearance, with a grave, intelligent countenance, and a reserved but gracious manner. In his family, he was a faithful husband and an affectionate father. As a man, he was free from many of the vices of princes, and was sincerely attached to the English Church. But it did not take his Parliament and people long to find out that he was headstrong, obstinate, and insincere ; and, like his father, filled with the notion that he ruled by Divine Right. His great vice was falsehood ; he would make solemn promises to his parliaments when in a strait, and then break them as soon as he thought himself out of danger. So in spite of his kingly manners, and his good private life, he was a much worse king than James I.

2. Early Troubles.—Charles soon got into a quarrel with his Parliament, which disliked the influence Buckingham had over him. Charles asked his first Parliament for a large sum to carry on the war, but instead of giving him what he wanted, it granted him less than half, and besides refused to give him, for more than a year, a tax called "Tonnage and Poundage." It had been the custom to grant this tax (which was so much on every tun of beer and wine, and on every pound of certain other articles) to the king for life, and Charles was so angry at Parliament that he soon afterwards dissolved it, when it began to enquire into Buckingham's conduct.

Buckingham now thought he would make himself and the king popular by sending a fleet to Spain to attack Cadiz. The expedition was not well equipped, and when it reached Cadiz Bay, the men, who went on shore, got drunk and had to be taken back to their vessels in a helpless condition. The fleet then returned to England, after failing to take some Spanish treasure-ships expected from America. So this expedition, from which the king and Buckingham hoped so much, ended in leaving them heavily in debt, and forced Charles to call another Parliament in 1626.

When Charles' second Parliament met, Sir John Eliot, a noble patriot, who spoke words which stirred the hearts of his fellow members, moved to have Buckingham impeached for wasting the king's revenues. The Commons were proceeding with the impeachment when Charles, to save his favourite, once more dissolved Parliament.

3. **Forced Loans.**—Charles now tried to get money without asking his Parliament's consent. He had much need of it, for urged by Buckingham, he had begun a war against France in aid of the French Protestants of La Rochelle. So he began to levy tonnage and poundage, and to force people to lend him money although he had no intention of ever paying it back. In this way he collected a large sum, although many refused to pay and were punished in various ways. Some were fined and imprisoned, others were forced into the army and navy, or had soldiers billeted in their houses. In this way Buckingham got money enough to raise an army and fleet to go to La Rochelle, where the English were so badly defeated and suffered so heavy a loss that they had to return home.

4. **Petition of Right.**—Parliament now had to be summoned to get supplies, and when it met, it at once began to complain of the way the king had collected money and imprisoned those who had refused to pay his forced loans. Sir John Eliot was again the chief spokesman, and under his guidance Parliament drew up a "Petition of Right," in which they demanded of the king that no man should be asked for a loan without consent of Parliament; that no man should be sent to prison without cause being shown; that soldiers should not be billeted in private houses, and that martial law should cease. The king did not want to agree to this petition, but he was so much in need of money that he finally yielded. On June 7, 1628, the Petition of Right became law, and the people were so delighted that they rang the bells and lighted great bonfires. Parliament, too, granted Charles the money he wanted; but it did not cease its attack on Buckingham, who now began to prepare another expedition for La Rochelle. This disturber of the peace of the nation was, however, to trouble them no longer. When on the point of leaving Portsmouth for France, he was stabbed to the heart by one John Felton, who had a private grudge against him, and blamed him for all England's woes.

The king wept at the loss of his favourite, but the people rejoiced and praised Felton for the deed.

5. Sir John Eliot.—Buckingham, whom all thought the cause of the king's bad government, was dead, yet matters did not mend. The king soon ceased to be bound by the Petition of Right, and began once more to raise money by illegal means, just as if he had never promised to wait the consent of his parliament. He also caused his people anxiety by making William Laud, Bishop of London. Laud wished to enforce greater strictness in the observance of forms and ceremonies in church worship, and he taught that Charles ruled by Divine Right, and could do as he wished without asking the consent of his people. What with Laud's efforts to make changes in the Church, and Charles' arbitrary rule, it was feared by the Puritans that England would lose her religion and her freedom. So when Parliament met in 1629, there was great excitement, and Eliot demanded that the custom-house officers who had taken away the goods of a member of Parliament should be punished. Charles sent down an order to Parliament to adjourn. Parliament refused, and to prevent the speaker or chairman from leaving his place, two members held him down while Eliot put a strong resolution to vote, condemning, as a traitor, any one who would make any changes in religion, or who should pay or take custom duties without consent of Parliament. The vote had scarcely been taken when the king's guard appeared and broke up the session. A few days later Charles dissolved Parliament and sent Eliot to the Tower, where three years and a half after he died, killed by the close confinement of prison life. Charles knew that Eliot was dying from the effects of imprisonment; yet he refused to release him.

6. Wentworth and Laud.—For eleven years Charles now ruled without a parliament. Weston was his Treasurer; Wentworth, who had deserted his old friends, was his chief adviser; while Laud, who became Archbishop of Canterbury, ruled the Church. Perhaps Charles did not, at first, intend to go so long without a parliament; but as the years passed he found it easier to have his own way without a parliament than with one. He had made peace with France, and Weston was a careful treasurer, so his expenses were light. Times, too, were better, and with the revival of trade came an increased revenue from customs; and Charles found it not at all difficult to make ends meet now that there was no war. The courtiers thought that the people were content to be governed in this way, and laughed when any one talked of the king's illegal rule. Wentworth, who formerly had stood by Eliot and Hampden for the Petition of Right, now aimed at making the king absolute. He wanted to raise a standing army, and force Parliament to do the king's will. The king was afraid to try such means, so Strafford (as Wentworth was now called) had himself appointed Lord-Lieutenant of Ireland, where he proposed to show Charles how a land could be ruled by fear. While Strafford was in Ireland he made the Irish Parliament do whatever he willed, and so ruled that there was peace and order under his heavy hand. He allowed no tyranny but his own, and raised a standing army, which could be used, if necessary, in England against the English. In every possible way he sought to create ill-feeling between the Irish and the English settlers in Ireland, and the fruits of this policy were soon to appear. One good thing he did he introduced the culture of flax and the manufacture of linen, an industry that has been very successful in Ireland.

In the meantime Laud was emptying the pulpits of Puritans, and filling them with new men who taught the doctrine of the Divine Right of Kings, and who believed in his ideas of public worship. This made the English people very anxious, for religion was more to them than civil liberty. Charles greatly increased the power of the Star Chamber Court, which was now used to fine and punish men who would not submit to his tyranny. Laud, to carry out his plans in the Church, used another arbitrary tribunal, the High Commission Court, before which the clergy who would not preach and do as he wished were brought and punished. The Puritans were very strict in keeping Sunday, and would not allow any games or amusements on that day. This gave Laud a chance to annoy them. He induced Charles to order the clergy to announce from the pulpits that games and sports were to be practised on Sunday after the Church service was over, as had been customary some time before. Many honest ministers refused to do his bidding, and were driven from their pulpits. The Puritans began to despair of recovering their religious freedom, and thousands during these dark days left England forever, and settled in New England. Not Puritans alone, but

Roman Catholics found homes in the wilds of North America. In 1634, Lord Baltimore founded the colony of Maryland, where one of the first laws was that religious liberty should be allowed to all.

7. Ship-money.—Charles now found a new way of raising money. A fleet was needed in the English channel to protect English trade, but Charles had no money to equip one. A lawyer told him that it was once the custom for the coast towns to provide ships, and the king saw in the suggestion a means of keeping up a fleet and army without any expense to himself. He, therefore, commanded the people living in the coast towns to provide him with ships. The next step was to get them to pay him money to equip a fleet, and then as the people living inland were benefited by this fleet protecting England's shores, he called upon them, also, to pay a tax. When John Hampden, who lived in Buckinghamshire, refused to pay, he was brought before the king's judges, who decided by a vote of seven to five, that the king had a right to collect this tax, although the Petition of Right said no tax could be levied without the consent of Parliament. Hampden lost his case, but his refusal to pay roused the people to a sense of their danger.

8. Laud and Scotland.—How long Charles would have ruled without a parliament, we know not, had not Laud by his excessive zeal brought him into conflict with the Scotch. Wentworth, who was in Ireland, and Laud had been writing letters to each other, and laying a plan by which the king was to be made absolute in the State, and the Puritans and Presbyterians were to be forced to submit to Laud's rule in the Church. This scheme which they called "Thorough," proposed that a standing army should be raised, and by it all opposition to the king's will crushed out. Wentworth was carrying out part of this plan in Ireland, and Laud was anxious to try the rest in Scotland. So he persuaded Charles to appoint bishops in Scotland, and to order that a Prayer-Book, much like the English Prayer-Book, should be used in all the Scotch churches. The Scotch did not use any Prayer-book, and when an attempt was made to read the new service in a church in Edinburgh, an old woman, Jenny Geddes, threw her stool at the preacher's head, and there was a riot, which led to the church being cleared. When Charles heard of this he commanded the Scotch to submit; but, instead of that, they signed the National Covenant, whereby they solemnly swore to defend their religion against all its enemies. Not content with that they gathered an army, and when Charles marched north to punish them, they at once crossed the Border, prepared to give him battle. Charles now found himself in a strait. His army would not fight against the Scotch, and he had to return to London. He sent for Strafford from Ireland to help him, and when Strafford came he advised Charles to call Parliament to get money for an army, and then went back to Ireland for his own troops.

9. **The Short Parliament.**—When Parliament met in April, 1640, it was in no hurry to give the king the money he wanted. It began to complain of Charles' illegal taxes, and refused to make a grant until its grievances were redressed. In the meantime the Scotch were quietly waiting in the north of England to see what was going to be done. Charles was very angry at Parliament and dissolved it, after it had sat three weeks. He then went against the Scotch with all the men he could gather; but his soldiers would not fight, and he had to make terms with the Scotch by promising them a large sum of money.

10. **The Long Parliament.**—To get this money, he called the famous "Long Parliament," in Nov. 1640, a Parliament which was not legally dissolved until after nineteen years had passed. It immediately began to undo, as far as possible, all the wrongful acts the king, Wentworth, and Laud had committed since the last Parliament had met. By one act it abolished the Star Chamber Court, the High Commission Court, and all other courts that had no right to exist. It then proceeded to punish Strafford and Laud for the bad advice they had given the king and for their tyrannical acts. Strafford was at first *impeached* by the Commons for treason; and when the impeachment seemed likely to fail, because it was hard to prove he had broken the law of treason, he was *attainted*, that is, a law was made condemning him to die, and causing his family to lose his title and property. Charles was asked to sign the bill of attainder, and at first refused, for he had promised Strafford he would not allow a hair of his head to be injured. But when the queen urged him to sign, seeing how the people gathered in angry crowds before the palace, and when Strafford sent word to his master not to spare

him, Charles yielded. Strafford was at once executed, and the throngs that came to see the great traitor die went home rejoicing. Laud was not executed till 1645, four years later.

11. The Grand Remonstrance.—Parliament was not content with removing the men who gave the king bad advice. It sought to prevent bad government in the future, and to make sure that Parliaments should be called it passed a "Triennial Act," by which it was ordered that a Parliament should meet, at least once in every three years. But through its fear of being dissolved, it went too far, and made Charles consent to a bill decreeing that Parliament should not be dissolved without its own consent. It passed laws against illegal taxation, and condemned the decision the judges had given in the case of Hampden and ship-money. The chief leaders in Parliament of those opposed to the king were Pym and Hampden; but a party arose that thought the king was being harshly treated, and that Parliament was exceeding its rightful authority. Pym and his followers wanted to take the command of the army and navy, and the appointment of great officers in the State, out of the king's hands, as they could no longer trust him. These demands caused a great many to go over to the king's side, and such moderate men as Lord Falkland and Edward Hyde became leaders of a party which wished to keep the king from acts of tyranny, and yet leave him his ordinary power and authority. Thus we see that now there were two parties in Parliament, and as time passed the feeling between them became very bitter. This feeling was increased by terrible news from Ireland. When Strafford returned to England, he left no one behind strong enough to keep peace, and to prevent the English and Irish from flying at each other's throats. A dreadful massacre took place in 1641, in which the English settlers, being few in number suffered most. The Irish leaders said that they were acting, under Charles' authority. This was not true, but many people believed it. This they did the more readily because Charles was very cool and unconcerned when the news of the rising and massacre reached him.

Pym and Hampden, seeing what a strong following Charles had in Parliament, determined to rouse the nation by bringing in a bill called the "Grand Remonstrance," in which all the king's misrule was recited, and a demand made for parliamentary control of appointments. An excited debate followed and lasted all day, after which, by the small majority of eleven, the "Grand Remonstrance" was passed.

12. Attempt to Seize the Five Members.—Charles was very angry when he heard of what had been done, and urged, it is said, by the queen, went down to Westminster with a company of Guards and armed gentlemen, to seize five of the leading members of the Commons—Pym, Hampden, Hollis, Haselrig, and Strode. Fortunately, the news of his coming was brought to Parliament, and when he entered the House he saw that the men he wanted had escaped. They had taken refuge in the City of London, where they were protected by armed train-bands and apprentice boys. The next week they returned to their seats in triumph, escorted by the citizens, who were strongly on the side of Parliament, and against the king, as Charles, some time before, had fined the city heavily because its people had built outside the limits allowed by law.

13. Civil War Begins.—And now it was clear that war was nigh at hand. Charles left London, and the queen went to Holland to collect arms, and raise money, taking the crown jewels with her for that purpose. In August, 1642, the king raised his standard at Nottingham, and called upon his friends to rally around it. He sent some men to seize the arms and ammunition in Hull, but Pym had given instructions to the governor of that city to close the gates, and so Parliament was able to begin the struggle with a supply of war material ready to hand.

The king was supported by most of the nobles, gentry, and clergy, while Parliament had the great mass of the middle classes, the small farmers, merchants, and artisans on its side. The north and west were with the king, and the east and south with Parliament. The King's followers were called "Cavaliers," because many of them were skilled horsemen and accustomed to arms. They wore their hair long, whereas the Puritans who fought in the Parliamentary army had theirs cropped close to the head, and so were called "Roundheads." The king had the best soldiers, but Parliament had the most money and the great advantage of having the rich city of London at its back. During the strife there were two Parliaments: the king's at Oxford, to which most of the peers went, and the Long Parliament at Westminster, composed of a majority of the Commons.

The early battles were favourable to the king; partly because his troops under his dashing nephew, Prince Rupert, were good horsemen and used to arms; and partly because the Parliamentary general, Earl Essex, was afraid to push the king too far. Two little skirmishes in 1642, at Powick Bridge and Edgehill, were somewhat against Parliament, and Charles' forces for a time threatened London.

14. **Principal Events of the War.**—The war was carried on in many quarters at the same time. The king was very successful in Cornwall and Devon; and Fairfax, the parliamentary general in the north, was hard pressed by the royalists. In a skirmish at Chalgrove Field, 1643, Hampden was killed, and in the same year, in a battle at Newbury, Lord Falkland fell, crying, "Peace, peace." Town after town passed into the hands of the king, and great fear was felt for London itself. Pym now sent Sir Henry Vane to Scotland, and by agreeing to accept Presbyterianism as the form of church government in England, obtained the aid of a Scotch army. The "Solemn League and Covenant," as this bargain was called, had scarcely been signed when Pym died.

And now appeared on the scene one of the greatest men England ever had. Oliver Cromwell, a stern, brave, Puritan gentleman-farmer of Huntingdonshire, had been for some time in Parliament and had watched the growing evils in the government of the country. When the war broke out he formed a regiment of horse which became known as "Cromwell's Ironsides," on account of the severe drill through which it passed. They were not common soldiers, but gentlemen farmers and sturdy yeomen who fought for their religion and freedom, and not for pay. Cromwell saw that the only way to fight the king was to match his cavaliers with strong men who knew what they were fighting for, and loved the cause of religion and freedom. It was not long before Cromwell had a chance to show what his "Ironsides" could do. For in 1644, at Marston Moor, in Yorkshire, Fairfax, aided by the Scots and Cromwell, met and scattered the king's troops under Prince Rupert. This was the first great battle of the war, and Cromwell proved that his "Ironsides" were more than a match for Rupert's cavalry.

Cromwell now pressed to have the army reorganized, and succeeded in getting Parliament to pass a "Self-Denying Ordinance," by which members of Parliament were not allowed to command in

the army. Fairfax was made commander-in-chief, and by special permission Cromwell was allowed to remain with him. Strict discipline was now enforced in the army, and the "New Model," as it was called, in a short time, proved how wise was Cromwell's advice and leadership by utterly defeating the king in a decisive battle at Naseby in Northamptonshire. This battle really ended the war, for Charles now fled to Wales, and thence to the Scotch army at Newark, where he hoped to be kindly treated. Parliament would have allowed the king to come back had he been willing to surrender the command of the army for twenty years, and to accept Presbyterianism as the form of religion in England. But Charles would not consent, so the Scotch gave him up to Parliament in return for the payment of £400,000 due them as expenses.

15. **Trial and Execution of Charles I.**—When Charles came back he was well treated, and might have been restored to the throne had he acted with sincerity towards Parliament and the army. He thought that they could not get along without him, and hoped by taking advantage of the quarrels between the officers and Parliament to recover all his lost authority. In consequence of one of those quarrels, the army seized the king, and offered to put him back on the throne, on much more reasonable terms than had been offered by Parliament. Charles pretended to treat with the officers, but at the same time was stirring up another civil war, hoping through the aid of the Scotch and Irish, to be able to make his own terms. Suddenly he escaped from the army and made his way to the Isle of Wight, where he was captured and imprisoned. Several risings took place in his favor, but they were soon crushed. Then the army sternly resolved that it would bring "Charles Stuart, that man of blood" to account for all the misery he had brought on the land. Parliament was purged of the members who would not consent to bring the king to trial; and then a tribunal of sixty-three men was formed, with Bradshaw a famous lawyer at its head, to solemnly impeach the king. Before this stern court, Charles was brought, and called to answer to charges of treason and murder. In these last trying moments Charles maintained all the dignity of a king, and refused to defend himself before judges having no legal authority. Nevertheless the trial went on, and having heard the evidence, the court condemned the king to die. Nine days later, on a scaffold outside a window of Whitehall Palace. Charles Stuart, calmly and bravely laid his head on the fatal block, Jan. 30, 1649.

CHAPTER XVII.

THE COMMONWEALTH.

1. England becomes a Republic.—England was now without a king, and, as the House of Lords was soon after abolished, the only authority left to govern was a part of the Long Parliament, composed of not more then eighty men. This "Rump Parliament," as it was coarsely called, promptly undertook the task of ruling, and elected a council of State of forty members, to manage the affairs of the nation. England was declared a "Commonwealth," and Parliament set to work to meet the dangers that threatened the young Republic. At foreign courts the execution of Charles was looked upon as a terrible crime. None of the European nations would recognize the "Commonwealth" and its council of State, for they thought Charles Stuart, Charles I's eldest son, was the rightful ruler of England. There was also much discontent at home, for many, now that the king was dead, began to look upon him as a martyr. This feeling was increased by the publication of a book, the "Royal Image," which professed to be an account by the king himself of his sayings and doings while a prisoner. It painted Charles in very flattering colours, and made him appear little less than a saint. The book was a forgery by a Presbyterian clergyman, Dr. Gauden; nevertheless it had a large sale, and made many regret that the king had been treated so harshly. In Ireland, too, there was danger to the Commonwealth. There the Duke of Ormond had united all classes of the population in favor of Charles II., who was invited to go to Ireland and become king. Prince Rupert was in the channel preying on English commerce with a number of ships which had taken refuge in Dutch harbours. Scotland was growing daily more discontented and was beginning to look for the restoration of Charles II. All the Scotch waited for was Charles' assent to the Covenant, after which they were ready to make him their king, and to aid him in recovering the English throne.

2. Cromwell in Ireland.—The most pressing danger was in Ireland, and to that unhappy land an English army was sent in 1649, with Cromwell as leader. Time was precious, and much had to be done before Cromwell could restore peace and English supremacy in the island. He and his men thought the Irish deserved little mercy on account of the massacre of 1641. The work of re-conquest began with the siege of Drogheda, and Cromwell ordered that no one bearing arms should be spared. The city was taken by storm and 2000 men were put to the sword; while of those who surrendered, every tenth man was knocked on the head, the rest being sent as slaves to the Barbadoes. A month later a similar massacre took place at Wexford, though not by Cromwell's orders. The effect of this terrible severity was soon seen, the other towns offering but little opposition to Cromwell's army. After nine months spent in Ireland Cromwell returned to England, leaving the task of completing the conquest to others. Sad was the fate of the poor Irish who had taken part in the strife. Many were put to death or exiled, and thousands were turned out of their homes and banished to the dreary wilds of Connaught, their lands being given to English settlers. The bitterest curse an Irishman can use to-day is the "Curse of Cromwell."

3. **Cromwell in Scotland.**—While Cromwell was thus subduing the enemies of the Commonwealth in Ireland, in England its affairs were being managed by men like Vane, who was at the head of the navy, with Admiral Blake as his chief officer. John Milton, the great Puritan poet, was Latin Secretary of the Council, and Bradshaw was its president. These were able and honest men; but many of the members of Parliament and the Council were selfish and corrupt, and used their positions to put their friends into fat offices, and to satisfy their own ambition and greed. They were unwilling to have a Parliament elected that represented the people, and were suspicious and jealous of the army and of all who had the interests of the country at heart. But any discontent with Parliament had to be put aside until a new danger which had arisen was removed. For Charles II. had agreed to become a Presbyterian, and to uphold the Covenant, and the Scotch had recalled him as their king. It would not do to allow Charles to march into England with a Scotch army, so Cromwell marched north with an English army into Scotland. The people fled at his approach, having heard of his doings in Ireland, and Cromwell found himself, when near Edinburgh, hemmed in between the hills and the sea

with no supplies for his army, save what could be brought from his ships which followed along the coast. When he reached Dunbar, it seemed as if he would have to put his men on board his ships and return, for David Leslie, the crafty Scotch general, had entrenched himself in the Lammermuir Hills, and cut off Cromwell's escape by land. Leslie for several days refused to come down from the hills and fight, preferring to starve his enemy out. At last, overborne by the urgent demands of some Presbyterian ministers in his camp, he left his vantage ground and moved down into the plain to give Cromwell battle. Cromwell was delighted, and early the following morning, September 3rd, 1650, before the Scotch were well awake, he flung himself on the Covenanters with the cry, "The Lord of Hosts, the Lord of Hosts." In one short hour the victory was won ; 3,000 men were killed, 10,000 were taken prisoners, and Leslie's army was a thing of the past. The war lingered for another year, for Charles had found support in the north, and Cromwell found it difficult to bring him to a decisive conflict. Finally, he left the way open into England, and at once Charles began to march southwards, hoping the Royalists would rise in his favour. But though Charles had many friends in England, they were afraid to give him any help, and so, when he reached Worcester, he found himself surrounded by 30,000 men, with only 16,000 at his back. Cromwell had pursued and overtaken him, and once more the terrible Puritan army dealt out death and destruction to their enemies. The battle was fought on the anniversary of that of Dunbar, and Charles' troops, after a desperate defence, were totally defeated. It was, as Cromwell said, "a crowning mercy," for no more risings against the Commonwealth took place as long as Cromwell lived. With great difficulty, Charles escaped to France, in a little collier vessel.

4. The Dutch War.—Foreign nations now saw that the Commonwealth could hold its own against its enemies, and began to treat it with respect. Blake had driven Rupert from the seas, and Sir Harry Vane determined to build up the English navy at the expense of the Dutch, who had aided Charles. So, in 1651, a "Navigation Act" was passed which forbade foreign vessels from bringing into England any goods other than the products of their own country. This Act was aimed at the Dutch who did a large carrying trade for other nations. So much ill-feeling was created by this measure that a war broke out, in which Van Tromp for the Dutch, and Blake for the English, fought several fierce naval battles. Van Tromp was killed in 1653, and the supremacy of the seas passed over to England, where it has remained ever since.

5. Expulsion of the Long Parliament.—One object of the Dutch war was to make the fleet strong at the expense of the army. The army was dissatisfied with Parliament, partly because it had not been paid, but, chiefly because its officers saw that the members were unwilling to have parliament dissolved and a new one, representing the people, elected. When it was clear that Parliament was not going to allow a new election except on terms that would give the old members the right to say who should sit with them, Cromwell decided to take prompt measures. Marching down to Westminster with a regiment of musketeers, he turned the members out, locked the doors, and put the key in his pocket. "Not a dog barked," as Cromwell said afterwards, at this daring deed; and the nation felt that what Cromwell had done was necessary and right.

6. Instrument of Government.—And now England had neither king nor parliament, and order had to be maintained by Cromwell and his army, until some form of government could be agreed upon. An assembly, chosen by the congregations of the Independents, was convened at Westminister by Cromwell, and it proceeded to arrange for a real Parliament. This assembly got the nick-name of "Barebone's Parliament" from Praise-God Barebones, one of its members. Its members were honest, zealous men, who tried to do much in the way of removing long standing evils, and so made many enemies. Finding that it could not carry out its good intentions, Barebone's Parliament resigned its power into the hands of Cromwell. Before doing so, however, it drew up a new Constitution called the "Instrument of Government," and made Cromwell Lord Protector. For the next ten months Cromwell ruled alone, and on his own authority made many good laws. He ended the war with Holland, and made treaties, favourable to English trade, with other countries. He was tolerant to all religious bodies, although he would not let the royalist clergy preach in the churches, nor allow the Book of Common Prayer to be used. He united Scotland to England, and the

Scotch said that his eight years of rule were "years of peace and prosperity."

In 1654 a new Parliament was elected, with members in it from Scotland and Ireland, and so was the first united Parliament of Great Britain and Ireland. This Parliament was chosen more fairly than most Parliaments, but Roman Catholics and royalists were shut out. It at once began to settle the affairs of the nation, and to make Cromwell's laws legal. Had it been left to carry out its will, England might have been spared many troubles; but Cromwell began to fear it would interfere with his authority, and, unwisely, dissolved it.

7. Cromwell Rules Alone.—Cromwell now ruled for a time without a Parliament, and though this rule was a tyranny, yet it was a wise and merciful tyranny. He knew many were discontented, and, to prevent risings, he divided England into military districts, over which he placed major-generals who were responsible for their order and good government. Cromwell would allow no persecution, and even the Quaker and the Jew found in him a protector and friend. It was at this time the Jews were allowed to return to England.

8. Petition and Advice.—Although Cromwell ruled by force, he did not wish to be a mere tyrant. He longed to see England once more contented and well governed; but he feared the royalists would take advantage of the quarrels in Parliament to bring about a restoration of the Stuarts. Nevertheless, he called a second Parliament, in 1656, but excluded all who had not a certificate from his Council. This Parliament offered to make Cromwell king, and Cromwell would have taken the title had not the army been so strongly opposed. Cromwell contented himself with the power of a king, which was given by a new Constitution, the "Petition and Advice," drawn up by Parliament. This Constitution provided for a House of Lords to be named by Cromwell, and Cromwell was given the right to choose his successor. For a short time there was peace, and then it was found that the Commons would not work with the Lords, and the republicans in the Parliament began to plot against Cromwell himself. Once more he dissolved Parliament, and for the rest of his life ruled alone, although he was planning to call a third Parliament when death came to him.

Never, except in the time of Elizabeth, had England been so respected abroad as in these years. Jamaica was taken from Spain, 1655, and France gave up Dunkirk as the price of Cromwell's aid against Spain. The Duke of Savoy, at Cromwell's command, was forced to cease persecuting the Vaudois, and in him oppressed Protestants everywhere found a powerful protector.

9. State of the Country.—But peace and power, while it brought prosperity, did not bring content. The Puritan rule was hard, cold, and joyless. Innocent, as well as harmful, amusements were suppressed. Cock-fighting and bear-baiting, to the Puritans, were no worse than dancing round the Maypole, and eating mince pies. Theatres were closed, and Christmas revels were forbidden. The Puritans tried to make everybody religious, earnest, and sober. This they could not do, and people began to long for the return of the good old days, and some began to wish for the death of Cromwell. Plots were formed to kill him, and in his latter days he wore armour constantly under his clothing.

10. Death of Cromwell.—But the end was near. Cromwell's health suffered much from his fear of assassination, and from his anxiety about the future of the nation. Then his favourite daughter, Elizabeth, died, and this broke the strong man's heart. Ague seized him, and although prayers went up everywhere for his recovery, he passed away on the anniversary of his great victories at Dunbar and Worcester, Sept. 3rd, 1658. He was buried with royal honors in Westminster Abbey, and no greater ruler was there laid to rest than the "uncrowned King of England."

11. Restoration of Charles II.—So great was the fear of Cromwell, even in death, that his eldest son, Richard, was allowed to succeed him as quietly as if he had been the rightful heir to a crown. Richard was a weak, good-natured, worthless man, and soon lost the respect of the army, which forced him to dissolve the Parliament which had just been elected, and to recall the fragment of the Long Parliament that Cromwell had driven out. But, as the Long Parliament could not agree with the army, it was again expelled. In the meantime, Richard, after holding office ten months, had to resign the Protectorship, and he gladly retired into private life. It was evident that England was drifting into anarchy, and that something must be done to save her from strife and civil war. General Monk, who commanded an army in Scotland, saw what was taking place and marched down into England. He kept his own counsel, and everywhere he went proclaimed his loyalty to the Commonwealth, but demanded a "free Parliament." General Lambert tried to stop his march but failed, and Monk entered London. The Rump now dissolved itself, and a Convention Parliament (one called without a king's writ), met, which immediately sent for Charles II. to come and rule. Monk had prepared everything, and Charles was waiting for the invitation. He had issued a proclamation from Breda promising religious freedom and a general pardon ; but he was allowed to return without any pledges for his future good conduct.

On the 25th May, 1660, he landed, and on the 29th he entered London amid the rejoicings of a great multitude. Cromwell's veterans looked on with sad hearts, remembering the cause for which they suffered so much, and then, a few months later, went quietly back to their farms and shops.

CHAPTER XVIII.

THE RESTORATION.

1. **Charles II.**—The English people were glad to have kingship restored, for they were tired of the hard, stern rule of the Puritans. Charles II. was also glad to get back to England, where he could get money to spend on his wicked pleasures. When on "his travels," as he humorously called his exile, his life had been full of hardship, for he was driven from court to court, and had to depend for support on his devoted adherents in England. Now when he came back, it was with the resolve never to leave England again. He loved pleasure above all things, and surrounded himself with a court that for open profligacy has no equal in English history. Beautiful and abandoned women were his chosen companions, and to gratify their whims and tastes the public money was lavishly spent. Charles was a shrewd, witty, talkative, easy-going

man, who cared little for Church or State, so long as he had his own way, and meddlesome people did not pry into how he squandered his subjects' money. His policy was to keep on the throne at all hazards, and never to allow public feeling to run so high as to imperil his position. Yet like all the Stuarts he loved power, and by occasionally yielding to great waves of popular indignation, he managed to do much as he pleased in spite of the efforts made to keep him in check. In religion, he professed to belong to the English Church, but he was secretly, if anything, a Roman Catholic, and used his position to favour that cause.

2. Clarendon's Adminstration.—Charles' first chief adviser was Edward Hyde, Lord Clarendon, a faithful follower who had been his tutor and companion in exile. He was a moderate royalist, and strongly attached to the Church. The Parliament that recalled Charles had in it many Presbyterians and moderate royalists, and was not disposed to go to extremes. It contented itself with putting to death thirteen of the men who had taken part in the execution of Charles I., and with taking from their graves in Westminster Abbey the bodies of Cromwell, Ireton and Bradshaw, and hanging them in chains. It then passed an Act of Indemnity, pardoning all offenders except Vane and Lambert. The king had promised Vane his life, but afterwards had him executed, coolly remarking that he was too dangerous to be allowed to live. The king's income was fixed for life at £1,200,000 a year, and he agreed to give up certain feudal rights which were vexatious to the landowners. The army was disbanded, but Charles, to make sure of his safety, kept 5000 men in his pay, and this was the beginning of a standing army in England. Then the Convention Parliament was dissolved, and a regular Parliament elected.

The new Parliament was composed mainly of Cavaliers, whose loyalty was so great that even the king found it troublesome. It was eager to avenge Charles I's. death, and many that were spared by the Convention Parliament were now punished.

3. State of the Nation.—A period of revelry and wickedness now began at the court and among those who were brought into contact with it. Theatres were again opened, and the most licentious plays were acted in the presence of the king and his friends, who applauded and rewarded the playwriters and actors. The old amusements of the people were restored, and once more the village green was the scene of mirth and jollity. It seemed as if Puritanism was dead, so great was the change from the days of Cromwell. Nevertheless, the sober middle class of England was still Puritan, and the earnestness and strong sense of duty which marked Puritan teaching left a lasting impression on the English people. Meanwhile many improvements had been introduced during the preceding fifty years. In James I's. reign, the post office for foreign letters had been established; silk-weaving had been encouraged; low-lying lands had been drained; and improvements had been made in agriculture. A little later, stage-coaches began to run between the chief towns, and letters were carried more frequently from place to place. The north of England was thinly inhabited, and highwaymen levied toll at pleasure from travellers over the lonely moors. Even judges had to be protected while going on circuit.

4. Religious Persecution.—And now the Puritans and Presbyterians were to find out how much truth there was in Charles' promise of religious freedom. In Scotland, where Charles had signed the Covenant, bishops were forced upon the people, and the Covenanters were fiercely persecuted and hunted down. The Cavalier Parliament was resolved that no form of religious worship should be allowed except that of the English Church in the time of Laud; so it passed, in 1661, a "Corporation Act" which compelled all officials in the towns and cities to take an oath of non-resistance to the king, and to receive the sacrament in the English Church. The next year, 1662, an "Act of Uniformity" was passed, which allowed no minister to preach or act as pastor unless he was ordained by a bishop, and used the Prayer-Book. So, on St. Bartholomew's Day, Aug. 24th, 1662, nearly 2,000 of the Puritan and Presbyterian clergy then in the English Church gave up their livings rather than comply with these conditions. They formed congregations of their own, which became known as "Dissenters," the name yet given to all Protestants in England who do not belong to the English Church.

Not content with these cruel laws, a Conventicle Act" was passed in 1664, forbidding the Dissenters from worshipping in chapels or conventicles; and in 1665, the "Five Mile Act" forbade their ministers from preaching or teaching within five miles of any town or village. This was done because most of the Dissenters lived in the towns and villages. Soon the prisons were filled with men who refused to stop preaching and ministering to their flocks. Among others who thus suffered was John Bunyan, the famous author of "Pilgrim's Progress." Bunyan spent twelve years in Bedford jail, earning a living for himself and family by making metal tags for laces, and employing his spare moments in writing books. It was in this reign, when old, poor, and blind, that John Milton, the great Puritan poet, wrote his "Paradise Lost." Bunyan and Milton are among the greatest writers of the 17th century, and both truly represent the best types of Puritanism. The fierce persecution of this time drove many to America, and among other colonies founded was that by William Penn, the Quaker, who bought from the Indians the right to settle in Pennsylvania.

5. **Dutch War.**—At the beginning of his reign Charles married Katharine of Portugal, and received as her dowry Bombay in India, and the fortress of Tangier in Morocco. This marriage displeased the English, as the queen was a Roman Catholic. In another way Charles angered his people: he sold the fortress of Dunkirk, which Cromwell had gained, to Louis XIV of France for money to spend on his low pleasures.

Not long after this, in 1665, a war broke out between England and Holland. These two nations were keen rivals for the supremacy of the sea, and Charles disliked the Dutch because they had driven him from their capital when he was in exile. One dispute led to another, until the vessels of the two nations came into conflict. A battle was fought off Lowestoft in Suffolk, in which the English won a victory; but they gained little by it, for the victory was not followed up by the Admiral, the Duke of York. The fleet was not kept in good condition for war; much of the money voted by Parliament being spent by Charles on unworthy favourites.

6. **The Plague and the Fire of London.**—And now a terrible calamity came upon London. The summer of 1665 was very hot, and the streets of London were very narrow and filthy. So when the plague travelled from the East to England, it found in London plenty of material on which to work. It broke out in May and raged till winter, during which time more than 100,000 people

died. Every person that could get away fled from London in terror, leaving but few to care for the sick and dying. To add to her misfortunes, a great fire broke out in London the following year, 1666, in which over 13,000 houses and public buildings were destroyed, among others St. Paul's Cathedral. The fire was a blessing in disguise, for it burnt down many old wooden houses, and helped to clear away the remains of the plague. After this better houses were built, the streets were made wider, and purer water was brought into the city.

Meanwhile the Dutch war went on. Charles neglected his fleet and spent the public money on his court, and when Clarendon asked for a grant to carry on the war, Parliament insisted on knowing what had become of former grants. Charles now thought it best to make peace with the Dutch, but while arranging the terms the Dutch fleet sailed up the Medway and burnt three men-of-war. This was looked upon as a national disgrace, and Clarendon became so unpopular that he had to leave the country.

7. **The Cabal.**—Charles now took for his chief advisers five men, the initials of whose names made the word "cabal." These were Clifford, Arlington, Buckingham, Ashley, and Lauderdale, and as their intrigues and base actions made them hateful to the people, the word "cabal" has ever since had a bad meaning. They were made the tools of the king, and many of their misdeeds were due to the secret intrigues of Charles with Louis XIV. of France. Louis was the most powerful king in Europe, and he had cast covetous eyes on the Netherlands which belonged to Spain. He wanted Charles to help him to get this rich territory, and to prevent England and Holland from interfering with his plans. Holland became alarmed at Louis' encroachments, and succeeded in 1668 in getting England and Sweden to join her in a "Triple Alliance," which for the time forced Louis to keep the peace. And now a most shameful thing was done by the king. Charles, in spite of the "Triple Alliance" treaty, made a secret treaty with Louis at Dover, in 1670, by which he agreed to help Louis against Holland and to declare himself a Roman Catholic, in return for a large pension from Louis and the aid of French troops in case the English people should rebel. Clifford and Arlington, who were secretly Roman Catholics, knew of this

treaty; but the other members of the Cabal were kept in ignorance. Then followed another disgraceful act. The goldsmiths and bankers of London had lent the king about £1,300,000, expecting to be repaid out of the revenue. Charles now refused to pay back this money, and so brought ruin on the lenders, who had borrowed the money from others. This money was not repaid till William III. came to the throne.

8. Declaration of Indulgence and the Test Act.—To carry out part of his agreement with Louis, Charles, in 1672, declared war with Holland, and issued a "Declaration of Indulgence," which allowed all Dissenters and Roman Catholics to worship as they pleased, and released from prison thousands of the victims of religious persecution. Bunyan was released at this time from his long imprisonment in Bedford jail. The war with Holland was not successful, for William of Orange, the brave young leader of the Dutch, opened the dykes of his native land, and let in the water from the sea. In this way he succeeded in forcing his enemies to retire.

Charles now had to summon his Parliament to get more money. The Commons were very angry that Charles should suspend the laws against Dissenters and Roman Catholics, and they forced him to withdraw his "Declaration of Indulgence," and to give his assent to a "Test Act" which compelled every man holding office to take an oath against transubstantiation, and to receive the sacrament according to the rites of the English Church. The Duke of York avowed himself a Roman Catholic, and had to give up his command of the fleet. Clifford and Arlington, also, had to leave the king's service. Ashley, now Earl of Shaftesbury, became the leader of the "country party" in Parliament, and sought to compel the king to give religious freedom to the Protestant Dissenters, but not to Roman Catholics.

9. Danby Administration.—Charles now thought it prudent to please the Church party, and therefore chose the Earl of Danby as his minister. He made peace with Holland, and allowed Danby to arrange, much against Louis XIV's wishes, a marriage between Mary, daughter of James, Duke of York, and William of Orange, her cousin. This pleased the people, for as Charles had no legitimate children, and James had no son, it was expected that Mary, who was a Protestant, would become Queen of England. Nevertheless, Charles continued to intrigue with Louis, and made the marriage a means of getting a larger grant from the French king. He even persuaded Danby to write to Louis a letter asking for money, and promising to prevent his Parliament from going to war with France.

10. **The "Popish Plot," 1678.**—Although these intrigues were kept secret, the people became uneasy and felt they were betrayed. While they were in this humour, a low scoundrel, called Titus Oates, who had been a Jesuit but had left that body, came forward with a strange tale. He said there was a plot to kill Charles and make the Duke of York king. Oates told his story to Sir Edmund Bury Godfrey, a London magistrate, and soon afterwards Godfrey was found dead in a ditch. How he came to his death no one ever knew; but people said that he was killed by the Roman Catholics to prevent the "Popish Plot" from coming out. This caused great excitement, which was increased by the discovery of some papers belonging to Coleman, the secretary of the Duchess of York, in which references were made to some hope of the Roman Catholics. Parliament, in its alarm, passed an act preventing Roman Catholics from becoming members; and Oates, Bedloe, and other perjured witnesses swore away the lives of many innocent victims. Judges and juries believed the most ridiculous tales of plots, and condemned the accused on the most trivial and contradictory evidence. The most illustrious victim was Lord Stafford, who perished in 1681. Charles did not believe these tales, but laughed at the whole matter, and allowed the popular frenzy to spend itself in putting to death men of his own creed. Shaftesbury helped the plot along for his own ends, and when, in 1679, Danby's letter to Louis XIV., asking for a pension for Charles, was laid on the table of the House of Commons, he had his revenge. Danby was impeached and driven from office, Parliament was dissolved for the first time in seventeen years, and Shaftesbury became chief minister.

11. **Exclusion Bill.**—Amidst this excitement a new Parliament was elected in 1679. Under Shaftesbury's leadership it brought in a bill to exclude James, Duke of York, from the throne. But Charles, to save James, dissolved Parliament, not, however, before

THE RESTORATION. 115

it had passed the famous "Habeas Corpus Act." This act, next in importance to Magna Charta, prevents people from being arrested without a proper warrant, and compels gaolers to show on what authority a person is detained in prison. Prisoners must be brought to trial within a reasonable time, and if their offences are bailable, they must be allowed their freedom.

Parliament met again in 1679, more determined than ever to exclude James from the throne. An "Exclusion Bill" was passed in the Commons, but thrown out of the House of Lords through the influence of Lord Halifax. Shaftesbury had made the great mistake of selecting the Duke of Monmouth, a natural son of Charles, as the king's successor. Monmouth was popular, but honest people thought it a shameful thing to exclude from the throne, Mary, Princess of Orange, for an illegitimate son of the king. Then began a great struggle, in which for the first time Charles stood firm against his Parliament. He refused to abandon James, although it looked, at times, as if there would be another civil war.

Men now divided into two great parties; one in favor of the exclusion of James, and the other opposed to it. The first became known as "Whigs," and the second as "Tories." *Whig* means whey or sour milk, and was a name given to some rebels in Ayrshire in Scotland. *Tory* means a bog-robber, and was the name applied to some outlaws in Ireland. These names, at first given in hatred and contempt, for a long time were used to denote the two great political parties in England; the one supposed to favour the *People*, the other the *Crown*. At last, Charles called a Parliament at Oxford, in 1681, and many of the Whigs went to it armed. This created alarm, and people began to ask if there was to be another civil war. Charles offered to make the Princess of Orange regent after his death, and this seemed so reasonable that many went over to the side of Charles and James. He now dissolved Parliament, and it met no more in his reign.

12. Rye-House Plot.—From this time onward Charles did much as he pleased. Shaftesbury was charged with treason, but the Grand Jury of Middlesex would not bring in a bill against him. Then Charles took away the charter of London, and appointed the Lord Mayor and sheriffs himself. Shaftesbury knew that the king's sheriffs would pack the jury against him, and he fled from the country. After he had gone a number of his friends formed a plot in favour of Monmouth; but, while they were arranging their plans, a band of desperate men formed another plot to murder the king and the Duke of York at the Rye House, a lonely spot in Hertfordshire. This latter plot was discovered, and the crown lawyers tried to make it appear that the Whig leaders were connected with it. They were innocent, but they knew the judges and juries would be chosen so as to convict them. Monmouth escaped to Holland, Essex killed himself, and Lord Russell and Algernon Sidney were executed. In those days a prisoner was not allowed to have a lawyer to defend him, and so Russell, aided by his devoted wife, who sat beside him at the trial and took notes, conducted his own defence.

13. Death of Charles II.—All opposition to James was now at an end, and he returned to England from Scotland where he had been hunting down and torturing the poor Covenanters. The charters of many towns were taken away, and this put the power of life and death, and the choice of members of parliament into the hands of the officers chosen by the king. Charles was again in the pay of Louis, and besides kept several thousand men as a standing army. The clergy preached the duty of "passive obedience" to the king, and it seemed as if English liberty was near its end. In this hour of her great peril England was saved by the death of Charles, in 1685. When near his end he received the rites of the Roman Catholic Church at the hands of a priest. His last words were an apology for "being so unconscionably long in dying," and a request not to let his favourite mistress, Nell Gwynne, starve.

So ended the reign of the "merry monarch" who

"Never said a foolish thing
And never did a wise one,"

unless we except the encouragement he gave to science by helping to found the Royal Society of England.

1. **James II.**—James, Duke of York, now became king. He promised to support the English Church, and people thought that as he had honestly acknowledged he was a Roman Catholic when the Test Act was passed he would be as good as his word. He was known to be stubborn and narrow-minded, but at the same time he was believed to be sincere and well meaning. His first Parliament was as loyal as he could wish, for it was elected at a time when the tide of public opinion had turned against his opponents, and had been chosen under the control of sheriffs appointed by the Crown in the towns and cities from which charters had been taken.

It was soon seen that James did not intend to support the Established Church, for before he was crowned he went publicly to mass in his own chapel. He told the Bishops they must stop the English Church clergy from preaching against the Roman Catholic religion, and he opened the prison doors to all who were confined for religion's sake. This last act was good in itself, but it was done against the law of the land, and proved that James did not intend to abide by the laws.

2. **Monmouth's Rebellion.**—When Parliament met it voted the King an income of two million pounds a year for life. It was anxious to show James how loyal it was, for a rebellion had just broken out to make Monmouth king. Monmouth and the Duke of Argyle had escaped to Holland toward the close of the reign of Charles II., and were now urged by their friends in England and Scotland to return. They were led to believe that most of the English and Scotch people would gladly join them in driving James from the throne. Finally, Argyle crossed over to Scotland, and a little later Monmouth landed in England. Argyle's clan, the Campbells, rose at his call, but the Covenanters were afraid to rebel, and the rising was soon crushed. Argyle was taken prisoner and executed; and his followers were cruelly punished, many being sold into slavery in America.

Monmouth landed at Lyme, in Dorset, and thousands flocked to greet the popular and handsome young Duke. He marched to Exeter, and thence to Taunton, where he was received with rejoicings by the lower classes. The gentry, nobles, and clergy were against him, for they hoped that when James died he would be succeeded by his daughter Mary, the Princess of Orange. Soon James' troops under Lord Feversham, and Captain Churchill, were moving against the poorly-armed followers of Monmouth. On the night of July 5th, 1685, Monmouth endeavored to surprise the royal troops at Sedgemoor. When he reached their lines he found they were protected by a deep trench, full of water, and although he had some success at first, James' soldiers soon rallied and easily routed his brave peasants and colliers. Two days after Monmouth was found concealed in a ditch, half-starved. He was brought to London, and, although he begged his uncle to spare him, his plea for mercy was not listened to, and he was executed.

3. The Bloody Assizes.—Perhaps nothing gives us a better idea of James' revengeful disposition than the events which followed the Battle of Sedgemoor. Colonel Kirke was left in command of some troops in the neighbourhood of the battle, and he at once began to hang whole batches of prisoners, without troubling himself to find out their share in the rebellion. To add to their miseries, the people of the western counties had Judge Jeffreys sent among them. His mission was to convict as many as possible, and to sentence them to death. In the "Bloody Assizes" which followed, 320 people were hanged, and over 800 sold into slavery in the West Indies. This brutal judge browbeat witnesses and juries to secure sentences against the prisoners, and made the unfortunate, and often innocent victims, the butts of his coarse jokes and his savage insolence. Among those who suffered at his hands was Alice Lisle, an aged lady, whose only crime was hiding two fugitives from the battle-field, thinking they were persecuted puritan preachers fleeing from their enemies. Some were spared through their friends bribing the judge and the queen's "maids of honor;" others were given to the courtiers to be sold into slavery.

4. James violates the Test Act.—Jeffreys was rewarded for his infamous conduct with the position of Lord Chancellor; and James thought it a favourable occasion to increase his standing army, and to put Roman Catholic officers in command. This was against the Test Act; but James cared nothing for the law, and replaced those advisers who found fault with his actions by men like Sunderland and Jeffreys. This made the English people uneasy, and when in October, 1685, Louis XIV. revoked the Edict of Nantes, and took away from his Protestant subjects their right to religious freedom, James' subjects became very much alarmed. Louis' persecution of the Huguenots was a good thing for England, for many of them found refuge there, and brought with them their skill in silk-weaving and other industries. When Parliament met it complained of the violation of the Test Act, but James, now grown bold, prorogued Parliament, and two years after dissolved it. This was the last Parliament that met in his reign. In this way he managed to get rid of an unpleasant opposition; but he could not prevent people from talking about the way the law was being broken to please Roman Catholics.

After Parliament was dissolved he asked his judges if he had the right to dispense with the Test Act, and when four of them said he had not, he dismissed them from the bench, and appointed others in their stead. He then had a test case brought before the judges, and they decided that James could, if he wished, do away with laws against Roman Catholics. James now felt free to make all the appointments he wished, and began to turn leading Protestants out of office, and to put Roman Catholics in their places. His own brothers-in-law, the sons of Clarendon, were dismissed because they would not change their religion to please him. Lord Tyrconnel was appointed Lord-Lieutenant of Ireland in place of the elder Clarendon, and the younger Clarendon was dismissed from his post of High Treasurer.

A new court was now called into existence to control the Church. This was the Ecclesiastical Commission, which had for its head Judge Jeffreys, and concerned itself with the acts of the English Church clergy. The king built Roman Catholic chapels in London, and expected his lords to attend him when he went to service; but most of them refused. Orders of monks began to settle in London, and a Jesuit school was opened. All these things made James' subjects angry, and to overawe the people of London, James placed an army of 13,000 men in a camp at Hounslow. He next published a "Declaration of Indulgence," in 1687, hoping to get, by his liberality, the support of the persecuted Dissenters. Some were glad to get their freedom, and praised James for his kindness and justice; but the more thoughtful saw that if the king could do away with one law, then he could do away with all laws, and this would make the government of England a despotism.

5. Attack on the Universities.—James' own friends saw that in his zeal for his church he was doing it harm, and advised him to be more prudent and cautious. But James thought he was right and would take no advice. His next step was an attack on the Universities of Oxford and Cambridge, about the only places in England where a good education could be obtained. The clergy and the sons of the nobles and gentry were educated there, but no student could take a degree or hold an office in these colleges unless he belonged to the English Church. James wished to open the Universities to Roman Catholics, and so placed at the head of one college a Roman Catholic, and when a vacancy occured in the headship of Magdalen College, he told the Fellows to elect Dr. Parker, also a Roman Catholic. The Fellows refused, and James drove them forth from the college walls. Cambridge University was also attacked, and men began to fear that the chief seats of learning would soon be under the control of the Roman Catholics.

6. Birth of James the Pretender.—It was at this time, in 1687, that Parliament was dissolved, and James began his preparations for a new election. He asked the Lord-Lieutenants and sheriffs in the counties to send up members who would vote to repeal the Test Act; and when he met with a general refusal, he dismissed them from their offices, and replaced them by others.

Many were disposed to bear patiently James' tyranny, in the hope that his reign would soon be at an end, and then his daughter Mary would undo all his tyrannical acts. But this hope disappeared when it was given forth that a son was born to James, in June 1688. It was now felt there was likely to be a succession of Roman Catholic kings, and in that event, there was great danger England would lose her religion and freedom. It was then resolved that William of Orange should be invited to come over with an army to help to drive James from the throne. The nation was afraid to rise against the king, for it remembered the terrible vengeance that followed Monmouth's rebellion. So messengers were sent to William to ask for his aid, and he promised to go to England if Louis XIV. did not invade his country. Louis, as it happened sent his army against Germany, and this left the way open for William to go to England.

7. Declaration of Indulgence.—In the meantime James had resolved on issuing another "Declaration of Indulgence," and, as his former " declaration " had been little heeded, he ordered that the clergy should read it from their pulpits. Most of the clergy refused, and seven bishops, with Archbishop Sancroft at their head, drew up a respectful petition to James asking him to withdraw his order to the clergy. When James read this petition he was so angry that he had the bishops charged with libel and sent to the Tower.

8. Trial of the Bishops.—The bishops were in due time brought to trial, and thousands came flocking to London to see they suffered no wrong. So great was the anxiety to hear the trial that crowds stood for miles around the court. Able lawyers, like Somers, defended the bishops, and showed that the petition was not a libel at all; and the jury, after a night's discussion, at last agreed upon a verdict of "Not Guilty." Such a scene of excitement as followed is seldom witnessed. Bells rang, bonfires blazed, the people thronged the churches, and returned thanks in sobs of joy. James' own soldiers in Hounslow camp took up the cheers of the multitude, greatly to James' dismay and chagrin.

9. The Revolution.—And now Admiral Herbert went in disguise to Holland with an invitation from Whigs and Tories, Churchmen and Dissenters, the Army and Navy, Peers and Commoners. William began to prepare an army and fleet, and issued a proclamation to the nation that he was coming to restore its rights and liberties. James was now thoroughly alarmed, and hastily began to undo his illegal acts; but it was too late. William landed, November 5th, 1688, at Torbay, with 13,000 men, and though, at first, coldly received, he was soon joined by the leading men of England. James thought his forces were strong enough to defeat his opponent; but, as the armies approached each other, Churchill took his troops over to William, and James saw he was deserted. Even his daughter Anne and her husband left him, and nothing remained for James but to send his wife and child to France, and

122 HISTORY OF ENGLAND.

make his own way there as best he could. William was glad to have him go, and left the way open for his escape. So, on Dec. 23rd, 1688, James found his way to the court of Louis XIV., and England saw him no more.

10. Declaration of Rights.—Before William reached London some rioting took place, and an assembly formed of some members of the Commons in the time of Charles II., the Aldermen of London, and a few others, joined the House of Lords in asking him to take charge of affairs and keep order until a Parliament could decide what was best to be done. William then called a Convention Parliament in January, 1689, which, after considerable discussion, agreed that William and Mary should be joint King and Queen, and that William only should rule. It was now thought wise to make the new king and queen agree to certain principles before they were crowned; and so Somers drew up for Parliament a "Declaration of Rights," which after William became king was changed into a law. This "Declaration," after reciting the misdeeds of James, declared that the king had no power to suspend or dispense with the laws, nor raise money, nor keep a standing army without consent of Parliament; that subjects may petition the king; that elections of members must be free, and that free speech in Parliament must be allowed; and that Parliaments should meet frequently to redress grievances. The Bill of Rights afterwards added "that no Papist should ever again hold the Crown of England."

William and Mary agreed to be bound by these conditions, and were crowned April 11th, 1689.

CHAPTER XX.

RETURN TO PARLIAMENTARY GOVERNMENT.

1. William III.—The "New Monarchy" was now at an end, and government by Parliament, as in the days of the Plantagenets, was at last restored. The Bill of Rights gave the crown to William and Mary, and their children (if they had any), failing which it was to go to the Princess Anne and her children. So we see that William's right to the crown was given by Parliament, and henceforth no sovereign ruled by any other title than a parliamentary one.

William III. was in every respect a remarkable man. He was an unfortunate general, yet one who succeeded by his calmness and courage in the hour of defeat in wresting gain out of his losses. He had been brought up in a land which had suffered greatly from religious persecution, and so had learned to be liberal and tolerant to people of all creeds. When quite young he had been surrounded by enemies who watched his words and actions, and he had formed the habit of keeping his own counsel and trusting but few. This, added to a disposition naturally distrustful, caused him to appear to the English people sullen and morose. When it is remembered that William suffered almost continually from ill-health, and that when in England he was living among men who constantly sought to betray him, we have an explanation of his being so unsociable and suspicious, and why he was so unpopular with his English subjects. Yet, while the English did not like his foreign ways and his foreign favorites, they knew that he alone stood between them and the loss of their religion and their political rights, and this caused them to give him their support in the days when he was most disliked.

2. **Early Difficulties.**—But William was not accepted as king by all his subjects. In England, some of the clergy who believed in the Divine Right of kings refused to take the oath of allegiance to him, and, in consequence, were turned out of their offices. They then formed themselves into a party called the "Non-Jurors," and for a century elected their own bishops. The "Non-Jurors" caused a good deal of trouble, for they joined with the friends of James, or Jacobites (from *Jacobus*, Latin for James), in plots to have the Stuarts restored.

In Scotland, Parliament agreed to accept William as king on the condition that Presbyterianism should be restored. The English Church clergy in Scotland would now have been severely treated by the Covenanters, had not William interfered to stop the "rabbling" that began with the downfall of James. In the Highlands, the people were mostly Roman Catholics, and there an old follower of

James and fierce persecutor of the Covenanters, Graham of Claverhouse, now Viscount Dundee, raised an army, which at the Pass of Killiecrankie, in July 1689, swept before it William's troops under General Mackay. But in the hour of victory, Claverhouse was killed, and then, the Highlanders collecting all the booty they could, separated for their homes. Troops were now stationed at different posts in the Highlands and order was once more restored.

3. Massacre of Glencoe.—The Highland chiefs were gradually won over to take the oath of allegiance, and were promised a full pardon if their submission was made before the 1st January, 1692. When that time came, it was found all had taken the oath of allegiance except chief Ian Macdonald, of the Macdonalds of Glencoe. He was too proud to yield till the last moment, and then he went to the wrong place to take the oath. So it was after the 1st of January when he made his submission; nevertheless he was assured that he would not be molested. But Dalrymple, Master (or Lord) of Stair, who ruled Scotland for William, thought it an excellent opportunity to make an example of this unruly clan, Macdonald. He got William to agree to send troops into the valley of Glencoe, to "extirpate this band of thieves." To make sure work, Dalrymple sent the foemen of the Macdonalds, the Campbells of Argyle. When the soldiers reached Glencoe they were treated with true Highland kindness and hospitality by the Macdonalds. Days were passed in feasting and dancing; and then, early one morning, in the depth of winter, the soldiers surrounded the huts of their hosts and began the work of murder. Soon thirty lay dead on the snow, and of those that escaped half-clad to the hills, the greater number perished of cold and hunger. This terrible deed has never been forgotten by the people of the Highlands, and William's fair fame received a lasting stain by his share in this cruel and teacherous massacre.

4. Civil War in Ireland.—Before James was driven out of England he had put Ireland under the control of Tyrconnel, who raised an army of 20,000 men to aid James in case his English subjects grew rebellious. Now that he was exiled, James crossed over from France to Ireland with money and officers lent him by Louis XIV. The Irish, as a people, gave him a hearty welcome, and he was at once recognized as king throughout the greater part of Ireland. The small body of English and Scotch settlers in the island was much alarmed at James' landing, for they feared another massacre such as had taken place in 1641. As many as could escaped to England; but in the north, they gathered together for mutual aid at Enniskillen, and at Londonderry on Lough Foyle. James proceeded to attack Londonderry, which was in a wretched condition to stand a siege. Nevertheless the people of the city, under the leadership of the Rev. Geo. Walker and Major Baker, were so brave and resolute in its defence that James had to fall back on the plan of cutting off its food supply. To prevent aid coming from England by sea, a boom made of logs of timber fastened end to end was stretched across the mouth of the Foyle. English vessels sailed up to the boom, within sight of the starving garrison, and then retreated. For one hundred and five days the siege lasted, until the garrison was reduced to eating hides and leather. At last, an order was sent from England that the vessels must make an effort to relieve the garrison. On the 30th July, 1689, two ships sailed straight for the boom which gave way, and then sailing up to the starving city, they threw in a supply of provisions. James now saw it would be of no use to continue the siege and retreated with his army. Almost at the same time, Colonel Wolseley defeated an Irish army at Newton Butler, and this freed the north of Ireland from James' troops.

James now went to Dublin, where he set up his government. As money was scarce he met his expenses with brass money, which was to be changed for gold when he once more became king of England. In the meantime William was busy elsewhere, and had to leave the war in Ireland to his general Marshal Schomberg. Early in 1690, Louis sent a large force to help James, and then William saw he would have to go to Ireland himself, and take an army with him. He crossed over in June, and on the 1st July, met James at the famous Battle of the Boyne, where William's daring and courage won him a great victory. James watched from a distance the battle going against his followers and then fled in terror to Dublin. Thence he crossed over to France, leaving his brave Irish soldiers to fight his battles for another year.

Led by French officers, the Irish were again defeated at Aughrim by General Ginkell, after which, under General Patrick Sarsfield, they took refuge behind the old battered and ruined walls of Limerick, which were so weak that the French general said they could be "battered down with roasted apples." Here for months the English strove in vain to capture the last stronghold of James in Ireland. At last General Ginkell agreed to allow Sarsfield to go out with all the honours of war, and to take his soldiers abroad wherever he wished. He also promised that the Irish should have the same freedom of religious worship they enjoyed in the time of Charles II. So Sarsfield took 14,000 men to France, and the Irish were left to become "hewers of wood and drawers of water" for their English masters. Parliament refused to be bound by Ginkell's promise to give the Irish religious freedom, and the Treaty of Limerick, in 1691, is looked upon by the people of Ireland as a glaring instance of English perfidy.

5. **Some Important Laws.**—While these wars were going on, important changes were taking place in England. In 1689, the Dissenters were permitted by the "Toleration Act" to worship in their own chapels ; but they were not given the right to hold offices in the army and navy or to become members of Parliament. The Roman Catholics were left under cruel and unjust laws, which, however, were not fully enforced. A revenue of £1,200,000 a year was voted William and Mary, but instead of voting it for life, as in the days of Charles II. and James I., only a part was granted, the rest being kept under the control of parliament. It was in this reign that the money needed for the public service began to be voted annually, and this made it necessary that Parliament should meet every year.

Another very important Act in 1689 was the "Mutiny Bill," which gave the officers of the army and navy power to form courts for the trial and punishment of offenders against discipline. This power was given at first for six months and then for a year at a time. This law also makes it necessary that Parliament should meet every year, otherwise there would be no means of maintaining order in the army and of paying the soldiers.

6. **War with France.**—For the first eight years of William's reign war was going on against France. A Grand Alliance was formed in 1690, of England, Holland, Germany, Spain, and some smaller states, to keep Louis XIV. in check. For a time little was done by the Allies, and Louis had everything much his own way.

RETURN TO PARLIAMENTARY GOVERNMENT. 127

The day before the Battle of the Boyne, England was disgráced by her admiral, Lord Torrington, standing aloof while a French fleet defeated the Dutch off Beachy Head. The French then sailed along the coast of England, and, landing, burned the little village of Teignmouth. Although there were many people in England who were discontented with William's rule, nevertheless, the thought of Frenchmen landing on England's shores roused a fierce indignation against the Jacobites, and made William much stronger in England than he was before. He now crossed over to the Netherlands to take command of the allied army which was fighting there against Louis' forces. William was not very successful, and he lost many battles. His losses encouraged the numerous traitors at that time in England to carry on plots against him, and to treat with James for his return. Churchill was one of the basest of these traitors, and Lord Russell, the admiral of the fleet, was known at the court of James to be unfaithful. Yet, when Admiral Tourville tried to cross the channel with a French army, Russell rather than allow the French to triumph in English waters, met him at Cape La Hague, in 1692, and inflicted so heavy a loss on the French fleet that France made no further attempts to invade England.

7. The National Debt and Bank of England.—But all this fighting made heavy taxes for the English people, who had to bear the heaviest portion of the expenses of the Allies. To lighten their burdens, William's Treasurer, Charles Montague, introduced the plan of borrowing what was needed from rich people, who received in return each year from the government interest on what they lent. It was not easy to borrow much at first, for there were no banks which could receive the savings of many people, and then lend them to the government. But in 1694, Patterson, a Scotchman, suggested the founding of a bank, and his plan was carried out by Montague. In this way the Bank of England, perhaps the strongest bank in the world, had its beginning. Montague carried out another reform, very much needed at that time. The coin of the realm had become so worn and clipped by dishonest men, that a shilling was often worth no more than sixpence. The rich people did not feel this much for they took the coins at what they were really worth ; but poor men had little choice, and their wages were often paid in this debased coin at its face value, while the coins they gave for what they bought were taken by dealers at sometimes less than their true value. Montague determined to give the nation good coin, and, at a great loss to the Treasury, he called in all the worn and clipped coins and gave coins of full weight in exchange. He also had the coins made with "milled" or ribbed edges, so that it could be easily seen whether a coin had been cut or clipped.

8. Rise of Party Government.—When William came to the throne he wished to have both Tories and Whigs among his advisers. He could not understand why they could not work together for the public interest; but he soon found out that the feeling between the two parties was too bitter to permit common action. So much trouble arose through their quarrels, that at length he listened to the advice of Earl Sunderland to choose his advisers from the party having the greatest number of supporters in Parliament. In this way our system of Party Government began, although it must not be supposed that it was carried out very thoroughly in William's reign, or in that of his successor.

9. Useful Laws.—With the introduction of Party Government began the passage of many useful measures. A "Triennial Act," which decreed that a new Parliament must be elected at least every three years became law in 1694; and the law which made it necessary that all books, newspapers, and pamphlets, should be licensed by a committee of the King's Council, was allowed to drop. Henceforth any man could publish what he wished, without asking for permission. This led to better newspapers being published, although it was a long time before it was safe to publish anything against the government of the day. In 1695 the law of treason was made more just and merciful, and for the future a man charged with treason could have a lawyer to defend him, and a copy of the charges brought against him.

10. Peace of Ryswick.—While England was thus improving her laws, William had to endure many sorrows and disappointments. In 1694, Queen Mary died of small-pox, and William was almost heart-broken. Their early married life had been unhappy, through William's sullenness and bad temper; and he had treated her with coldness and neglect. She bore all his harshness and unfaithfulness with patience, and after a time her truth, constancy, and loving disposition so melted his coldness and drove away his suspicions, that he became one of the most loyal and devoted of husbands. It is said he never recovered from the shock of her death. Then a plot was formed in 1696 to murder him; but its discovery had the effect of making his subjects more loyal. The war against Louis had been generally unsuccessful, until 1695, when William won a great victory by taking the strong fortress of Namur.

At last Louis was tired of war, and he agreed to a peace in 1697. The Treaty of Ryswick was signed, and by it Louis gave up most of his conquests and consented to acknowledge William as king of England. The nation was glad to have the war ended, and Parliament began at once to reduce the number of men in the army and navy. It even went so far as to send William's Dutch Guards back to Holland, an act that William felt to be both ungrateful and insulting. Besides he thought a strong army was still needed, for he foresaw in the near future a new danger to the peace of Europe.

11. Spanish Succession.—This danger arose out of the sickly condition of Charles II. King of Spain, who was not expected to live many years. He had no children, and his great possessions in Spain, Italy, the Low Countries, and America, were coveted by his near relations. Louis XIV. had married Charles' eldest sister, but he had solemnly renounced all claim to the Spanish throne on behalf of himself and his children. The Elector of Bavaria had a good claim to the throne of Spain, so also had the German Emperor Leopold. William considered it dangerous for the Emperor or one of the French royal family to become king of Spain; and so he entered into a treaty with Louis by which the greater portion of the Spanish possessions should go to the Elector of Bavaria. The Elector, however, died, and a second Partition Treaty was framed, which gave the Spanish crown and most of the Spanish territory to the Archduke Charles, the second son of the Emperor. In all these arrangements the Spanish people were not consulted; and when the facts came to light, they were very angry, and Charles II., acting under the advice of his friends, made a will and left all his dominions to Philip of Anjou, grandson of Louis XIV. The temptation to break the Partition Treaty was too strong for Louis, and he accepted the Spanish crown on behalf of his grandson, and put garrisons in the Spanish fortresses in the Low Countries. William was indignant, but for the time being he was powerless. His troops were few, and England refused to go to war; and so, very unwillingly, he had to assent to Louis' breach of faith.

12. The Act of Settlement.—The English were more concerned about who should reign after Anne, than who should be king of Spain. William had no children, and the last of Anne's nineteen children had just died. The fear was strong that James II.'s son would be hosen if the succession was not settled in time. So, in 1701, an "Act of Settlement" was passed, which arranged that the throne after Anne's death should go to the Princess Sophia of Hanover and her heirs. Sophia was the grand-daughter of James I., and daughter of Elizabeth, the wife of the unfortunate Elector Palatine. Her claim by birth was not very strong, but she was the nearest Protestant relation of the royal family.

The Act of Settlement also enacted, among other things, that in future judges should hold office for life or good conduct. Henceforth judges could not be dismissed at the king's whim or pleasure, as in the days of the Tudors and the Stuarts.

13. Death of William.—And now an event took place which made the English people as eager for war as a few months before they had been anxious for peace. James II. was visited on his death-bed by Louis XIV., and Louis promised to recognize his son James as the king of England. The English could not endure that the French king should choose a ruler for them, and at once they cried out for war. William now found no trouble in getting Parliamen to vote all the men and money he wanted. But the war was not to be waged under William's command. His life was near its close, and an accident, by which he broke his collar bone, hastened his end. He knew no one fit to lead the armies of the Allies against Louis' generals save Churchill, the Earl of Marlborough ; and Churchill had been banished from his court some time before for his base treachery to William. He was now recalled, and trusting to his ambition to keep him faithful, William named him Captain-General of the allied armies. Then, on the 20th February, 1702, passed away one of England's greatest kings and truest friends. He had his faults both as a man and as a ruler. He did not fully understand the English people and the English form of government, and he often acted without the consent of his Parliament in matters of grave importance. But his prudence, foresight, tolerance, and courage, saved England from the loss of her religious and political freedom at a time when England seemed powerless to save herself.

CHAPTER XXI.

THE LAST OF THE STUARTS.

1. **Queen Anne.**—William was succeeded by Anne, the second daughter of James II. The nation was glad to have once more an English sovereign, and "Good Queen Anne" was, throughout her reign, popular with all classes of her subjects. She was a dull but kind-hearted woman, who had won the pity and sympathy of her people by losing all her many children. Her inclinations and feelings were on the side of the Stuarts and against the line of Hanover, which was to come after her. It would have pleased her much if her brother James, the Pretender (as he was called), had consented to give up his Roman Catholic faith and become a supporter of the English Church. This James refused to do, and Anne felt compelled, through her love for the Church, to refuse her assent to his claim to the throne.

Anne was much under the influence of Sarah, the Duchess of Marlborough, a beautiful but violent-tempered woman, who had been Anne's friend from early years. They were on very familiar terms, and called each other "Mrs. Morley" and "Mrs. Freeman." This friendship had a great deal to do with the politics of the time, for in consequence of it Anne, though a Tory at heart, kept a Whig government in office for many years, because the Whigs supported the war in which the Duke of Marlborough was the chief commander. Marlborough himself, and Godolphin, the High Treasurer, were Tories, but they had to join the Whigs as the Tories were bitterly opposed to the war against France.

2. **War of the Spanish Succession.**—This war was to prevent Louis XIV. from placing his grandson on the throne of Spain. William had formed a Grand Alliance, the principal members of which were England, Holland, Portugal, Savoy, Prussia, Austria, and a small portion of Spain. Louis had Bavaria and nearly all Spain on his side. The chief leaders among the Allies were Marlborough, Prince Eugene of Savoy, and Heinsius of Holland, while the Earl of Peterborough during the early years of the war did good service for them in Spain. Louis, on the other hand, had

large armies and great generals, and his troops had been successful in many battles during the preceding half century.

Marlborough had many difficulties to overcome abroad and at home. The Allies were not always willing to do as he wished, and the Tories in England put obstacles in his way. Yet he never lost patience, and by his tact and winning manners gradually succeeded in getting the Allies to follow his advice and leadership. His ability as a commander was not fully known until this war began; but he soon proved himself to be one of the greatest generals in all history. He was calm and heedless of danger on the battlefield, and his readiness of resource was equal to every occasion. He was great, also, as a statesman and diplomatist; but he was faithless and cold-hearted, and his love for money amounted to avarice. The pleasantest feature of his character and career was his love for his wife.

Marlborough could not do much during the first two years of the war, on account of the timidity of the Allies, and the hindrances their quarrels placed in the way. Meanwhile the Tories in England were trying to prevent, by an "Occasional Conformity Bill," the Dissenters from holding any office. Some of the Dissenters, in order to get into parliament, would take the sacrament in the English church, and then attend worship in their own chapel. This the Tories sought to stop; but the Bill they brought in was defeated by the Whigs in the House of Lords.

Not until 1704 was the war carried on with much vigor. A large French army was then sent by Louis to Bavaria to attack Austria. Marlborough saw the danger, and, by a stratagem, managed to get his Dutch allies away from their own frontier. He then marched straight to Bavaria, where he joined Prince Eugene near the little village of Blenheim. Then was fought one of the most important battles of modern times. With an army not so numerous as that opposed to him, Marlborough defeated, with terrible loss, on the 13th of August, 1704, a veteran French force commanded by one of France's best generals. Henceforth the French soldiers were no longer thought to be invincible. The same year the great rock fortress, Gibraltar, was taken by Admiral Rooke, and it has remained in England's possession ever since. Marlborough's great victory made the Whigs very popular in England, and Marlborough himself became the idol of the people.

In 1706, the Allies under Marlborough won another great victory over the French at Ramillies in Flanders, and took nine strong fortresses along the Flemish frontiers. While these victories were being won in Flanders, Peterborough was carrying on a spirited campaign in Spain. By a clever stratagem he took Barcelona, and succeeded in proclaiming the Archduke Charles king at Madrid. All these losses made Louis anxious for peace, but the Allies were so elated with their successes that they would not listen to the fair terms he offered. Marlborough and the Whigs knew that their power depended on the continuance of the war.

3. State of the Nation.—It so happened that England was very prosperous at this time, and her people did not feel the heavy expense of the war. Money was borrowed freely to pay the Allies, and the debt of the nation grew to over £50,000,000. This debt was useful in keeping the Pretender off the throne, for those who had lent money to the government were afraid if he became king their money would not be repaid. The Bank of England was doing a good work in helping trade and commerce; large towns like Manchester and Leeds were springing up, and Liverpool was fast becoming a great city. But the growth of large towns was at the expense of the country districts. The yeomanry of England began to disappear, as the small farmers found it paid better to sell their farms to rich men and put their money into trade in the towns than to till the soil.

4. Union of England and Scotland.—Much more important than all Marlborough's victories was the Union of England and Scotland, which took place in 1707. The two nations had never been on very friendly terms, although, since the time of James I., they had been ruled by the same sovereign. The Act of Settlement had said that Anne was to be succeeded in England by the House of Hanover; but the Scotch Parliament had not agreed that it should reign in Scotland. The Scotch were angry with the English because they would not allow Scotland to trade freely with England, or in English foreign ports. So, when a Scotch colony on the Isthmus of Darien failed, the Scotch blamed the English laws, and the Scotch Parliament, in 1703, passed a Bill that when Anne died Scotland should not have the same sovereign as England. English statesmen foresaw this would lead to war, and they offered Scotland good terms if she would agree to unite with England. The Scotch people did not like to give up their independence ; but their Parliament was bribed, it is said, to consent, and Scotland and England became one nation with a common flag and a common Parliament. The terms were that Scotland was to keep her own Established Church —the Presbyterian—and her own peculiar laws and courts. She was to send forty-five members to the House of Commons and sixteen elected peers to the House of Lords. Trade was to be free at home and abroad between the two peoples, and Scotland was to get a sum of money to make her coinage as good as that of England. The Union proved a great boon to both nations, although, for many years, the Scotch and English did not understand each other, and this led occasionally to bitter feelings.

5. **Party Struggles.**—While England and Scotland were settling their difficulties, the war against France was going on. In 1708, Marlborough defeated the French at Oudenarde and Lille; but the Allies lost ground in Spain after Peterborough was recalled. France was now greatly exhausted, and Louis again offered fair terms of peace, which the Allies would not accept, because Louis would not agree to help to drive his grandson out of Spain. The war again went on, and France at a great sacrifice put another large army in the field. In 1709, the Allies under Marlborough once more met the French and defeated them, this time at Malplaquet, in the north of France. The loss was very heavy on both sides; but the Allies suffered more than the French, and gained little by their victory.

The English had now become tired of the war, and they began to think that it was carried on to please Marlborough and the Whigs. What the people thought was shown very clearly when the Whig Government impeached Dr. Sacheverell for preaching a foolish sermon on "Divine Right" and the sin of resisting a rightful king. Had the Whigs been wise they would have paid no attention to Sacheverell ; but they thought his sermon was an open attack on the right of Parliament to choose the sovereign, and so had Sacheverell tried before the Lords, who ordered his sermon to be burnt, and condemned him to cease preaching for three years. This made him a popular hero, and great crowds after the trial cheered him, rang the bells, and lit bonfires, to show their approval of his conduct, and their dislike of the Whigs.

THE LAST OF THE STUARTS. 135

The queen, who was in sympathy with the Tories, had just quarrelled with the Duchess of Marlborough, and had taken a new favourite, a Mrs. Masham, the cousin of Harley, a leading Tory statesman. Through Mrs. Masham's influence, Anne now dismissed her Whig ministers and chose in their stead Tories, the chief of which were Harley and Bolingbroke, the latter a brilliant speaker and writer. A general election followed, which resulted in the Tory party gaining a large majority in the House of Commons. Marlborough was dismissed from his command of the army, and charged with taking wrongfully some of the public money given for the army. He was forced to leave England, and never again held any high position. So ended the career of England's greatest general—one who never lost a battle nor besieged a fortress he did not take.

6. Peace of Utrecht (1713).—The new Tory ministry was very anxious for peace, for it knew that the war could not succeed without Marlborough. So it offered, secretly, good terms to Louis, and peace was agreed upon without the knowledge of England's allies. It was a disgraceful act, although there was nothing to be gained by continuing the war. Louis gave up all his conquests in the Low Countries and Germany; Austria obtained Naples, Milan, and the Netherlands; while Philip of Anjou kept Spain and her possessions in America. England obtained Gibraltar, Minorca, Hudson's Bay and Straits, Newfoundland, and Nova Scotia. Louis, further, promised to acknowledge Anne and her Hanoverian successors, and never again to help the Pretender. But after all this bloodshed to drive Philip from Spain, he was allowed to remain king.

7. Death of Anne (1714).—The Peace of Utrecht was scarcely concluded when Anne died. The Princess Sophia died a few months before her, and George, Sophia's son, was Anne's successor. George was not in England at the time of the queen's death: Anne's dislike of her successor being so great that she would not allow him to visit England. A short time before Anne died, Bolingbroke, Harley (now Earl of Oxford), Ormond, and other Jacobites began to intrigue to restore the Pretender. Bolingbroke thought he had everything in readiness to place the Pretender on the throne; but the sudden death of the queen, and the prompt action of the Whigs and the Duke of Shrewsbury ruined his plans, and George I. became king without any opposition.

8. **Literature of the Age of Anne.**—The latter part of the 17th century, and the beginning of the 18th, are rich in great poets and prose writers. We have already mentioned Milton and Bunyan; but, besides these, there were Addison, Steele, and Swift, satirists and essayists; Bishop Burnet, the historian of his own times; Locke and Hobbes, great writers on philosophy and politics; the poets Cowley, Dryden, Pope, and Butler; De Foe, the author of *Robinson Crusoe*; and Pepys, the author of a *Diary*, which tells us what was going on in London at the court and among the people. These writers, excepting Milton, were not so great as those of the age of Elizabeth; but they wrote in simpler language and in plainer sentences, because their writings were read by people many of whom were not scholars, whereas, in the time of Elizabeth, few read much except educated men and women.

CHAPTER XXII.

THE WHIG NOBLES RULE ENGLAND.

1. **George I.**—The first king of the line of Hanover, was past middle age when he came to the throne, and cared much more for Hanover and its people than for his English crown. As a man he had few good and no great qualities; but as a king he did fairly well, because he left the government of the country much in the hands of his ministers. He knew little or no English, and brought his companions and associates with him from Germany; some of them as gross and licentious as the favourites of Charles II.

Almost his first act was to dismiss the Tory ministers, and appoint Whigs in their stead. Bolingbroke, Oxford, and Ormond were impeached for treason, and for their share in the Treaty of Utrecht. Bolingbroke and Ormond fled to France; Oxford stood his ground, and after an imprisonment of two years was released.

2. **The Rebellion of 1715.**—The year after George's accession, the Jacobites in Scotland and in the north of England rose in rebellion. The Earl of Mar raised an army in the Highlands, but he was defeated by the Duke of Argyle at Sheriffmuir, on the same day that

the Jacobites in England were compelled to surrender at Preston in Lancashire. The Pretender landed after the rebellion was over and, finding his cause was lost, returned to France with the Earl of Mar. Several persons were put to death after this rising, among whom was the Earl of Derwentwater, a leader of the Jacobites in the north of England.

The rebellion led to an important change in the time a Parliament can last. The Whigs were afraid that if an election took place at this time they might be defeated, and they changed the law so that a Parliament could remain in existence *seven* years instead of *three*; and the Septennial Act, as the new measure was called, has remained law to the present. The worst feature of this change was that the Parliament which made it continued to sit for the new term, although it was elected for but three years.

In 1715 Louis XIV. died, and was succeeded by his great-grandson Louis XV. The new king was a mere lad, and the Duke of Orleans acted as Regent. Orleans was friendly to England, and when Spain tried, in 1718, to recover a portion of her lost territory in Italy, France and England united to force her to keep the peace.

3. **South Sea Bubble.**—The National Debt had now grown so large that Aislabie, the Treasurer, proposed to Parliament a scheme for its easy payment. This was to accept the offer of the South Sea Company, which promised, if given the sole right of trading with South America in slaves and other commodities, to pay off a large share of the public debt. When the proposal was made the Bank of England also made an offer, and then the two companies began to bid against each other, until, at last, the South Sea Company offered to give £7,500,000 to the Government, in addition to what it had first proposed. The offer was accepted in 1720, in spite of the warnings of Robert Walpole, a rough but shrewd Norfolk squire, who showed clearly that the Company could not carry out its agreement. No sooner was the scheme adopted than every person who had any money to invest rushed to buy the shares of the Company. In a short time shares rose from £100 to £1000; and then almost as quickly the public lost confidence in the Company, and the anxiety to sell caused the shares to fall in price until they were nearly worthless. Thousands of people of all classes were ruined, and public wrath was turned against the

King's ministers, some of whom were found to have taken bribes from the Company to further its scheme. They had to resign, and Walpole, who had spoken against the scheme, was now called upon to lessen the evil effects of the failure and panic.

4. Walpole.—Walpole became chief minister in 1721, and continued in office till 1742. He was the first to be called "Prime Minister," and held that post longer than any other man in English history. He was a rough, coarse man, who enjoyed foul talk, eating, drinking, and fox hunting. He lived a licentious life, such as was very common in the 18th century among men in high positions. He kept himself in office by buying the support of members of Parliament, and by paying great attention to trade and commerce, of which matters he knew more than most men of his time. He did good service to Britain by keeping the country at peace, and by the steady support he gave to the House of Hanover. In his day the nation made great progress in extending its trade, increasing its manufactures, and in employing better methods of tilling the soil. He was tolerant to the Dissenters, but was too much afraid of the Church party to repeal the Test and Corporation Acts, which prevented them from having their rights as citizens.

All through the reigns of George I. and George II. the Whigs were in office, and when one Government went out, it was replaced by another of the same political opinions. The Whig nobles were very powerful in the country where they owned large estates, and they banded themselves together to keep in power. They bought up the right to send members from boroughs where there were few voters, and by this means always had many supporters in Parliament. Then, again, the Tories were suspected of being Jacobites, and of wishing to bring back the Pretender, and so every man that had lent money to the Government supported the Whigs fearing, if the Tories got into office, he would never be repaid. By such means as these the Whig nobles managed to have things all their own way for nearly fifty years.

5. George II.—Beyond a slight plot, in 1722, by Bishop Atterbury, in the interest of the Pretender, and a brief excitement in Ireland over the coinage of some half-pence, nothing of interest took place in the last six years of George I.'s reign. George died, while abroad in Hanover, in 1727, and was succeeded by his son, George

II. The new king had been opposed to Walpole while his father, George I., was living, and Walpole expected to be turned out of office as soon as he came to the throne. Perhaps he would, had not Queen Caroline, a shrewd and wise woman, used her influence with her husband to keep him in his post. George II. was a thorough German, and knew very little more about the English language and the English people than his father. He was a stubborn man, and too fond of war, for he was a brave soldier and a good general. Fortunately his queen had great influence over him, and through her Walpole was able to get the king to do much as he wished.

6. Walpole's Policy.—The first ten years of George II.'s reign had few stirring events. The nation was kept at peace, and Walpole gave his attention to helping trade and commerce, and to lessening the public debt. He took the duties off a great many articles that came into the country as well as off many that were sent out of it. He allowed the colonies in America to trade with other countries, and by so doing Georgia and Carolina were able to sell their rice in foreign markets. He saw that he could prevent a great deal of smuggling by making goods pay duty when they were sold in the country instead of when they were brought into ports of entry. So in 1733, he brought in an Excise Bill, which aimed at collecting the duties on certain kinds of goods by making them pay a tax when they were sold, instead of when they were brought into the sea-ports. The first duty is called *excise*, and the second *customs*. But Walpole was too much ahead of his time. People were afraid of his scheme, and so great an outcry was raised against the Excise Bill that Walpole, rather than have any bloodshed, abandoned it.

Walpole had one weakness which helped to bring about his downfall. He wanted to have all the power of the government in his own hands, and was so jealous of other able men, that he forced them one by one to leave his ministry, until he had for associates none but inferior men who would do his bidding. In this way there grew up gradually a strong "Opposition" composed of men who had formerly supported him, the leaders of which were Pulteney, Carteret, Chesterfield, and, later on, William Pitt, the grandson of a former governor of Madras. The younger members of this party grew tired of Walpole's method of ruling, and of his peace policy, and in their speeches talked a good deal about "Patriotism," or love of country. Hence they were, in derision, called the "Patriots," and Walpole sneered at them, and said that when they grew older they would become wiser.

7. The Family Compact.—In spite of all the "Patriots" could do, Walpole continued to hold his ground, until a war with Spain broke out in 1739. This was caused by France and Spain forming a secret "Family Compact" (they both had members of the Bourbon family on their thrones) against England. Spain was to get the aid of France in recovering Gibraltar from England, in return for her giving France the sole right to trade with her colonies in America. English merchants, after the Treaty of Utrecht, had been permitted to trade slightly in the South Seas, and finding the trade profitable, had managed to increase it a good deal by smuggling. When the smugglers were caught by the Spanish authorities, they were imprisoned and otherwise punished. Tales of Spanish cruelty were spread abroad throughout England, and Parliament and the people began to clamour for war. Walpole was very much against going to war, as he knew that England was not prepared, and besides, feared a Jacobite rising, aided by France and Spain. But the feeling of the nation for war was so strong, that Walpole unwillingly gave way, and declared war in 1739. When the bells began to ring at the news, Walpole said, "They may ring their bells now, but they will soon be wringing their hands."

8. Fall of Walpole.—It did not take long for Walpole's words to come true. The war was badly managed, and England had little success. Walpole was blamed for this, and perhaps he deserved the blame, as he was not fitted for the duties of a war minister. To make matters worse, crops failed, and bread became dear. People began to cry out against Walpole, and he was forced to resign, in 1742. He was made Earl of Orford, and given a pension. He never again held office, but for years had influence enough with the king to say who should be the king's ministers.

9. War of the Austrian Succession.—And now another war sprang up in which England, rather unwisely, took part. The German Emperor, Charles VI. (the Archduke Charles of the war of the Spanish Succession) had no son, and desiring to leave his hereditary dominions in Austria and Hungary to his daughter Maria Theresa, persuaded the strong nations of Europe to sign an agreement, called the "Pragmatic Sanction," by which the crown of Austria and Hungary should go to his daughter. When he died in 1740, it was soon seen that there was a plot to rob Maria Theresa of her dominions. Frederick II. of Prussia seized Silesia, the Elector of Bavaria claimed the Imperial Crown, and was supported by France and Spain in his claim. England and Holland alone remained true to their promises, and George II. put himself at the head of an army and defeated the French at Dettingen on the Maine, in 1743. The French, to draw off the English troops, sent Charles Edward, son of James the Pretender, into Scotland, to claim the crown of Great Britain and Ireland. Fifteen thousand men were to assist him, but a storm wrecked the French fleet, and the French troops never landed. The French were, however, more fortunate at Fontenoy, in 1745, where under Marshal Saxe they defeated the English with heavy loss.

10. **The Rebellion of 1745.**—Charles Edward landed, July 1745, in the Highlands, and soon was at the head of a large number of clansmen, who were eager to fight against the Duke of Argyle, and the king he supported. A little later, "Prince Charlie" was in Edinburgh, where he proclaimed his father king. On September 21, his Highlanders met and defeated Sir John Cope at Prestonpans. Had he now marched into England he might have had a chance to recover the throne for the Stuarts, for just then there were few troops in England to oppose him. But he lingered at Edinburgh enjoying the smiles and favours of the ladies of the gay Scotch capital, for the Young Pretender was a handsome, daring young fellow, who won many hearts by his pleasant ways. At last he started south with 6,000 men, mostly Highlanders, expecting to get aid on his march from the Jacobites in England. The people turned out to look at his army as it passed by, but did not give him much help in either men or money. At Derby he was advised to return to Scotland, as the king's troops were on the march to meet him. At Falkirk, 1746, he defeated General Hawley, and then many of his men deserted him and returned home. With a brave remnant of his followers, he made a stand at Culloden, in Invernesshire, against a large and well-armed force under the Duke of Cumberland, but his men were cut to pieces, April, 1745. For

five months Charles Edward wandered through the Highlands, seeking a way of escape, and carefully concealed from his enemies by his few faithful friends, the most famous of whom was the heroine Flora Macdonald. Then, in September, he left Scotland's shores for ever, and went back to France.

The Jacobites made no further attempts to restore the Stuarts. The Duke of Cumberland earned the title of "Butcher" Cumberland, by his cruelty to the Highlanders after the Battle of Culloden, and three Scotch nobles were put to death for treason. Efforts were now made to prevent further risings in the Highlands, and laws were made forbidding the chiefs of clans from exercising their ancient rights over their clansmen. The Highlanders were not allowed to carry arms or wear their tartans, and roads were made through the Highlands so that troops could easily march from point to point. All these changes made the proud Highlanders very unhappy and restless, and it was not till 1758, when William Pitt allowed Highland regiments to be formed under the command of their own chiefs, with their own peculiar uniform and music, that peace was restored among these brave and high-spirited people.

11. **Religious Revival.**—Meanwhile, England had sunk into a condition in which it seemed as if all religion and morality were dead. The lower classes were ignorant and brutal, and no one seemed to care for their moral and spiritual welfare. The middle classes were given up to money-making, and had lost nearly all interest in religious matters. The upper classes were steeped in vice, profanity, and infidelity; while the clergy, as a rule, neglected their duties. The country vicars were the boon companions of the squires in their sports and revels. Bishops often paid more attention to winning the favour of the king's German mistresses, through whom they expected promotion, than to looking after their dioceses. In fact, all classes seemed stricken with moral deadness, and with a desire to enjoy merely earthly pleasures.

The "darkest hour before the dawn" had been reached in English social life, when three English Church clergymen, John Wesley, Charles Wesley, George Whitfield, and a few others, began a religious movement which has gone on, with almost undiminished vigor, to the present day. The movement began at Oxford among a few earnest students, and after a few years spread throughout the land. The Wesleys and Whitfield went through the length

THE WHIG NOBLES RULE ENGLAND. 143

and breadth of England, preaching in the open air to great throngs of colliers, and to the neglected poor among the people, and arousing earnest and deep resolves among them to lead better lives. For a time fierce persecution from those opposed to the movement was met with by the preachers; but in the end the value of their great work was recognized, and all classes and Churches reaped the benefit of this remarkable revival. A new and powerful denomination, the "Methodists," arose out of John Wesley's preaching and wonderful power of organization, a denomination which now has its adherents all over the world. Among other important results of this revival was the new intesest aroused in moral reforms, and the beginning of earnest efforts to lessen the misery and ignorance of the poor and the oppressed.

12. East India Company.—The war of the Austrian Succession came to an end by the Peace of Aix-la-Chapelle, in 1748, when Henry Pelham was Prime Minister. England gained nothing beyond an increase in her national debt, and Maria Theresa lost Silesia to Frederick II. of Prussia.

In 1751, Frederick, Prince of Wales, died, and this left his son, George, as the heir to the throne. In the same year, the *time* of the nation was put right, by taking eleven days out of the year, the 3rd of September being henceforth counted the 14th. This was owing to the year having been hitherto too long, and this made the clock of the nation too slow. After this the year was made shorter, and no change in the *time* has since taken place.

And now England was on the eve of wars which were to greatly increase her territory and her influence in Asia and America. In the year 1599 Queen Elizabeth granted a charter to a company to trade in the East Indies. This was the East India Company which gradually founded factories and small trading posts on the coasts of India. In this way Fort St. George, or Madras, was established. Bombay was acquired by the marriage of Charles II. to Katharine of Portugal, and Fort William (now Calcutta) was founded by another English trading company in the reign of William III. In 1702, the two companies united. They kept at each trading post a small body of native soldiers, or *sepoys*, and they paid rent to the neighbouring native prince or ruler for the land they occupied. These rulers of small districts owed allegiance to a higher ruler, who in turn was supposed to obey the Great Moghul of India.

The French also had a company in India which had built a fort at Pondicherry. The English and French traders were very jealous of each other, and sometimes their mutual dislike led to fighting, even when England and France were at peace. At last, Dupleix, the Governor of Pondicherry, formed a scheme of driving the English out of India, and of obtaining for France the control of Indian affairs. His plan was to take advantage of the frequent quarrels among the many native rulers of India, to play off one ruler against the other, and so, in the end, get the control of Southern India. To carry out his plans, it was necessary that the English should be driven out of the country, and this he proceeded to do by attacking and capturing Madras. For a time it seemed as if the English must submit, when the whole aspect of affairs was changed by the skill in war and vigor of a young man in the East India Company's service, Robert Clive. Clive had been sent to India as a clerk, his friends in England in this way hoping to rid themselves of a wild and troublesome youth. He now gave up his clerkship, and putting himself at the head of a few English and native troops defeated the French at Arcot, in 1751, and held the fort until assistance came. From that time onwards the French were driven back until Dupleix was recalled, and peace was made in 1754.

13. French and English in America.—A similar struggle for power and supremacy had been going on for many years in America between the English and French. Though there were intervals of peace between the French colonies in Canada and Acadia, and the English colonies to the south of them, yet an almost constant border warfare was carried on in which the North American Indians took an active part. The English and French colonists both wanted the sole right to trade in furs with the Indians, and often when England and France were at peace their colonies were keeping up a cruel warfare, and making attacks on each other's settlements. The French settlements were in what we now call Quebec and Nova Scotia, and in Louisiana, at the mouth of the Mississippi; while the English had thirteen colonies scattered along the eastern coast of North America. The French claimed the right to all the land west of the Alleghanies, and as that would have shut out the English fur-traders from a profitable trade with the numerous tribes of Indians in the north-west, the French claim was disputed by the English colonists. The French established themselves at Fort Duquesne, in a fork of the Ohio river, and the English sent George Washington to build another fort near at hand. By mistake Washington fired into a party of French soldiers sent to warn him off French soil, and this led to a general war which did not end till the French were driven out of Canada. These events occurred in 1754, and the next year General Braddock, who was sent with a large force to take Fort Duquesne, through his own obstinacy and rashness, was surprised in a narrow pass in the woods, when near the fort, by a party of French and Indians, and most of his army destroyed. Braddock was killed, and for a time the French had matters all their own way.

14. Seven Years' War, 1756-63.—The year after Braddock's defeat, a great war broke out in Europe and lasted seven years. This war was caused by Maria Theresa's determination to recover Silesia from Frederick II. called the Great, of Prussia. In this she was aided by France, Russia and Saxony, while Frederick had no ally save England. When England entered into this war, she found herself without either army or general fit to take the field. The Duke of Newcastle, a weak, corrupt man, was now Prime Minister, and for a time nothing but disaster followed every effort of the English army and navy. France seized Minorca, and when Admiral Byng, who was sent to retake it with a weak fleet, retreated without striking a blow, the people were so angry that Newcastle, to save himself, had Byng tried by court-martial and shot. Soon after this terrible news came from India. Suraj-ud-Daula, the ruler of Bengal, marched on Calcutta, and taking the English inhabitants prisoners thrust them, 146 in number, into a small room not more than twenty feet square. There, in the "Black Hole of Calcutta," with but one small opening to admit air, they spent the hot sultry night, enduring the agonies of thirst and suffocation. When morning dawned, only twenty-three were found alive. In Europe, the Duke of Cumberland made an agreement with the French, allowing them to occupy Hanover, and disbanding his army. These were dark days for England. Despair settled on the nation, and men exclaimed, "We are no longer a nation."

15. William Pitt, the Great Commoner.—And now England

was to learn what a great man could do in rousing the nation by giving it his own courage and confidence; for it was now that William Pitt, the leader of the "Patriots," came forward to save his country. Pitt believed in himself, and his self-confidence was so great that he said he could save the country, and no one else could. He was a great parliamentary orator, and very outspoken and vehement in his attacks on wrong-doing in any form, caring little whom he pleased or offended. The Duke of Newcastle tried to rule without him by means of bribery and family influence ; but the people asked for Pitt. Finally Pitt and Newcastle ruled together, Pitt as Secretary of State and War Minister, and Newcastle as Prime Minister. By this division of power the government had a strong support, for Pitt was popular with the people, and Newcastle kept Parliament faithful by bribery, which Pitt himself scorned to use. Pitt came into office in 1757, and in a short time a great change took place. The army was organized, the navy equipped, good officers were put at the head of English troops, and, best of all, hope and courage brought back to soldiers and citizens. The Duke of Cumberland was recalled, and Ferdinand of Brunswick put at the head of the army in Germany. Frederick the Great, now supported strongly by Pitt, defeated the French at Rossbach, in 1757, and won victory after victory in face of heavy odds.

16. Conquest of Canada.—If we now turn to America, we will find that there also Pitt's wise and vigorous policy was bearing good fruit. He roused the English colonists to fresh endeavours, and formed a plan for driving the French out of America. Men, (including Highland regiments), arms, and money, were freely sent to the aid of the colonists, and never was Pitt's knowledge of men better shown than in choosing the officers who were sent to command.

Abercromby was for a time Commander-in-Chief, but he was soon replaced by an abler man, General Amherst, who had under him, Wolfe, the hero of Quebec, Townshend, Murray, and others. The first great success was won at Louisbourg in Cape Breton, where Wolfe greatly distinguished himself in taking that strong fortress. Step by step the French were driven back, until they made their last stand at Quebec under General Montcalm, a brave and skilful officer. It fell to the lot of Wolfe to make the effort to capture this Gibraltar of America, in the summer of 1759. The

French had fortified Quebec and the steep banks of the St. Lawrence so well, that Wolfe, who was seriously ill, almost despaired of success. At last on the night of Sept. 12, Wolfe and his men climbed up a narrow path, on the face of the cliff above Quebec, unobserved save by a small French outpost. There on the Plains of Abraham the early dawn found him with his troops drawn up in order of battle. Montcalm, who was below Quebec when the news of Wolfe's landing reached him, in great haste marched to meet the enemy. Passing through Quebec, he at once attacked the English, who quietly waited until the French were close at hand, and then poured a deadly volley into their ranks. This was followed by a fierce charge of bayonets before which the French troops gave way. In the hour of victory Wolfe was mortally wounded, but he lived long enough to know that his task was successfully accomplished. The brave Montcalm also fell, and the following night died within the walls of Quebec. Five days after Quebec surrendered.

The war went on another year, and then Montreal surrendered, and with it, in 1760, passed all Canada into the hands of England.

17. **Clive and India.**—In these days news of victories won on land and sea came thick and fast to cheer the hearts of the English. At Minden, in Westphalia, Duke Ferdinand won a great victory over the French, while Admiral Hawke and Admiral Boscawen won victories at sea over the French fleet, the first at Quiberon Bay, and the second at Lagos.

But equally important with Quebec and Minden, was Clive's great victory at Plassy, in Bengal. Clive had just returned to Madras from England, when news came of the horrible tragedy at Calcutta. He at once proceeded to retake Calcutta, and meeting Suraj-ud-Daula on the Plains of Plassy, he, with 3,000 men, routed an army of 60,000 natives, with little loss to his troops. Suraj-ud-Daula was now dethroned, and a ruler more friendly to the English put in his place. This was the beginning of the English conquest of Bengal, and one step led to another, until the East India Company, in 1765, held the chief power in the most important provinces of Hindostan.

18. **Close of Seven Years' War.**—In 1760 George II. died, and was succeeded by his grandson, George III. The young king did

not like the Whigs and Pitt, and to get rid of them he used his influence to bring the war to a close. Pitt was opposed to peace, for he knew Spain had secretly promised to aid France; but George managed to get Parliament on his side, and Pitt resigned. Newcastle, too, was driven by slights and insults from office, and Lord Bute, the king's tutor, took his place as Prime Minister. Nevertheless the war with Spain took place, as Pitt had foreseen, and lasted a year. England now refused to help Frederick the Great further, and he made a peace with his enemies, by which he kept Silesia. A general peace was signed at Paris, in 1763, between France, England, Spain and Portugal, and the "Seven Years' War" came to an end. England kept Canada and Florida; Minorca was restored by France; while, in India, English influence and power was henceforth fully recognized.

CHAPTER XXIII.

PERSONAL INFLUENCE OF THE KING.

1. **George III.**—George III. began his reign with the resolve to allow the king's ministers to rule no longer for the king, as was the custom in the days of George I. and II. His mother had early and constantly taught him to "Be a King;" and his tutor, Lord Bute, had strengthened the impressions his mother's teachings had made on his naturally narrow mind and stubborn disposition. Few English kings were so unfit to rule as George III., and few did so much injury to England at home and abroad. Yet he came to the throne with many things in his favour. He had been born and educated in England, and so was the first English king who reigned since the Revolution of 1688. It pleased the people to have once more an Englishman on the throne, and it pleased the Scotch when he said he was not merely an Englishman, but was also a "Briton." With these advantages on his side he was at first popular, and so he might have remained had he not used his position to recover the authority lost by his predecessors—George I. and George II. Instead of ruling by the advice of his ministers he sought to make them

the mere instruments of his will. In spite of his many faults as a ruler the people respected him for his pure domestic life, and for his frugal and simple habits. Old "Farmer George" was always, even in the days when his stubbornness and ignorant self-will were injuring the nation, a king that many people loved and revered.

2. Growth of Industry.—The latter part of the 18th century was a time when Great Britain made great strides in wealth and population. This was due, mainly, to the invention of many labor-saving machines, such as the "spinning-jenny" and "mule," for spinning yarn, by Hargreaves and Crompton, and the steam-engine by Watt. During this time it became known that pit-coal could be used to smelt iron ore, and this, taken with the discovery of the steam-engine, soon led to large iron-works being founded in the north of England. Goods could now be manufactured in great quantities; and the difficulty of taking them to market was overcome by improving the roads, and especially by building numerous canals. The first canal, from Worsley to Manchester, was proposed in 1758 by the Duke of Bridgewater, and was successfully completed by the great engineer Brindley. The population of the towns and cities now increased very rapidly, so that with more people to feed, and heavy duties on wheat and other articles of food, bread became much dearer. This led to more land being tilled, and much that had hitherto been considered waste and worthless was now enclosed and made to give good crops. Between 1760 and 1774 numerous Enclosure Bills were passed by the British Parliament in favour of the large landowners, who had a great deal of power in Parliament. The fencing in of so much waste land was very hard on poor people, many of whom had been wont to use these *commons* for pasturing a horse or cow. Pauperism was fast becoming a great evil, and a burden on the working portion of the community.

3. Wilkes.—George III., as has been stated, was anxious to rule himself, through his ministers, and that was why he got rid of Pitt and Newcastle at the beginning of his reign, and made Lord Bute Prime Minister. It was the king's policy to break down the power of the Whig nobles, for he knew that he could not have his own way so long as the great Whig families were kept in office. His plan was to form a party of his own, the "King's friends," neither

Whig nor Tory, which would look to the king for guidance and support. In this he succeeded very well, for the Tories, who had long been out of office, and the Jacobites, who had given up all hope of restoring the Stuarts, were glad to be taken into the young king's favour. Besides the Tories and Jacobites, he managed by means of bribes in the shape of money, titles, and offices, to win over many of the supporters of the Whigs. Nevertheless, it is doubtful if he could have carried out his policy, had not the Whigs been split into factions which made war upon each other. Their quarrels gave the king the chance he desired, and he soon became so powerful that he made and unmade governments at his pleasure.

Lord Bute, who succeeded Pitt and Newcastle, did not hold his position very long. He was a Scotchman, and a great favourite of the king's mother, and these things made him hated by the people. Besides he had no experience in politics, and the people knew he was a mere puppet in the king's hands. He became so thoroughly hated, that he had to keep a bodyguard of prize fighters about him when he walked through the streets of London. Frightened at last by the evidences on every side of popular hatred, he resigned, and George III. had again to take a Whig for his minister. This was George Grenville, a conscientious, hardworking man, who made himself disliked by both king and people by his narrowness and obstinacy. His first trouble was with a newspaper, the "North Briton," which very violently attacked the king and his ministers. The editor of this paper was John Wilkes, a member of Parliament. He was a clever, witty, but profligate man, who by a strange fate had a great deal to do in bringing in some much-needed reforms. Grenville, acting under instructions from the king, issued a "general warrant," that is a warrant in which the name of no person was given, for the arrest of the publishers and editors of the offending paper. Wilkes, along with several others, was arrested and put in prison; but by appealing to the courts, he got his release, and then proceeded against the Government for arresting a member of Parliament contrary to law. The courts decided in his favour, gave him damages, and condemned "general warrants" as illegal. Parliament now charged him with libel, and Wilkes seeing that he had little chance of fair play fled to France, and was outlawed for not standing his trial. Nevertheless, no more "general warrants" have been issued since his time.

4. Stamp Act, 1765.—And now Grenville's meddlesome disposition led to a more serious difficulty than that with Wilkes. The English colonies in America had long felt that the Mother Country, by her trade policy, was injuring them for her own benefit. The colonies were not allowed to trade freely with other countries, but were expected to buy the manufactures they needed from England, and in return were given special privileges in the sale of their raw produce in England. The colonists had found it profitable to evade this law, and to carry on a trade with the Spanish colonies in America. This Grenville now tried to stop, and at the same time put a tax on the colonies to lessen the burden of the British taxpayers. The British Parliament said that much of the expense of the war in America was for the benefit of the colonies and, therefore, they should help to bear the burden. The tax was to be levied by making the colonists use *stamped* paper for notes, leases, and other legal documents. These stamps had to be bought from the British Government, which got a profit from their sale, although the money thus raised was spent in the colonies. The colonies were angry at this attempt to tax them without their own consent, and said that while they were willing to tax themselves for the good of the Mother Country, they were not willing that a Parliament in which they had no representatives should force them to pay taxes. They sent a petition against the "Stamp Act," but at first their remonstrance met with no attention. They then refused to buy any English manufactures, and this caused the English merchants and manufacturers to ask for the repeal of the Act. Meanwhile Grenville had displeased George III., and had been forced to give way to Lord Rockingham, the leader of the other section of the Whigs. Rockingham, aided by Pitt, did away with the Stamp Act, but Parliament, while removing it, took the opportunity of asserting its right to tax the colonies at pleasure.

A short time after this there was another change in the Government, and Pitt, with the title of "Earl of Chatham," came back as chief member of the Grafton Ministry. But ill-health forced him to leave the management of colonial affairs in other hands, and

Parliament, in 1767, placed duties on tea, painters' colours, glass, and a few other articles going into America. This aroused the colonies once more, who were now more than ever determined that they would not submit to arbitrary taxation, and began to take steps to defend their rights.

5. The Middlesex Elections.—The same obstinacy and love of power which caused George III. to drive his American subjects to revolt, led him to use his influence with the House of Commons to invade the rights of the electors of Middlesex. In 1769, Wilkes returned from France and was elected member for Middlesex, a county in which there were more electors than in most constituencies. George was angry, and through his Government had Wilkes arrested for his old offence, libel, and put in prison. The House of Commons was induced to expel him on account of the libel; but Wilkes was again elected by the people of Middlesex. Three times was Wilkes elected and expelled, and then the House of Commons declared Wilkes incapable of being elected, and persuaded Colonel Luttrell to oppose him in Middlesex. Wilkes received 1,143 votes and Luttrell only 296, nevertheless the Commons declared Luttrell elected. This high-handed and unjust act, by which the people were deprived of their right of election, caused great indignation, and when Wilkes came out of prison, the people of London showed their sympathy by electing him an alderman of the city.

6. Liberty of the Press.—The following year, 1771, Wilkes was engaged in another contest with Parliament, in the interest of the people. Although the press had now a right to publish without asking permission from any one, nevertheless it was against the rules to report the debates in Parliament. In spite of a "standing order" to the contrary, garbled reports were published, and at last, the Speaker of the Commons, ordered the arrest of a number of printers. Two of them appealed to the law, and Wilkes and another London alderman acting as magistrates, freed them as being guilty of no offence. The Speaker's messenger was arrested for trying to carry out the will of the Commons, and so serious was the quarrel that the Mayor of London was sent to the Tower while the session lasted. Meanwhile the printers were left at liberty, and though no decision was reached as to the right to publish debates, the press has ever since been permitted to report Parliamentary proceedings. This led to better newspapers being published, and more interest in public affairs being taken, and it helped to put a stop to the practice of bribing members of Parliament. Wilkes was allowed to take his seat in 1774, and in 1782 the House of Commons admitted that it was wrong in seating Colonel Luttrell in 1769.

7. The American Colonies Win Their Independence.—In 1770, George III. succeeded in getting a Prime Minister to his

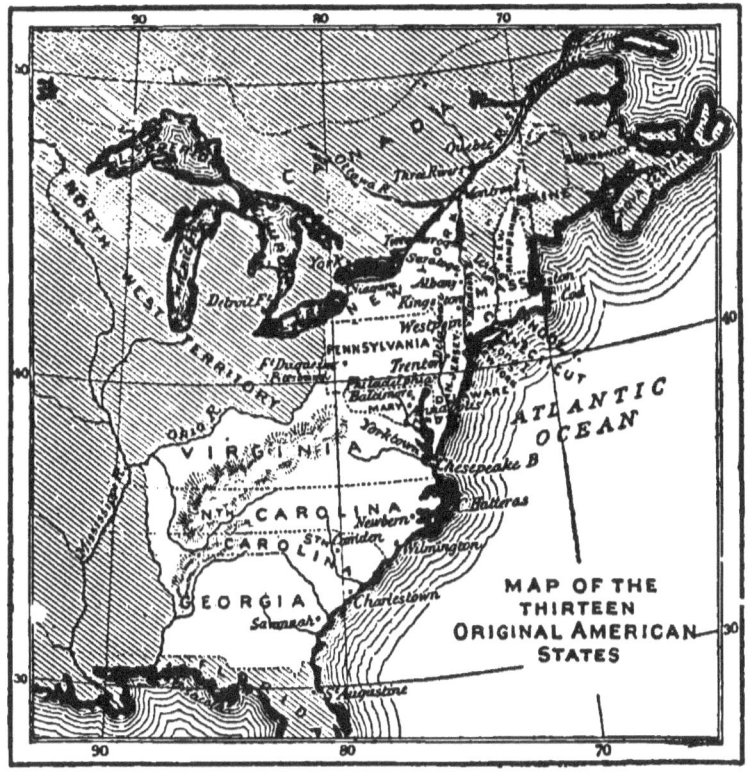

MAP OF THE THIRTEEN ORIGINAL AMERICAN STATES

taste. This was Lord North, an easy-going, good-natured Tory, who was quite content to take his orders from the king. Now that George was "king" as he wished to be, he resolved to make his American subjects feel his authority. In 1770, Lord North took off all the obnoxious taxes, except that on tea, and this George III.

retained, for the purpose of asserting his right of taxation over the colonies. Meanwhile, the feeling in America was growing stronger every year, and the colonists resolved not to buy any tea until the tax was removed. This resolve was carried out, and the East India Company began to suffer. In 1773 some ship-loads of tea entered Boston harbour, and an effort was made to land the cargo. A number of colonists resolved to prevent this, and dressed as Indians went on board the ships and threw the chests of tea into the water. For this act of violence Parliament closed the port of Boston, took away from Massachusetts its charter, and demanded that the offenders should be sent to England for trial.

War was now near at hand. In 1774, all the colonies, except Georgia, sent delegates to Philadelphia, where a congress was held to decide on what action should be taken for the protection of their rights and liberties. They resolved to trade no more with England until the charter of Massachusetts was restored, and they made preparations for resistance, if such should be needful. In 1775, at Lexington, near Boston, the first encounter took place between the British troops and the farmers and mechanics of Massachusetts. The following month, a more serious encounter took place at Bunker's Hill, also near Boston, and there the American militia showed George III. that the Yankees could fight. In the meantime George Washington, of Virginia, had been chosen commander-in-chief of the American forces, and at once began to make such preparations as he could to meet the coming storm. No better choice could have been made. Calm, patient, devoted to his country, for eight years he bore the heavy burden of what at times seemed an almost hopeless struggle, and finally secured the independence of the colonies, an independence largely due to his unflinching courage and endurance, and to his power to cheer and animate his followers.

Early in the war the British troops were forced to leave Boston and retire to New York, where the feeling in favour of the Mother Country was strong. Canada was invaded in 1775 by American armies, under Generals Montgomery and Arnold, in the hope of inducing the people to rebel. Montreal was easily taken, but Quebec resisted all attacks, and Montgomery was killed in an assault upon its defences. The Americans shortly afterwards retreated, and Canada was troubled no more. The colonists now finally decided to separate from the Mother Country, and Thomas Jefferson, on behalf of Congress, drew up a solemn "Declaration of Independence," which was approved and accepted July 4th, 1776. Hitherto, the war had gone against the colonists, and a large British army under General Burgoyne, in 1777, marched from Canada down to the Hudson River, to cut off New England from the rest of the colonies. Great alarm was felt at this movement, and the American militia flocked in from all quarters to check Burgoyne's march. Soon Burgoyne found himself hemmed in, and to save his army from utter destruction, surrendered with six thousand men. This was the turning-point in the fortunes of the colonies. The next year, 1778, France came to the aid of the young Republic, and sent men, money, and a fleet, all of which were sorely needed. The war went on for several years after this with varying results. Washington had been defeated at Brandywine River, 1777, and forced to give up Philadelphia to the British, and British generals won many victories in the Southern States. Nothing but the heroic courage and patience of Washington saved the colonies at this time from yielding in despair. The war was carried on with extreme bitterness, arising from the employment by England of hired German soldiers and North American Indians. In 1781, the fortunes of war changed in favour of the Americans, until the crowning victory was won at Yorktown, where Lord Cornwallis, cut off from supplies by an American army and a French fleet, surrendered with several thousand men, After this the British people saw that all hope of keeping the colonies was gone. Britain was now at war with Spain, which, in 1779, joined France against her, and made a desperate effort to retake Gibraltar. The fortress was defended for three years by General Eliot, who drove the besiegers back by pouring red-hot shot into their fleet. Russia, Sweden, and Denmark were also hostile, having banded themselves together against Britain, to prevent her from searching their ships. So, when the news of the surrender of Cornwallis came to England, people began to despair. Lord North, now thoroughly unpopular, resigned in 1782, and was succeeded by Rockingham. Pitt had died in 1778, his last speech being a plea against giving up the colonies, and a defiance to his old enemy, France. Nothing now remained but to make the best terms possible with France, Spain, and the colonies. Fortunately, a great victory won by Admiral Rodney over the French fleet enabled Britain to conclude an honorable peace. By the Treaty of Versailles, in 1783, the independence of the United States was recognized, France gained nothing, while Spain had to be content with Minorca and Florida. To Britain there remained in America, Canada, Nova Scotia, and Newfoundland.

8. Home Rule in Ireland.—While England had her troubles abroad, she was not without them at home. In 1780, a great riot took place in London, because Parliament removed some of the harsh laws against Roman Catholics. Lord George Gordon was the leader of a mob of 60,000 men, who came to Parliament with a petition against the measure. Not content with presenting their petition, the excited people broke out into acts of violence, burning Roman Catholic chapels, and destroying public and private property. Finally 10,000 troops had to be called out to restore order in the city.

A much more serious trouble was the demand made by the Protestants in Ireland for the right to manage their own affairs by an Irish Parliament. While the war with the colonies was going on, all the troops in Ireland were taken to America, and as France threatened an invasion, a large Protestant volunteer force, 100,000 in number, was raised to defend the country. This was Ireland's opportunity, and the Protestant leaders in the Irish Parliament, of whom the chief was Henry Grattan, demanded that Ireland should have the right to control her own trade and commerce, and that Poyning's law, which gave the English Parliament the right to prevent Bills passed in the Irish Parliament from becoming law, should be repealed. Lord Rockingham had no choice but to submit, and so, in 1782, Ireland got "Home Rule." Nevertheless, only a very small portion of the people of Ireland governed her, as Roman Catholics and Dissenters could not be members of Parliament, and this gave all the power into the hands of a few Protestant families belonging to the English Church in Ireland.

9. Warren Hastings.—Though England had lost ground in America, she was extending her possessions in Asia and Australia. In the latter country a convict settlement was formed in 1788 at Sydney, in New South Wales. For many years none but convicts were sent out, but, as we shall find, these were the pioneers of what promises to be a great Anglo-Saxon nation. In India, Clive did much to bring about a better treatment of the natives, who were

oppressed and robbed by English traders after the East India
Company had gained so much control in the land. Clive returned
to England and through his influence Warren Hastings, the
Governor of Bengal, was made, in 1773, Governor-General of
Bengal, Bombay, and Madras. When Hastings went to India he
made great changes in the administration of affairs, in spite of
a very bitter opposition from some members of his own Council.
He had to wage a war against the Mahrattas, the roving free-
booters of Central India, and against Hyder Ali, a military
adventurer who had desolated the Carnatic with fire and sword.
In spite of all the difficulties which his Council, the native princes,
and the French put in his way, Hastings held for England all
she had won, and laid the foundations of her present great Indian
Empire. He returned to England in 1784, expecting to be rewarded for his services, but instead was impeached before the
House of Lords by the Commons, for his cruel and unjust treatment of the natives. He was charged with selling the services of his
English troops to a native prince, who used them to conquer and
enslave the Rohillas, an Afghan tribe. He was also accused of ex-
torting money from native rulers, and for putting a native to death
illegally. Hastings did not think he had done anything wrong, for
he knew that the offences he was charged with had been committed
in the interest of the East India Company. His trial lasted eight
years, and ended in his acquittal in 1795, although the three greatest
orators of his time, Burke, Fox, and Sheridan, were employed to
press the charges against him. Although acquitted, the trial had the
result of making the English in India more just and merciful to the
natives, and led to the better government of the country.

10. The Coalition Government and Its Overthrow.—When
Lord Rockingham died, Lord Shelburne became Prime Minister.
Among the followers of Rockingham was Charles James Fox, an able
orator and statesman, who for years had spoken strongly against
Lord North's government. Fox was a very amiable, liberal-minded
man ; but he was very much given to gambling and other vices.
King George hated him, because he was the boon companion of
George, Prince of Wales, and the king blamed him for corrupting
his son and heir. Fox quarrelled with Shelburne, and to drive him
from office united with Lord North in what was called a Coalition,

that is a union of people holding different opinions. The followers of Fox and North together were now more numerous than those of Shelburne, and they succeeded in turning him out of office. What is known in history as the "Coalition" government of Fox and North was now formed. It had a large following in Parliament, but people outside thought it was wrong that Tories and Whigs, who had been abusing each other so bitterly for so many years. should go into the same government. The king, too, was displeased, partly because he hated Fox, and partly because the ministry was too well supported. At first he could do nothing; but when Fox brought in a Bill for the better government of India, the king induced his friends in the Lords to throw it out, and then made this an excuse for forcing his ministers to resign. He now called on William Pitt, a young man of twenty four years of age, to become Prime Minister. Pitt was the second son of William Pitt, the great Commoner, and although young in years was old in knowledge, ability, and self-confidence. In vain, Fox and North outvoted him in Parliament, and tried to force him to resign. The king gave him his influence and support, and when, a few months later, the king dissolved Parliament, and called upon the people to elect their representatives, it was found that the nation was so strongly with Pitt that few of the followers of Fox and North were able to keep their seats. Pitt was now Prime Minister with a large following in Parliament and in the country, and the king was content to let him rule. For seventeen years without a break, from December 1783 to February 1801, he remained in power, guiding and controlling the affairs of the nation as no man had done since the days of Walpole.

CHAPTER XXIV.

THE STRUGGLE AGAINST NAPOLEON BONAPARTE.

1. William Pitt the Younger.—One of Pitt's first acts was to pass an India Bill, in 1784, which gave the Government control over the political acts of the East India Company. This was done

THE STRUGGLE AGAINST NAPOLEON BONAPARTE.   159

by appointing a Board of Control, the president of which was to be
a member of the Government. But Pitt had a great many other
reforms in view. He saw that Parliament did not represent the
people, and he tried to do away with some of the small and rotten
boroughs, and give more members to large cities and towns, and
to populous counties. In this he failed, as too many powerful
persons wished to keep things as they were. He also sought to
make trade freer between England and other countries. Pitt had
studied and accepted the views of a famous book called the "Wealth
of Nations," published in 1776, the author of which was Adam
Smith, a Professor in a Scotch University. Pitt partly carried out
Smith's doctrines by lowering the export and import duties on
many articles. In this way he checked smuggling, and the public
revenue was increased. He saw that Ireland was suffering from
poverty, because she had no markets for her products, and he
offered to admit Irish goods into English markets if the Irish
Parliament would allow England to send her goods into Ireland.
This the Irish Parliament refused to do because England did not
propose to give to Ireland the right to trade in all her ports at home
and abroad. Pitt was much disappointed at the refusal of his offer,
but he succeeded in making trade freer with France. Pitt also
put a stop to the practice of borrowing money from political friends
at high rates of interest, and of giving them the privilege of doing
work for the Government at their own prices. So, in many ways,
he saved the public money, and began to lessen the public debt.

2. French Revolution.—Under such a wise and careful minister,
who kept the country at peace and encourged trade and commerce,
the people were very prosperous, and the population and wealth of
the nation grew rapidly. But in 1783 it looked as if Pitt's power
would soon be at an end. George III. had an attack of insanity
which lasted so long that Parliament began to take steps to have
his son George, the Prince of Wales, appointed Regent. The
Prince of Wales was a great friend of Fox, and Pitt and Fox both
expected that when the Prince became Regent, Pitt would go out of
office, and Fox would come in. So when a Regency Bill was brought
in which proposed to state what the power of the Regent should be,
Fox wanted the Prince to become Regent at once with all the
power of the king, but this Pitt would not allow. While the two
parties were disputing the old king recovered, and then the Bill was

no longer needed. The next year saw the beginning of the French Revolution, and from this time onward Pitt's plans for lessening the debt and carrying out great reforms at home had to be dropped. The causes of this Revolution may be traced a long way back. For many years the French people had been very badly governed, the poor and the working classes having to pay all the taxes, while the nobles and clergy did nothing but spend the earnings of the peasants, labourers, and artisans. But the time came when the heavy expenses of the French court could not be paid out of the taxes of the poor, and then the French king, Louis XVI., called together the French Parliament, or "States-General," to get money from the nobles and clergy. There were three branches of this States-General; for the nobles, the clergy, and the commons, sat and voted in separate chambers. When the Parliament met the commons would do no business until the nobles and clergy consented to meet and vote in the same assembly with them. The new assembly thus formed became known as the "National Assembly." The National Assembly soon began to make many changes giving the people more freedom, and taking away much of the power of the king, nobles, and clergy. In July, 1789, the Paris mob attacked and took the Bastille, a great stone fortress and prison on the Seine, where many innocent people had met a mysterious fate. A little later the king was forced by the mob to leave his palace at Versailles and take up his abode in Paris, where he was kept a kind of prisoner. Once he tried to escape, but his flight was discovered and he was brought back. Then Austria and Prussia made war upon France to put Louis in his old position, and this so enraged the Paris mob that it broke into the prisons and murdered a great number of royalist prisoners. This was in September, 1792. A few months afterwards, Louis and his queen, Marie Antoinette, were put to death for plotting the invasion of France by Austria and Prussia. While these events were taking place in France the English people looked on quietly. Pitt, at first, was pleased with the Revolution, as he thought the French were trying to get the same kind of government as existed in England. Fox was delighted; but Edmund Burke spoke and wrote against the revolutionists with all his great genius and eloquence. Burke's speeches had little effect for a time, but when the French went from one excess to another, then Burke's writings began to be widely read, and people grew alarmed lest a revolution should break out in England. War with France now became popular. Austria and Prussia had not been successful in their invasion of France, for after the first fear had passed away the French Republicans drove their enemies back, and in their turn invaded the Austrian dominions in the Netherlands. The French now wanted all other nations to become republics, and when they began to take steps to invade Holland, which was under the protection of England, peace could no longer be maintained, and in Feb. 1793, France declared war against England, Holland, and Spain.

3. **War with France.**—In the war that followed England had, at first, as allies, Spain, Holland, Austria, and Prussia. England had to provide much of the money for the war, which owing to bad generalship and lack of energy was full of disasters for the Allies. The French drove the English out of Toulon, captured Amsterdam, and seized the Dutch fleet. Prussia soon made peace, while Spain cast in her lot with France against England. Against these reverses, we must place a victory by Lord Howe over the French fleet at Brest, and the seizure of the Dutch colonies at the Cape of Good Hope, in Ceylon, and in Malacca. So unsuccessful was the war, and so heavy the burden placed upon the English taxpayer, that Pitt was anxious to bring about an honorable peace. But the French were so elated with their victories, that no reasonable terms could be made, and in spite of bad harvests and great distress among the poor and the working classes, the war had to go on. To make matters worse, a foolish terror had seized upon the ruling and middle classes, who imagined they saw plots and conspiracies in every meeting held, and society formed, to obtain better government and a better representation in Parliament. Cruel and unjust laws were passed to prevent public gatherings and political writings. The *Habeas Corpus* Act was suspended, and innocent men on the most trivial evidence were imprisoned and banished.

4. **Trouble in Ireland.**—In the meantime affairs in Ireland were growing worse and worse. The Irish Parliament did not represent the Irish people, and all offices and places of trust were given to the friends of a few ruling families. Shut in to Ireland by heavy duties against their products in English markets, the Irish were growing restless under the combined forces of grinding poverty and

political injustice. Pitt had tried to remedy some of their wrongs, but between the Irish Parliament and George III. he had failed. In 1790, Orange lodges (so called from William, Prince of Orange), were formed in the North of Ireland, and in 1791, a body of Roman Catholics and Protestants, known as the "United Irishmen," began to agitate for their civil and religious rights. Some of the leaders of this body, Wolf Tone, Hamilton Rowan, and others, asked the French for help, and the request was answered by sending a body of French troops under General Hoche, who attempted to land, but failed owing to a great storm at sea. At last the Irish rose in open rebellion, and formed a camp at Vinegar Hill, in Wexford, where they were attacked and defeated by General Lake, in June, 1798. A French force, under General Humbert, landed after the battle, and had a brief success, but was soon hemmed in and defeated. This rising was attended by horrible acts of cruelty, committed by both the Orangemen and the rebels, and by the different secret societies that sprang up over the land.

5. **Naval Victories.**—While Ireland was in this troubled condition, France, under its republican rulers, the "Directory," was extending her conquests in Italy and elsewhere. Her great success was largely due to the wonderful genius for war of a young and rising general, Napoleon Bonaparte, a native of Corsica. He had helped to drive the English out of France, had saved the French Directory from the Paris mob, and had been given command of an army which won victory after victory over the Austrians in Italy, and forced them to yield up their Italian possessions. France now planned to invade England, with the aid of the fleets of Holland and Spain, but Admiral Jervis defeated the Spanish fleet off Cape St. Vincent, in 1797, and drove it into Cadiz Harbor. Nelson, who was to win such great renown on the sea, was in this battle, and displayed great daring and skill. It was fortunate for England that this victory was won, for now the sailors, goaded to desperation by bad pay, bad food, and cruel treatment, mutinied, first at Spithead and then at the Nore. Their grievances were partially righted, a few of the ringleaders were punished, and then the men returned to their duty. They soon afterwards proved their loyalty and courage by defeating, under Admiral Duncan, the Dutch fleet at Camperdown, October, 1797.

But the British navy was now to win a still more famous victory, under her greatest naval commander. Bonaparte, having humbled the Austrians, got permission to take a fleet and an army to Egypt. Admiral Horatio Nelson was sent with an English fleet to overtake him, but failed for some time to find his whereabouts. At length he got the necessary information, and sailed at once for Egypt, where he found Napoleon had landed, and had won a great victory over the Mamelukes, at the Battle of the Pyramids. But Napoleon's fleet lay anchored in the Bay of Aboukir, and, though it was six o'clock in the evening, Nelson sent some of his ships between the French fleet and the shore, and began a battle which raged nearly all night. The morning found most of the French fleet destroyed, and Napoleon's army without the means of return. The Battle of the Nile, which was fought August 1, 1798, brought great joy and relief to England, for France was now without a fleet. From Egypt, Bonaparte crossed over to Syria, besieged and took Jaffa, but was repulsed at Acre by the Turks and the English, and then returned to Egypt. Hearing that his interests could be best served by his return, he escaped in a vessel back to France, leaving his army behind him. He was now made First Consul, and once more led a French army against the Austrians in Italy, defeating them at Marengo in 1801. The same year his army in Egypt was defeated by Sir Ralph Abercromby, and his soldiers made prisoners.

6. Union of Great Britain and Ireland.—After the rebellion of 1798 in Ireland, Pitt saw that the only way to save the island from anarchy was to bring about a Union between Great Britain and Ireland. This he succeeded in carrying out in 1800, by bribing the Irish members of Parliament, and by promising the Irish Catholics to repeal the laws which deprived them of their rights as citizens. So, on January 1st, 1801, the Irish Parliament ceased to exist, and Ireland became represented in the United Parliament at London, by one hundred members of the House of Commons, and by twenty-eight peers. But Pitt's promise of civil and religious freedom for the Roman Catholics could not be carried out. When George III. heard that Pitt was preparing a Bill to give Roman Catholics their rights, he declared he would resign his crown rather than assent to it, and, Pitt who had pledged himself to this act of justice, felt it his duty to resign in 1801.

7. Peace of Amiens.—Addington, the Speaker of the Commons, now became Prime Minister, and was supported by Pitt. In April of the same year, the English attacked the Danish fleet at Copenhagen, the Danes having shown signs of hostility. Sir Hyde Parker was the English Admiral, but Nelson did the fighting and won a hard-fought battle. Once during the struggle Parker signal led Nelson to retire, but Nelson put his telescope to his blind eye, and said he could see no signal, and went on fighting. Bonaparte, to serve his own ends, was now ready to make a truce, and so in March, 1802, the Peace of Amiens was signed. England gave up most of her conquests, and France restored the south of Italy to Austria.

8. Trafalgar.—The Peace of Amiens was but a hollow peace and Napoleon soon found a pretext for renewing the war. In defiance of the treaty he seized Parma and Piedmont, and placed an army in Switzerland. He found fault with England for not restoring the island of Malta to the Knights of St. John, and for harbouring French refugees. In 1804, his ambition was gratified by being made Emperor of France, and he was now eager to extend his empire, and dictate to Europe. To do this he saw he must first crush England, and to this end he began to gather a large army at Bolougne which was to be carried across the Channel in flat-bottomed boats. When news of Napoleon's designs reached England, nearly 400,000 volunteers offered their services to defend their country, and formed themselves into companies and regiments for purposes of drill and discipline. But Pitt who had been called back to his old post, in 1804, depended on England's navy, and it did not fail her in this hour of danger. Napoleon hoped to draw the English fleet away from the Channel, by sending it in pursuit of the French and Spanish fleets which sailed, apparently, for the West Indies. The plan partially succeeded, for Nelson went in pursuit of them, but after a while found that they had turned back, for the purpose of escorting Napoleon's army across the Channel. The Spanish fleet was, however, met by an English fleet at Cape Finisterre and driven into Cadiz, and Nelson having found out his mistake, returned in great haste, and coming up with the French fleet at Cape Trafalgar, October 21st, 1805, fought and won the greatest naval battle of the war. When the action was about to begin, Nelson gave the signal, "This day England expects every man to do his duty," and nothing more was needed. Nelson, against the advice of his friends, exposed himself fearlessly to the French marksmen, one of whom shot him down while standing on the deck of his own ship, the *Victory*. He lived long enough to know that the battle was won, and that all danger of a French invasion of England's shores was at an end. The English people rejoiced at Nelson's last and greatest victory, although the price at which it was bought brought sorrow and mourning into every household.

Soon after this, Napoleon, who had turned away from England to attack Austria, met and defeated the armies of Austria and Russia at Austerlitz, December 2, 1805, and the news of this disaster "killed Pitt." At the early age of forty-seven, in January 1806, this worthy son of a noble sire passed away, full of sorrow and anxiety for the country he had served so well.

9. Abolition of the Slave Trade.—It had been Pitt's wish, when he returned to office in 1804, to have the aid of Fox in his Government, but George III. would not hear of it. Now, after Pitt's death, Fox was taken in, for all parties were united in fighting England's battles against Napoleon. It was hoped that Fox would, on account of his known friendliness to France, be able to bring about a peace, but this was not realized, and Fox soon followed his great rival to the grave, dying in 1806. It was at this time, 1807, that England took her first step in ridding herself of the curse of slavery. Ever since the revival under the Wesleys and Whitfield, a deep interest had been taken in the poor, the ignorant, and the oppressed. In 1773, John Howard was drawn into the work of visiting English jails and prisons, and his reports of their wretched and filthy condition, and of the vice and misery that prevailed in them, led Parliament to take steps to reform some of the more glaring abuses. In 1788, Clarkson, Wilberforce, and Zachary Macaulay, began a crusade against the slave trade between Africa and America, and against slavery itself. Pitt and Fox sympathized with the movement and lent it their aid, but the strong opposition of the merchants of Liverpool and others who made gain by the wrongs and sufferings of the poor negroes, prevented Parliament from doing justice until 1807, when the *slave-trade* was made *piracy*, and abolished.

10. The Berlin Decree.—The Battle of Trafalgar had taught

Napoleon that England could defend her own shores against all attempts at invasion. He next sought to ruin England through her trade and commerce. In 1806, he defeated Russia and Prussia at Jena, and he was now the dictator of continental Europe. He used his power in an endeavor to close the ports of the continent against English ships. By a decree issued from Berlin, he forbade all European nations to trade with England. This was a severe blow to British merchants, and the British Government retaliated by forbidding other nations to trade with France, and ordering foreign vessels to touch at British ports on pain of seizure. Between these two decrees, the vessels of neutral nations found it impossible to carry on their commerce, and the United States of America, which had hitherto a large carrying trade, was so vexed at England's harshness and obstinacy that it declared war against her in 1812. The Americans complained, also, of English vessels claiming the right to search American vessels for deserting seamen. The war that followed was waged principally in Canada, and ended in 1815, by the matters in dispute being left unsettled. Nothing was gained by either nation in this unnatural and foolish war.

11. Peninsular War.—Napoleon had become so puffed up with his successes, that he began to make and unmake kings at pleasure. His brothers and relations had kingdoms carved out for them in different parts of Europe, at the expense of the old ruling families. His pride and arrogance carried him so far that at last he dethroned the King of Spain and put his own brother Joseph in his place. This was more than the Spaniards could endure and they called on England for aid. The rising man at this time in English politics was George Canning. He was Minister of Foreign Affairs, and he determined to help the Spanish people. Sir Arthur Wellesley, who had distinguished himself in wars in India, and Sir John Moore were sent with a small force to Portugal. Wellesley defeated Marshal Junot at Vimiero in Aug. 1808, but a foolish "Convention," or agreement, was made at Cintra without his consent, by which the French were permitted to leave Portugal. Wellesley was recalled to England, and Sir John Moore advanced into Spain. He found the Spanish troops that he was sent to aid utterly unreliable, although they would fight well enough in small "guerilla" bands. Moore learned that Bonaparte himself was marching on Madrid with 70,000 men, and as he had only 25,000 he prudently retreated towards the coast where he expected to find his ships. He was pursued at first by Napoleon, and afterwards by Marshal Soult, with a large army, in the hope of overtaking him before he reached the coast. When Moore arrived at Corunna the vessels in which he meant to embark his men were nowhere to be seen, and while waiting for them, the French army attacked his small force. On the

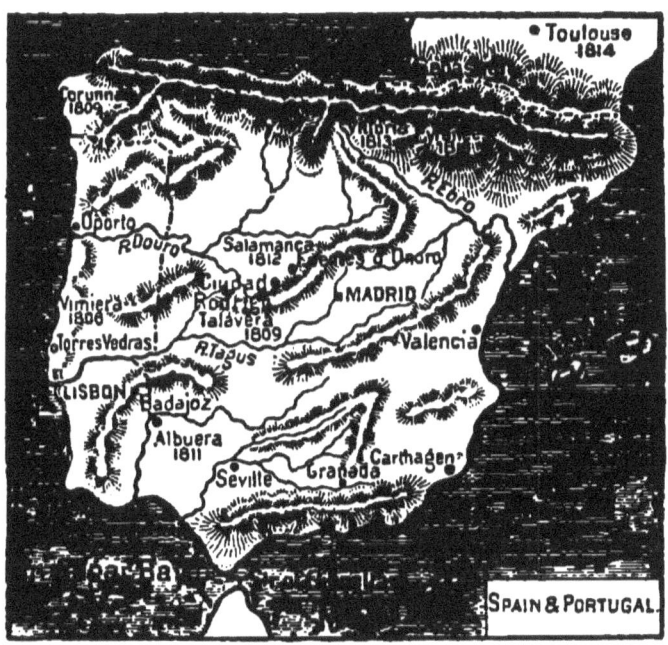

16th Jan. 1809, was fought the famous battle of Corunna, in which Moore, perhaps the most promising general in the British army, was killed. The French were defeated with a loss of 3,000 men, and Moore's army was allowed to embark without molestation. Moore himself was buried by his sorrowing comrades on the battlefield. So ended England's first effort to drive the French out of Spain.

But Canning was not dismayed. He sent Wellesley back again, but with an army altogether too small, and too badly supplied, for such a campaign as he had to carry on. For four years did Wellesley struggle against large French armies, with little support from his friends in England, or from his Spanish allies. In spite of tremendous difficulties he drove the French out of Portugal, and won victory after victory over them in Spain. In 1809, he defeated Marshal Soult at Oporto, and Marshal Victor at Talavera. He then retreated before a large army under Marshal Massena, and constructed a strong line of defences at Torres Vedras, near Lisbon, and on the coast of Portugal. Massena found he could not pass Wellesley's fortifications, and he had to retreat with great loss, for Wellesley had caused the whole country to be laid bare of cattle and food, and when Massena's army began to retreat the stragglers were cut off in great numbers by the enraged Spanish guerilla bands. Wellesley, now Viscount Wellington, followed up the French retreat and won many battles. He took by storm the two strong fortresses of Cuidad Rodrigo and Badajos in 1812, defeated the French at Salamanca and Vittoria in 1812 and 1813, and drove Joseph Bonaparte out of Spain. The successful siege of St. Sebastian in 1813, was followed in 1814 by the battle of Toulouse, the last battle of the Peninsular War.

12. **Russian Campaign.**—In 1812, Napoleon started with an army of half a million into Russia, to conquer that country. The Russian emperor had been on friendly terms with Napoleon for a few years, but Napoleon's Berlin decree, by which Russia was not permitted to trade with England, proved a great hardship to the Russian people, and they soon began to import English manufactures, against Napoleon's orders. This led to the breaking up of the alliance between Russia and France, and to Napoleon's invasion. At the battle of Borodino, in September 1812, the Russians were defeated after a fierce struggle, and then Napoleon pressed on to Moscow, the chief city in Russia. Rather than permit the French army to winter there, the Russians set fire to the city, and Napoleon, without food or shelter for his troops, had to begin a retreat. Winter now came on, and the retreating French, without proper clothing and food, died daily by the thousand. The Russians hung on the rear, cutting off the weary stragglers as they fell behind the main body of the army. So out of the great host that went with light hearts to an easy conquest, only 20,000 returned. Encouraged by Napoleon's misfortunes, Austria and Prussia now rose against the tyrant, and joining their forces with those of Russia, met and defeated him after three days of fighting, at Leipzig, in October, 1813. Step by step Napoleon was now driven back, until the armies of the allies entered Paris in 1814. Napoleon

THE STRUGGLE AGAINST NAPOLEON BONAPARTE.

had to give up his throne, and be content with ruling over the little island of Elba, which was given him as his kingdom by his victorious foes.

13. **Waterloo, 1815.**—Louis XVIII., the brother of Louis XVI., was now made King of France, and the Allies began to re-arrange the map of Europe, which had been thrown into sad confusion by Napoleon's conquests. Before they had made much progress, they were startled by the news that Napoleon had, after eleven months absence, returned to France, and was making his way towards Paris. His old soldiers gladly rallied around him, Louis XVIII. fled from Paris, and Napoleon was once more on the French throne. The Allies hastened to gather their forces to crush him, and England and Prussia soon had armies in the field. Napoleon saw that his only chance was to defeat the English and Prussians separately, before they could unite their forces. He marched north into Belgium, and on June 16, 1815, met and defeated the Prussians at Ligny. The same day the English and Belgians under Wellington were attacked at Quatre Bras by Marshal Ney. Wellington repulsed Ney, but hearing of the Prussian defeat at Ligny, he fell back to the field of Waterloo, nine miles from Brussels, to keep up his line of communication with Blucher, the Prussian general. There, on the 18th of June, 1815, Wellington and Napoleon met for the first and only time on the battlefield. Wellington's army was largely made up of Belgians and Germans, while his English troops were, many of them, raw levies and untried in battle. In numbers the armies were nearly equal, but Napoleon had with him the veterans of his army, besides being much superior to Wellington in cavalry and artillery. Wellington's hope was to hold the French at bay until Blucher and the Prussians could arrive in the early afternoon. Napoleon, on the other hand, hoped by the deadly play of his artillery, and the fierce charges of his cavalry to break the British ranks. As the day wore on, and Wellington saw his thin lines growing thinner under the desperate charges of the French cavalry and the fire of their artillery, he began to long for "Night or Blucher." At last, about five in the afternoon, the sound of distant firing was heard, and a little later it was seen that the Prussians had arrived, and were attacking the flank of the French army. Napoleon saw that but one chance remained, and that was by a desperate charge of his Old Guard to break the British lines

before help from the Prussians could reach them. These trusted veterans came gallantly forward, but when near the British lines they met with such a deadly volley of musketry, followed by such a fierce bayonet charge of the British infantry, that they wavered, turned, and fled. The victory was won, Napoleon's career was ended, and Europe was saved. The Prussians pursued the fleeing French far into the night, cutting down the fugitives without mercy. Napoleon himself fled to Paris, and a little later surrendered to the captain of a British man-of-war. He was banished to the lonely and rocky island of St. Helena, where six years after he died, May 5, 1821. Louis XVIII. came back to the French throne, and the great struggle for European freedom was over.

14. Condition of the Nation.—The long war was ended, and the nation found itself with over 800 millions of debt, much of it contracted in paying great sums to the Allies to keep their armies in the field. No nation had suffered so little from this desperate struggle as England, partly because she was free from invasion, and partly because she was the mistress of the sea, and controlled the carrying trade of the world. Her manufactures were sold in every European market and her industries suffered little check, until the poverty of other nations became so great as to prevent them from buying. But now that the war was over thousands of men were thrown out of employment, and when the crops failed in 1816, the high duty on wheat made food so dear as to cause a famine. The labour-saving machines were blamed for taking away employment from starving workingmen, and riots followed in which organized efforts were made to destroy the new and hated machinery.

The war had so fully taken the attention of the king's ministers and of Parliament, that all political reforms had ceased. George III. had become permanently insane in 1810, and his son George was appointed Regent. The Regent was a worthless profligate, and his base actions made him unpopular with the people. So, for some years after the war, there was great distress and much political discontent among the people, which was increased by the harsh laws passed by Parliament against freedom of speech.

15. Literature and Inventions.—George III. died in 1820, after the longest reign in our history, and was succeeded by his son George IV. The chief features of this eventful reign have been sketched; but no mention has been made of the great men who made England famous by their writings and scientific discoveries. For it was during this time that Robertson wrote his histories of Scotland, Spain, and America, that Gibbon composed his *Decline and Fall of the Roman Empire*, and that Adam Smith gave to the world his *Wealth of Nations*. Samuel Johnson wrote essays, criticisms, and poems, but he is best remembered by his *Dictionary*, published in the reign of George II. Goldsmith, who talked like "Poor Poll," wrote charming tales and essays. His name will never be forgotten while the *Vicar of Wakefield* retains its well deserved popularity. But the most remarkable feature of all this literary activity is the long list of great poets who lived and wrote during the latter half of the 18th and the beginning of the 19th century. For this literary outburst we must give some credit to the hopes and fears aroused by the great upheaval in the social and political life of France. Cowper, Burns, Shelley, Keats, Byron, Campbell, Coleridge, Southey, Wordsworth, Moore, and Scott, are names of poets second only to those of Spenser, Shakespeare, and Milton. But Scott (Sir Walter) ranks higher as a novelist than as a poet, and the author of the *Waverley Novels*, still holds the first place among the novelists of all climes and ages.

Towards the close of the reign, in 1807, two Americans, Fulton and Livingston, moved a vessel up the Hudson River by steam, and a little later, in 1813, steam-navigation was tried on a small scale on the Clyde. Scientific discoveries were made by such men as Herschel, Davey, and Priestly, while Josiah Wedgewood taught the people of Staffordshire the art of making beautiful and graceful pottery.

CHAPTER XXV.

A PERIOD OF REFORM.

1. **George IV.**—The last of the four Georges had been the acting king for ten years before his father's death, and the nation knew him too well to expect much in the way of good from his hands. His admirers called him "The First Gentleman in Europe," by which

they meant that in polish of manner and external grace he was a very fine gentleman. Nevertheless, he was, all through his life, a cowardly, licentious man, who would stoop to any act of meanness and treachery. Fortunately, his personal influence was small, and beyond raising a storm of national indignation at the beginning of his reign by trying in vain to force a Bill through Parliament to secure a divorce from his wife, Queen Caroline, his occupancy of the throne made little difference in English affairs.

2. **Holy Alliance.**—There was considerable unrest and discontent at the beginning of this reign, arising almost entirely from hard times, and the harsh laws passed by the Government against the right of the people to meet and discuss public affairs. One outcome of this feeling was an attempt, called the Cato Street Conspiracy, to murder the ministry, in 1820. The conspirators were seized, some were put to death, and others banished for life.

Abroad, the Emperors of Russia and Austria, and the Kings of Prussia, France, and Spain, formed an alliance, called the "Holy Alliance," to crush out any efforts that might be made by their subjects to increase their freedom, or secure their rights. This alliance was the result of the fear aroused by the French Revolution, and of the growing feeling in Europe in favour of liberty. The British Government, and Lord Castlereagh, the Foreign Secretary, in particular, were charged with being too friendly to the Holy Alliance, and too hostile to the oppressed people of other nations. But Castlereagh's suicide, in 1822, removed one obstacle to a more liberal policy, and henceforth the tide of Reform began to flow more strongly, and with fewer interruptions.

3. **Canning, Peel, and Huskisson.**—After Castlereagh's death, George Canning, a brilliant and liberal-minded statesman, became Foreign Secretary. Unlike Castlereagh, he was a friend of the oppressed everywhere, and while he managed England's foreign affairs, her influence was thrown into the scale of freedom. He would not aid the Turks, who were trying to crush out a revolt in Greece, nor the Spanish, when their colonies in America rose to gain their independence. He saved Portugal from an attack from France and Spain, when Portugal sought to introduce Parliamentary Government. Nor was Canning indifferent to wrongs nearer

home. He was an earnest advocate of the rights of Dissenters and Roman Catholics, as well as of the slaves in the West Indies.

While Canning was using his influence abroad and at home in the interests of the wronged and oppressed, Robert Peel, the Home Secretary, was busy reforming the Criminal Laws. Sir Samuel Romilly, in the early part of this century, had tried earnestly to get Parliament to lessen the number of crimes punishable with death, and had succeeded in getting pocket-picking removed from the list of capital offences. There was, it is said, over 200 crimes for which a person could be hanged. To steal five shillings from a shop or a fish from a pond, to injure Westminster Bridge, was to incur the death penalty, and to be put into the same list with the forger and murderer. At last men saw the folly and cruelty of the Criminal Law, and Peel, in 1824, managed to get Parliament to consent to remove more than 100 of the smaller offences from the list to which the death penalty was attached.

Not less useful than Canning and Peel in carrying out reforms was Huskisson, the President of the Board of Trade. He saw that England was suffering from her trade and navigation laws, and from the unwise restrictions placed upon workingmen. He succeeded in reducing the duties on silk and wool, and had the laws repealed which prevented workingmen from travelling to seek employment in other parts of the country, as well as the law which gave a magistrate the power to fix the wages of labouring men. Besides, he paved the way for freer trade by offering foreign vessels special advantages in English ports, on the condition that the same privileges were given by foreign nations to English vessels.

The years 1825-6 were years of scarcity, and following as they did a commercial panic arising out of foolish speculation, there was much distress, and some rioting. The high duties on food had now to give way for a time, and Huskisson passed a law by which the duty on wheat *fell* as the price *rose*, and *rose* as the price *fell*. This was the famous "sliding scale" of duties, which lasted till free trade came in. The distress and lack of employment led to a large emigration to Canada, Australia, the Cape of Good Hope, and the United States.

4. The Australian Colonies.—New South Wales in Australia was now a flourishing colony, and although at first settled by convicts it began about this time to receive a different kind of settlers. Many of the well-behaved convicts were given their freedom, and they and their descendants became good citizens. Other colonies were gradually founded, such as Queensland, Western Australia, and South Australia. Victoria now one of the most important colonies was once a part of New South Wales, and became a separate province in 1851. Large cities, in time, grew up, such as Sydney and Melbourne, the latter being founded in 1835.

5. Repeal of Test and Corporation Acts, 1828.—Lord Liverpool, the Prime Minister, died in 1827, and Canning was chosen to succeed him. Much was expected from such a liberal and clear-sighted man, but Canning died a few months after taking office, and shortly afterwards the Duke of Wellington became Prime Minister with Sir Robert Peel as the leader in the House of Commons. Wellington was not a liberal or far-seeing statesman, but he was thoroughly honest and unselfish. And now after a century and a half of injustice, Roman Catholics and Dissenters were to have their wrongs righted. The Test and Corporation Acts had prevented Dissenters from holding offices in the towns and cities. In 1828 Lord John Russell brought in a Bill to do away with these laws and the measure was carried. Although willing to relieve Protestant Dissenters, the Government would not consent to repeal the laws shutting Roman Catholics out of Parliament. The laws against Roman Catholics were not so severe as they had been, for in 1817 they were allowed to enter the army and navy, and they had the right to vote for members of Parliament. Perhaps at this time the majority of the English people were as unwilling as Parliament and the Government to do justice to the Roman Catholics. But what a sense of justice would not do, necessity forced on the nation. Daniel O'Connell, an exceedingly clever and eloquent Irish barrister, persuaded the people of Clare County, Ireland, to elect him as a member of Parliament, although he knew he could not take his seat. In the meantime a large "Catholic Association" had been formed in Ireland, to agitate for the rights of the Catholics, and this Association became so powerful under O'Connell's guidance, that the Government began to fear another civil war in Ireland, if measures were not taken to quiet the excitement.

6. Roman Catholic Emancipation Bill, 1829.—The Government, Parliament, and the majority of English people were all opposed to giving Roman Catholics their rights, but Wellington, who knew what war was, saw it was his duty to yield. The House of Lords, on more than one occasion had prevented justice being done, and now Wellington used his great influence with that body to have a Roman Catholic Emancipation Bill passed in 1829. Wellington and Peel had done their duty, but in so doing had made themselves unpopular with the English people. In 1833, the Quakers were allowed to become members of Parliament, and in 1858 the same measure of justice was meted out to the Jews.

7. William IV.—In June, 1830, George IV. died. His only daughter, the Princess Charlotte, had died in 1817, and this left William, Duke of Clarence, as his successor. William IV. had been a commander in the navy, and hence was called the "Sailor King." He was a frank, hearty, well-intentioned man, who, in spite of the fact that his private life was none too pure, was popular with the people. He came to the throne at a time of great excitement in Europe. Revolution was in the air. The French drove out Charles X., and put Louis Philippe on the throne, and Belgium separated from Holland and became an independent nation. Had there been an unwise or unpopular king in England at this time, the excitement in favour of political reform might have led to another revolution.

8. Reform Bill of 1832.—While the war with Napoleon was going on, the English people had too much to think about to pay much attention to Parliamentary Reform. Now, however, that the war was over, a more liberal government in office, and the dread of a revolution passed away, intelligent people began to see how unjust it was that large cities like Manchester, Birmingham, and Leeds should have no representatives in Parliament, while many small towns had the privilege of sending one or two. Still worse, quite a number of places that once had a population, but had lost it, continued to send members. In some cases there were only a dozen or a score of voters, and it is stated that in a county in Scotland, only one man voted, and he elected himself. Then there were a great number of small villages that sent members at the command of the land-owners, on whose estate the villages were built. If the land-owner was in need of money, he sold the right to the seat to some man who wished to be a member of Parliament, and these "nomination" boroughs soon came to have a regular market value. In other boroughs, the voters were so few that a rich candidate could easily buy their votes. So it can easily be seen that the British Parliament did not really represent the British people. Yet many men, some of them intelligent and honest, dreaded any change, fearing that it would be the beginning of a revolution, or that good and able men would find it difficult to be elected, if votes were given to the people. One of these was Wellington, who thought that everything was just right, and that the system in use could not be improved.

It was the custom then to have a general election soon after a new sovereign came to the throne, and the election that took place in 1830, showed that Wellington and Peel had lost their popularity on account of the Roman Catholic Emancipation Bill. Soon after the new Parliament met the Government had to resign and Lord Grey became Prime Minister, with Lord John Russell as leader in the Commons. Russell lost no time in bringing in a Reform Bill, but it made so many changes that it passed its second reading by a majority of only one, and a little later an important change was made in it, when it came up again for discussion. The ministers now persuaded the king to dissolve Parliament, and have a new election. Although very few people had votes, yet the feeling was so strong throughout the country among the merchants, manufacturers, artisans, and workingmen that the election resulted in giving the Bill a large majority. A second Reform Bill was now introduced in the Commons and carried by a majority of 109, but when it went before the House of Lords it was thrown out. This caused intense indignation, and great meetings were held in different parts of the country to denounce the Lords and to encourage the supporters of the measure. In some places there were riots and burnings, and people began to fear that a revolution was near at hand. Once more did the Government bring in the measure, and once more it was carried by a large majority in the Commons, and rejected in the Lords. Lord Grey and his colleagues now resigned, and Wellington tried to form a Government, but failed. Grey was recalled, not, however, before he had secured a pledge from the king, that he would, if necessary, create sufficient new peers to carry the

Bill through the Lords. This alarmed the Lords and when the measure came before them in June, 1832, many stayed away from the House and in this manner the Reform Bill became law.

The changes made by this celebrated Bill were two-fold. First, it took away from many (56) small boroughs the right to send members to Parliament and it reduced the members of thirty other boroughs from two each to one. The members thus taken from small boroughs were given to large towns, cities, and counties in England, Scotland and Ireland. Secondly, the number of voters was greatly increased, for those who paid £10 a year rental in towns, and £50 a year in counties were given votes. Besides these, votes were given to copy-holders and lease-holders. The class that benefitted most by this change was the middle class, the labouring classes having to wait many years before the franchise was given to them. After the Reform Bill the old political parties changed their names, taking now the titles of *Conservative* and *Liberal*, instead of *Tory* and *Whig*.

9. **Other Reforms.**—Now that a reformed Parliament was elected, a great many much needed reforms were carried out. In 1833, after a struggle of fifty years, against slavery in the West Indies, Wilberforce died, but not before he saw it practically abolished, at a cost of £20,000,000 to the British nation. The same year laws were passed to protect children from over-work in factories, and a grant of money was made to schools for the poor. In 1834, the Poor-Law, which had become a great burden on the industrious portion of the population, was amended by compelling those who could not work or support their families to go to places called *work-houses*, where work was given them if they were able to do it. The change from *out-door* to *in-door* relief soon had a great effect in reducing pauperism.

Other important changes at this time were the Municipal Act (1835) providing for the election of the mayor and aldermen of towns and cities by the ratepayers, and a Bill (1836) permitting Dissenters to be married in their own chapels.

Nor must we forget improvements and reforms of another kind that were taking place. The need of better means to carry goods to market led to the making of *Macadamized* roads, that is roads made of broken stone, and introduced by a Scotchman called Mac-

Adam.. Nevertheless, good roads and canals were not sufficient to meet the demands of English industry, and it was not till George Stephenson, the son of a poor collier, had overcome the difficulties of moving waggons along iron rails by means of a locomotive or steam-engine, that English products could find easy conveyance to their markets. The first railroad was built in 1830, from Manchester to Liverpool, and the train travelled at the rate of thirty-five miles an hour.

Besides these, other improvements were going on, such as founding Mechanics' Institutes, reducing the price of newspapers, building schools and colleges, and providing asylums for the insane. It is sad to think that, while so many things were being done to improve the lot of the poor, a great many were suffering from want, part of which was caused by the many improvements in labour-saving machines. So, in the year 1837, when William IV. died, there were many families in England that could scarcely afford to buy the coarsest food and clothing.

CHAPTER XXVI.

HISTORY OF OUR OWN TIMES.

1. Victoria.—William IV., like George IV., left no child as heir to the throne. He was succeeded by Victoria, the daughter of the Duke of Kent, fourth son of George III. The young queen at the time of her accession was but eighteen years of age, nevertheless, she had been so carefully trained and educated under her mother's watchful eye that, when she came to the throne, it was with a deep sense of the duties she had to discharge, and with a fixed resolve to keep the good of her people always before her. During the fifty-five years of her rule, she has earned the love and respect not of her subjects alone, but of the people of all nations, by her pure domestic life, and by her faithful discharge of every private and public duty.

Her accession to the throne made it necessary to separate Hanover from the Crown of England, the laws of Hanover not permitting a woman to rule. The queen's uncle, the Duke of Cumberland, now became King of Hanover, and England was no longer in danger of being drawn into European wars on account of this German kingdom.

2. **Rebellion in Canada.**—One of the first difficulties to be dealt with in this reign was a rebellion in Lower Canada. Canada had been divided into two Provinces, in 1791, by a measure known as the Constitutional Act. This Act also gave each Province a Parliament, composed of a Governor, a Legislative Council, and a Legislative Assembly. As Fox foresaw and pointed out at the time, the Act was full of defects, for it did not give the elected Assembly the full control of the revenue, and it did not make the Legislative Council and the Executive responsible to the people. The Act had many other defects besides these mentioned, and resulted in so much bad government in Lower and Upper Canada that some of the more hot-headed and impulsive of the people began a rebellion. The first risings were in Lower Canada, and thence the rebellion spread into Upper Canada in 1837. Lord Durham was sent out to inquire into the cause of the trouble, and he gave a report which pointed out very clearly the evils under which Canada was suffering, and outlined the proper method of dealing with the colony. Durham's report became, soon after, the basis of a new and better policy towards the colonies. The rebellion did not last long, but its fruits were the union of Upper and Lower Canada in one province in 1840, and the beginning of true responsible government in Canada. The two Provinces remained united till 1867, when owing to a deadlock between the two great political parties of the colony, the British North America Act was passed, which established a Federal form of government in British North America, leaving the different Provinces the control of their own local affairs, and establishing a Federal Parliament for the management of the general business of the Dominion of Canada. Beyond appointing the Governor-General and arranging treaties of commerce England now leaves Canada to look after her own interests, and interferes as little as possible with her affairs.

3. **Rise of the Chartists.**—The early years of this reign are marked by the introduction of the electric telegraph, Morse in America, and Wheatstone and Cooke in England, dividing the

honour of the invention between them in 1837. In 1838 steamships crossed the Atlantic, and in 1839 Sir Rowland Hill succeeded in getting the Government to carry letters to any part of Great Britain and Ireland for a penny. All these changes were in the interest of trade and commerce, and cheap postage was a great boon to the poor; nevertheless, work was scarce, food was dear, and there was much distress among the working classes. The Reform Bill had given political power to the middle classes, but had left the great mass of workingmen without any voice in the affairs of the nation. They began to think that their troubles were mainly due to the bad laws made without their consent, and an agitation began for further reforms. In 1838, at a great meeting in Birmingham, a formal demand was made for the "People's Charter." This charter asked (1) that all men should have votes; (2) for annual Parliaments; (3) for voting by ballot; (4) that a man might be a member of Parliament without owning any land; (5) that members of Parliament should be paid; (6) that the country should be divided into equal electoral districts. Most of these demands have since been granted, but at that time the upper and middle classes felt no inclination to share their power with their less fortunate countrymen.

4. **Anti-Corn Law League.**—Meanwhile it was beginning to be felt that one cause of the poverty of the working classes was to be found in the laws which placed a high tax on food and the raw material of manufactures coming into this country. We have seen that Walpole, Pitt, and Huskisson had each done something to lessen duties and make trade freer. The landowners, however, were very powerful in Parliament, and to keep up their rents they had heavy duties placed on wheat coming into the country. Whenever crops failed, bread became dear, and the poor were often on the verge of starvation. At last, Richard Cobden, a cotton printer, took the lead in forming a league which had for its object the removal of the taxes on food, and the lowering of duties on other imports. This league was formed in 1838, and under the guidance of Richard Cobden, and John Bright, a carpet manufacturer, it soon made its influence felt all over the land. Cobden and Bright were very clear-headed, able men, and by their speeches and writings they convinced the people that the taxes on food were unjust to the poor

and the cause of most of the distress that prevailed so frequently. Nevertheless the landowners and farmers bitterly opposed the movement, and it took eight years to convince the government that a change would be in the interests of the nation.

5. Troubles at Home and Abroad.—The Liberal party, which carried out so many reforms between 1832 and 1837, gradually lost its popularity; many people growing tired of, and others being offended by, so many changes. The Government at the beginning of the queen's reign had, as its head, Lord Melbourne, an easy-going, good-natured man, who proved a good friend to the young queen, although he was but an indifferent statesman. In 1841 his ministry had become so weak that it was obliged to resign, and give way to a Conservative government under Sir Robert Peel. In 1840 the queen was married to her cousin Prince Albert of Saxe-Coburg, a prince who proved a devoted husband, and a true friend to the people among whom he cast his lot.

Meanwhile, in 1839, a war had started with China, because English traders insisted on selling opium to the Chinese against the order of the Chinese government. The war came to an end in 1842, by the Chinese being compelled to open their ports to this wicked traffic.

At home, there was trouble in Ireland, and a religious agitation in Scotland. In Ireland O'Connell had begun to agitate for a Repeal of the Union, and so dangerous seemed the movement that O'Connell was at length arrested and tried for sedition in 1843-44. In Scotland the Presbyterian Church was rent by an agitation against the State controlling the Church, an agitation which ended in the "Free Church" being founded in 1843. Nor was England free from excitement and unrest. The Chartists were busy trying to make converts to their views, and the Anti-Corn Law League was equally zealous in showing the evils of the Corn Laws.

But all these troubles seemed small compared with a dreadful disaster which, in 1841, befell British troops in Afghanistan. The English had been gradually extending their territory in India towards the Indus and Afghanistan. This country lies between India and the Russian possessions in Asia, and the English were afraid that its ruler, Dost Mohammed, was too friendly towards Russia. Lord Auckland, the Governor-General of India, therefore sent an army to Cabul, the capital of Afghanistan, dethroned Dost Mohammed and put another chief in his place. This led to the fierce and treacherous Afghans murdering the English ambassador, and to a rising under Akbar Khan against the British troops. General Elphinstone, who commanded the army, resolved to retreat to India, and was promised protection for himself and his men, and for the women and children they were forced to leave behind. But when the army, in the depth of winter, tried to go through the rocky and narrow Cabul Pass, the Afghans attacked them so savagely and continuously, firing into and cutting down the wretched and weary soldiers, that only one man succeeded in reaching India alive. Dr. Brydon, the sole survivor of 4,500 soldiers, and 12,000 camp followers, told the sad tale to Sir Robert Sale at Jellalabad, and at once vengeance was determined upon. General Pollock and Sir Robert Sale marched into Afghanistan, retook Cabul, and rescued the women and children that had been left behind.

6. Repeal of the Corn Laws.—Let us now see what success Cobden and Bright were having in their crusade against the Corn Laws. For a time the speeches and pamphlets of the leaders of the League produced little effect, but the distress among the poor, and the failure of the harvest in 1845 helped along the movement for cheap food. Peel was gradually being convinced that Cobden was right, and when, in 1845, the crops failed so seriously in England and Scotland, and the potato blight destroyed the chief article of food of the Irish, he saw that he had to choose between leaving thousands of people to die of starvation, and taking off the duty on food. Peel had now become fully convinced that the corn laws should be repealed, and as his Ministry did not agree with him, he resigned his post, and advised the queen to call in Lord John Russell. Russell could not form a strong Government, and Peel had to return to office. Aided by the Liberals, and a portion of the Conservatives, he brought in a Bill, in 1846, to repeal the Corn Laws, which was carried in both Houses. The Corn Laws were repealed, but Peel's political career was ended. He had made bitter enemies of many of his old supporters, who looked upon him as a deserter, and they took their revenge by joining the Liberals to defeat him in 1846, on a "Coercion" Bill for Ireland. Lord John Russell now became Prime Minister.

7. End of the Chartist Agitation.—The duties on food were gradually reduced, and, in 1849, the Navigation laws were repealed. Step by step England removed the duties on nearly all the articles brought into the country, until now her revenue from that source is raised on a few luxuries such as tea, tobacco, and liquors of all kinds.

The repeal of the Corn Laws helped to make the poor more contented with their lot, and gave a great impulse to British manufactures and commerce. It was well that it did for, from 1846 to 1849, stirring events were taking place abroad and at home. In 1847 there was a dreadful famine in Ireland and millions died or emigrated to America. The poverty and misery of the Irish led to a rising under Smith O'Brien, but it was soon put down. In England, the Chartists drew up a monster petition to be presented to Parliament. It was said to be signed by five millions of people. Fergus O'Connor, the weak-headed leader of the Chartists, called a great meeting to be held on Kensington Common, and proposed that the people should go to the House of Commons to back up the petition. So loud were the Chartists in their boasts of what they would do, that all London grew alarmed, and 200,000 men were sworn in as special constables for the occasion. Wellington posted soldiers at various points to defend the city, and everybody awaited the great procession. But when the day came only 25,000 assembled, and the procession did not take place. The petition when presented was found to have less than two million names attached, and of these many were forged. This ended the Chartist agitation, although many of the reforms demanded were afterwards granted. Cheap food had killed the Chartist movement.

8. Extension of Territory.—Meanwhile, in India, Britain was extending her empire. Sir Charles Napier conquered Scinde in 1843, and in 1845 a war began with the brave Sikhs of the Punjaub, which ended in the annexation of that fine territory in 1849.

The discovery of gold, in 1851, in Victoria, Australia, led to a large emigration to that colony, which greatly increased its population and resources. In Africa, too, British territory was extending, and Natal and Cape Colony became important colonies. New Zealand began to be colonized in 1839, and in spite of fierce wars with the Maori chiefs the whole island became a British possession.

In 1850 a Bill was passed giving self-government to the Australian colonies, and, in 1852, New Zealand was given the same boon.

9. The Eastern Question.—The year 1851 was noted for the first great Exhibition of the industries of all nations. It was very largely an idea of Prince Albert, who, with others, thought it would bring about an age of peace and good-will among all peoples. It was held in London, and although many greater Exhibitions have since been held, yet none aroused so great curiosity and so much hope for the future.

The same year Prince Louis Napoleon, the President of the French Republic, by a treacherous massacre of his opponents in the streets of Paris, succeeded in obtaining the control of French affairs, and a year later made himself Emperor. He was the nephew of Napoleon Bonaparte, and the British naturally feared that this second Napoleon might try to imitate the policy of his uncle, and plunge Europe into another reat war. Their fears led to regiments of volunteers being formed in 1852, and so we have the beginning of the volunteer system now so popular and useful.

Napoleon, however, was friendly to England, and it was not long before France and England were figh ing side by side to save Turkey from the ambition of Russia. Russia had for many years looked with longing eyes on Constantinople, and when a quarrel broke out, in 1852, about the rights of the Greek and Latin Churches over the Holy Places in Jerusalem, the Emperor Nicholas of Russia, thought it a good opportunity to demand the right to protect the Greek Christians that lived in the Sultan's dominions. Nicholas wished England to join Russia in making a division of Turkey's possessions, but this England would not do. Then, when Turkey refused to admit Russia's claim to protect the Sultan's Christian subjects, Nicholas took the law into his own hands, and sent troops into the Turkish provinces on the Danube.

10. The Crimean War.—War now began and the Turks, who when aroused are brave soldiers, defeated the Russians near the Danube. France and England, in 1854, came to the aid of the Turks, for England feared Russia's influence in Asia, and the Emperor Napoleon thought a successful war would make the French forget the loss of their freedom. England had not taken part in a great war for nearly forty years, and she was wholly unprepared for such a conflict as she was now entering upon. Lord Aberdeen, the Prime Minister, was a lover of peace, and not fitted to manage affairs at such a time. The chief seat of the war was the Crimea, on the Black Sea, although the Baltic, the White Sea, and Russian Armenia were the scenes of strife. Kars, a fortress in Armenia, was bravely defended by the Turks under General Williams (afterwards the commander of the British troops in Canada), but at last surrendered with honorable terms near the close of the war.

It was the beginning of September when the Allies reached the Crimea, and not long after, September 20, they defeated the Russians at the River Alma. The Russians now retreated to Sebastopol, a strong fortress in the Crimea, and the delay of the Allies gave them time to strengthen its defences. The French were commanded by Marshal St. Arnaud, and the English by Lord Raglan. Both commanders died before the war ended, and were replaced by General Pélissier and General Simpson. The siege of Sebastopol began, but it was found that the Russian engineer, Todleben, had done his work well, and the Allies were for nearly a year held at bay. At times the Russians strove to drive the Allies back, and at Balaclava a fierce contest took place, which served to bring out the heroic qualities of the British soldier. Lord Cardigan, the commander of the Light Brigade, was ordered to charge the enemy and retake some guns which had fallen into their hands, but he mistook the order, and, instead, commanded his men to charge the main body of the Russian army. His men knew it was almost certain death, but not a man hesitated. Six hundred men rode headlong into the midst of the Russian army, cutting down the Russian gunners on their way, and then rode back amid a deadly hail from Russian muskets and artillery. Six hundred went into that "valley of death," less than two hundred returned to the ranks of the British army. This was on the 25th October, and on the 5th November a bloody battle was fought at Inkermann, in which the British private showed that his intelligence was more than a match for the brute force of the brave but ignorant Russian soldiery.

The siege of Sebastopol went on throughout the winter in spite of the terrible sufferings of the British soldiers. Mismanagement at home and in the Crimea left the soldiers without proper clothing shelter, and food. Shiploads of food were sent, which never reached the men. A cargo of boots did reach the half-shod men, but the boots were found to be all for one foot. These are but illustrations of the management of the war. The soldiers fell sick and could not be properly nursed and cared for. The result was that many died whose lives might have been saved under proper care. At last, Miss Florence Nightingale and a band of devoted women went out to nurse the sick and wounded. Very soon there was a marked change for the better in the condition of the patients, and from that time the value of women in army hospitals has been fully recognized. As time passed the war was better managed; there was less sickness among the soldiers, and better means were found of providing them with the necessary food, clothing, and shelter. In England, the discontent with the way things were going on led to Lord Aberdeen resigning, and to Lord Palmerston becoming Prime Minister. The siege of Sebastopol still went on, and at length attempts were made to carry it by storm. The first assault failed; the second was more successful. The French carried the Malakoff Tower, and although the English were repulsed at the Redan, the Russians blew up the forts, and left Sebastopol to the Allies, September, 1855. Soon after, in March, 1856, peace was made, and Russia, in the Treaty of Paris, agreed not to rebuild the fortifications of Sebastopol, and not to keep a fleet on the Black Sea.

11. The Indian Mutiny.—Scarcely was the Russian war ended, when a more serious trouble arose in India. The natives of India were not kindly treated by the English, and the discontent aroused was such that some fresh grievance was all that was needed to cause an outbreak. This grievance was found in the introduction of greased cartridges for the rifles of the Sepoys or native soldiers. The Sepoys thought it a great sin to use grease in any way, and when the Government found how much they were excited, they changed the greased for smooth paper. It was of no avail, the feeling grew that the English sought to make the soldiers lose their caste. Gradually the discontent increased, until three Sepoy regiments mutinied at Meerut near Delhi, and marched to Delhi, where an aged native king lived. Him they took out of his palace and made emperor. The rebellion now spread rapidly through Upper India, and the few thousand Englishmen in the country had to defend themselves against a host of enraged natives. Lord Canning, the

Governor-General, was a brave, capable man, and he was supported by able officers and brave soldiers. Sir John Lawrence sent his Sikhs and a few British troops to besiege Delhi, and Sir Henry Lawrence the Governor of Oude, gathered the British residents into the Governor's residence at Lucknow, where it was hoped they could hold out till relief came.

At Cawnpore, Nana Sahib, a native prince, when he heard Sir Henry Havelock was coming to the rescue, massacred the men, women, and children of the Europeans, July 15, 1857, The news of the horrible cruelties of Nana Sahib filled the British troops with a burning desire for revenge, which was with difficulty restrained by Canning. Soon the tide of war changed against the Sepoys. Delhi was taken, and Lucknow was relieved by Havelock, after a four months' siege. Highland regiments came on the scene under Sir James Outram and Sir Colin Campbell, and gradually the rebellion was crushed. The brutal massacre at Cawnpore was avenged by blowing from the cannon's mouth several of those who had taken an active part in that dreadful tragedy.

12. India under the Crown.—The Mutiny had some important results. Havelock, the brave Christian soldier, and the hero of the war, died of the hardships of the campaign. The British Government now resolved to take away from the East India Company its right of governing India. In 1858 India was placed under the Crown, and from that time has been governed by a Viceroy and Council under a Secretary for India, who is a member of the British Cabinet. The result is better government, and greater attention is paid to the feelings and prejudices of the natives, who are an intelligent and sensitive people.

13. Recent Wars.—Since the Indian Mutiny, Britain has been engaged in no great war. Several minor wars have, however, taken place, of which the following are the most important : (1) a war with China in 1855, and another in 1860, which led to opening up more of the Chinese ports to foreign trade ; (2) an invasion of Afghanistan in 1879-80 to avenge the murder of an English envoy, Sir Louis Cavagnari ; (3) two wars against the Zulus and Boers in South Africa in 1879-81 in which there was great loss of life ; (4) a war in the Soudan in 1884-5 to support the Khedive, or ruler of Egypt, against the Arabs. It was in this war that General

Gordon lost his life while defending Khartoum, and that Canadian boatmen helped to take a British army up the Nile in boats.

14. Reform Bills.—Let us now turn from these events in other lands and see what changes were taking place at home. While Lord Palmerston lived great reforms were not encouraged, but after his death the question of giving more political power to the working classes came to the front. Lord John Russell tried to pass a Reform Bill in 1866, and failed. Then Mr. Disraeli took office and, under his leadership, the Conservatives helped in carrying through a Reform Bill much more radical than that of Lord John Russell. The Reform Bill of 1867 gave votes to householders and lodgers in boroughs who paid rates and £10 rent, while in counties those who paid £12 rates were allowed to vote. Voting by ballot was made law in 1872, and a third Reform Bill was passed in 1884, by Mr. Gladstone, which gave votes to nearly every man, whether in town or county, and added 2,500,000 voters to the roll of electors. In 1885 a Redistribution Bill divided the country into more equal electoral districts, and increased the number of members for Scotland. In 1858 the volunteers were more thoroughly organized, and, in 1860, Cobden succeeded in making a treaty with France which encouraged freer trade between the two countries.

14. American Civil War.—In 1861 a civil war broke out in the United States of America, which led to great suffering among the operatives in the cotton factories of Lancashire. Most of the raw cotton used by England was brought from the Southern States, and as the war closed the ports of the South, its cotton could not find its way to the English markets. Thousands of workers were, in consequence, thrown out of employment when the mills were closed for want of raw cotton, and large sums of money had to be raised to keep the families of the operatives from starving. Nor was this the only bad effect of the war. Some of the British people were in sympathy with the South, and their desire to see the revolt successful led to allowing the Southerners to have ships built in British dockyards. One of these, the *Alabama*, did a great deal of injury to the merchant vessels of the North, and when the war was over England had to pay a heavy bill of damages for allowing the *Alabama* to escape from British ports.

15. Important Acts.—The year 1861 is memorable for the

death of Prince Albert, and 1863, for the marriage of the Prince of Wales to Alexandra, daughter of the King of Denmark. In 1869, a long delayed measure of justice was meted out to Ireland. The English Church in Ireland was disestablished and its revenues, after making due provision for the existing clergy, were set aside for the relief of the poor in Ireland. This Act was followed in 1870 by an Irish Land Act, which gave the tenants a more secure hold on their land, and did not leave them so much at the mercy of their landlords. They had henceforth a right to compensation for improvements they might make, in case they were turned out of their holdings.

A very important measure was the Education Act of 1870, which was brought into Parliament by Mr. Foster. It provided for the building and support of schools at the expense of the ratepayers, where there were not enough schools to educate all the children of the parish. Before this Act was passed, the masses had to depend for their education on private schools, and on schools under the control of the different Churches. To carry out this law School Boards were formed, the members of which were elected by the people. A few years later, parents were compelled by law to send their children to school; and, very recently, steps have been taken to make the education of a child in the Public Schools nearly as free as in Ontario. Religious tests, too, were done away with, in 1871, in the Universities of Oxford, Cambridge, and Dublin, so that all classes and creeds can attend these great seats of learning and get the advantage of a university education. Quite recently, in 1888, a measure was passed which gave the people of England a greater control over their own local affairs. These are perhaps the most important measures that have been passed in recent years, most of them under the leadership of Mr. Gladstone. In May, 1886, this great statesman joined Mr. Parnell, the leader of the Irish members, in a demand for Irish "Home Rule," that is, a demand for a Parliament in Dublin to look after Irish affairs. A "Home Rule" Bill was introduced into Parliament, but it failed to carry, and in the general election that followed Mr. Gladstone was defeated and gave way to Lord Salisbury. Mr. Parnell, the Irish leader, died in 1891, but "Home Rule" is to-day the great question in British politics.

16. Advances in the Last Fifty Years.—The history of the reign of Victoria is the history of great advances in art and science, and of remarkable inventions of time and labour-saving machines. Ships now cross the Atlantic ocean in less than six days, and trains travel at marvellous rates of speed. By the aid of the electric telegraph messages are carried across oceans and continents with the speed of lightning, while the more recent invention of the telephone enables us to carry on a conversation with friends many miles away. The phonograph keeps a record of the voices of the living and the dead, while the photograph keeps fresh in our memory the features of the absent. Electricity is now extensively used as a motive power to drive machinery, to propel trains, and to furnish light for our homes, shops, and streets. Science has made wonderful progress in nearly every department of human knowledge. Geology, biology, chemistry, history, political economy, language, medicine, theology, and politics, have each and all felt the influence of the scientific spirit and its methods of discovery and investigation. The age has been particularly great in writers of history, such as Hallam, Macaulay, Grote, Green, Froude, Freeman, Gardiner Lecky, and Carlyle. In fiction, we have had Thackeray, Dickens, George Eliot (Mrs. Cross), Charlotte Brontë, and a host of others only second to these great names. Tennyson (still living), the poet Laureate, and Robert Browning are great names in the realm of poetry, while Matthew Arnold has taught us the art of a true and lofty criticism of life and literature.

17. Conclusion.—These are a few, and only a few, of the names of English writers of the present century. So widespread has education become, and so numerous the fields of human activity, that where, a century ago, ten men distinguished themselves in art, science, or literature, a thousand now can be found.

We have followed the stream of English history down from its small beginnings in the first century to the present day. We have seen the gradual rise of parliamentary government and the steady growth of political freedom under the Plantagenets and the Lancastrians. We have seen, also, the struggle against despotism and tyranny under the Tudors and Stuarts, and the recovery of lost liberties by the Revolution of 1688. We have watched the steady increase in wealth and material prosperity under the Georges, and we have rejoiced at the success of the great moral movement in the 18th century, which roused England from spiritual deadness, and gave her strength to free herself from the shackles of political and social corruption. We have seen England standing almost alone against the giant power of Napoleon, fighting the battles of the world's freedom, undaunted by reverses, and gloriously successful through the courage and steadfastness of her sons. Not less interesting to us has been the marvellous growth of Britain's empire in the last hundred years. Her colonies and possessions are found on every continent, and her flag floats on every sea. She is still "Mistress of the Sea," and her navy carries British goods and manufactures to every land. Her commerce is great beyond comparison, and her language and civilization are finding a sure foothold in every nation. But better than all, England's influence for truth, justice, and righteousness, is greater than ever. She still leads all peoples in the struggle against vice, ignorance, and tyranny. Her shores are still a safe refuge for the oppressed of all nations, and from her the patriots of all lands derive hope and encouragement. At no period in her history have her people been so earnest in the pursuit of great moral reforms, and in removing the wrongs of centuries of misrule, as at the present day. After nineteen centuries of strife and struggle, England stands in the fore-front of nations, fresh and vigorous, every pulse throbbing with a healthy national life, her "eyes not dim and her natural strength not abated."

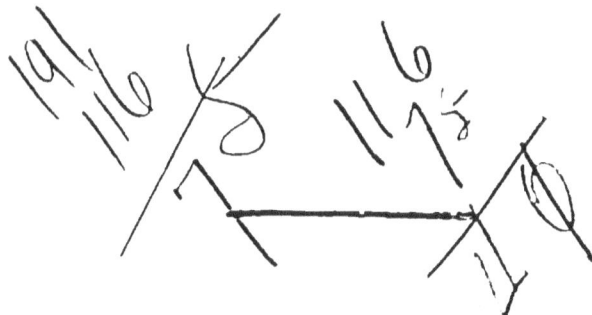

PUBLIC SCHOOL
HISTORY OF CANADA.

CHAPTER I.

EARLY SETTLEMENT OF CANADA.

1. Dominion of Canada.—If we take a map of North America we shall find that by far the greater part of its northern half is named the Dominion of Canada. On the east there is the Atlantic Ocean, on the west the Pacific, on the south the Great Lakes, and on the north the Arctic Sea. The only parts of this vast territory not in Canada are Alaska, a portion of Labrador, and the Island of Newfoundland. Its area is about 3,500,000 square miles, and is somewhat larger than the United States lying south of it. But the name Canada, has only very recently been applied to this territory, for less than twenty-five years ago that name was used to point out the Provinces marked Quebec and Ontario on the map. Then the Provinces of Nova Scotia, New Brunswick, Prince Edward Island, Manitoba, and British Columbia were from time to time added, and these with the great North-West Territories make up the present Dominion of Canada.

2. Early Inhabitants.—Who the first inhabitants of America were, we do not know, but we do know that they were not English, French, or the ancestors of any of the white or black people now living in Canada and the United States. Nor were the people now known as North American Indians the first to inhabit this Continent, as many remains exist of a more civilized race. Heaps of earth of curious shapes are found all over North America, (many of them in the neighborhood of Lake Superior) and these "mounds," as they are called, contain the bones of men and other animals, stone axes, copper tools, well shaped pottery and a variety of other articles, made with a great deal of skill and taste. Then on the shores of

Lake Superior we find old mines where copper has been taken out in large quantities a great many years ago. Large trees have grown over the rubbish that fill these mines, and this shows that a long time has passed since the miners were at work. Whence these clever and industrious people came we do not know, but it is thought they were originally from the south of Asia.

3. **North American Indians.**—The "Mound Builders" were followed by a fiercer and ruder people that cared for little except hunting and fishing, making war and roaming the forests. Very little interest was taken by them in tilling the soil, a few tribes growing small quantities of maize or Indian corn in clearings in the dense forests which covered most of the country. The principal tribes were the Algonquins, inhabiting the region from the Atlantic to Lake Superior; the Hurons, principally found in the Georgian Bay District, and the Five Nation Indians or Iroquois, occupying the middle and western part of the State of New York. These tribes were much alike in their appearance, manners and customs. Tall, sinewy, copper-colored, with straight black hair, black eyes, high cheek bones—they were keen of sight and hearing, swift of foot, fond of war, cruel to their enemies and generally true to their friends. The Algonquins lived almost entirely by fishing and hunting, dwelt in wretched tents called wigwams, and were often on the verge of starvation. The Hurons and Iroquois tilled the soil to some extent, and laid up stores of corn for the seasons when game was scarce. They often lived in villages, in large bark houses occupied by several families, and were much more comfortable and prosperous than the Algonquins. Indian women did all the work and drudgery; the men when not hunting, fishing, or fighting, lived a lazy life, and spent their spare hours sleeping, gambling, and story-telling. Such were the people the first European settlers found in the greater part of North America.

4. **Discovery of America.**—Little was known of America, until Christopher Columbus, a native of Genoa in Italy, persuaded Isabella, the Queen of Castile in Spain, to give him ships to find his way to India, by sailing westward instead of round the Cape of Good Hope. This was in 1492, A.D. Long before this, in the tenth century, the people of Iceland had made their way to the north-eastern coast of America, and seemed to have sailed south as

far as Massachusetts. These visits did not lead to any settlements being made, and were very soon forgotten, so that Columbus is the *real* discoverer of America. After a long voyage he came to an island and thought he had reached India. This mistake led to the group, of which this island is one, being called the West Indies. But Columbus did not reach the mainland as soon as John and Sebastian Cabot, two navigators sent out by Henry VII. of England, who explored the coast of Labrador and Newfoundland in 1497-98. A little later a Florentine named Amerigo Vespucci visited the New World and wrote an account of his travels. This led to the new continent being called America.

5. **Jacques Cartier.**—France, unlike Spain and England, did not take much interest in the work of exploring America until 1534, when Francis I. sent out from the sea-port of St. Malo, the famous sea captain, Jacques Cartier. Cartier sailed to Newfoundland, entered the straits of Belle Isle and passed into the Gulf of St. Lawrence. He landed at Gaspé, and erected a cross bearing the arms of France, to indicate that he had taken possession of the country for the French King. The next year he made another visit and entered the Gulf on St. Lawrence's Day, and for this reason he named the Gulf and the great river which empties into it the St. Lawrence. Sailing up the river he came to an Indian village, Stadacona, situated near where now the city of Quebec stands. Continuing his voyage he reached another Indian village, called Hochelaga. This village was situated at the foot of a beautiful mountain covered with trees, and he named it Mont Royal—hence the name of our great commercial city Montreal. After a short stay Cartier returned to Stadacona, and spent the winter there. His men suffered terribly from cold and scurvy, but were treated with the utmost kindness by the Indians. In the spring he returned to France, taking with him by force a number of Indian chiefs who were never permitted to go back to their own people—a base reward for their hospitality. Six years after, Cartier and Sieur de Roberval made an attempt to colonize Canada, but their efforts were fruitless ; and France, occupied with matters of greater interest at home, sent out no other expedition for nearly fifty years.

6. **Champlain.**—At last in 1603, Samuel De Champlain, a distinguished naval officer, and Pontgravé, a merchant of St. Malo,

were sent out to open up a trade in furs with the Indians and at the same time to attempt to civilize them and convert them to Christianity. They found no traces of the Indian villages Stadacona and Hochelaga and after a short stay, having reached the rapids of St. Louis, returned to France with a cargo of furs. For the next few years the efforts of the French were directed to establishing a colony in Acadia (now Nova Scotia), at Port Royal. Failing in this attempt, Champlain and Pontgravé were despatched to the St. Lawrence to build a fort at a suitable point for trade with the Indians. This led to the founding of the city of Quebec at the foot of the cliff Cape Diamond, in 1608. Champlain then proceeded westward, and meeting a war party of Algonquins and Hurons, was induced by promises of profitable trade to join an expedition against the Iroquois. He ascended the Richelieu river and discovered Lake Champlain, and near Lake George had his first encounter with the Iroquois. Again in 1615, he joined a war party of Hurons against the Iroquois; but was unsuccessful in the attack, notwithstanding the advantage of fire-arms. These unprovoked assaults taught the Iroquois to hate and distrust the French. Later on, when the Iroquois obtained possession of guns and were skilled in their use, a terrible revenge was taken on the weak Canadian colony. In nearly all the wars that followed between the English and French settlers in America, the brave and adroit Iroquois were found fighting on the side of the English. Champlain spent much time in exploring the country to the north and west, making his way up the Ottawa across to Georgian Bay, and thence down to Lake Ontario.

7. **Company of One Hundred Associates.**—So many companies were anxious to engage in the profitable fur trade of Canada, and so much rivalry and ill-feeling existed among them, that Cardinal Richelieu, the principal minister of Louis XIII, decided in 1627 to give the sole right to engage in the trade to a company known as that of the "One Hundred Associates." Besides the fur trade, this Company was given the control of the coast and inland fishing. In return for these grants, the Company bound itself to bring out six thousand colonists and settle them in Canada, at the same time making provision for the support of a Roman Catholic clergy who were to look after the religious welfare of the colonists, and to

labor to convert the Indians. Tradesmen and mechanics were to be taken out to Canada to build houses and make all necessary articles for the use of the settlers. Champlain was made governor of the young colony, but did not keep his position long; for war broke out between England and France, and England sent Sir David Kirke with a fleet to take Quebec. Twice Kirke appeared before the fort, and on the second occasion, in 1629, captured it. For three years England held Canada, and then, peace being restored, gave it back to France, not considering the country of much value. Champlain again took charge of the colony, and labored unceasingly to make it prosperous, and to bring the Indians to a knowledge of Christianity. In this he was partially successful, but his work was cut short by death, A. D. 1635. Champlain is rightly considered the Founder of the colony of New France or Canada*.

CHAPTER II.

CANADA UNDER FRENCH RULE.

1. Indian Missions.—To understand the history of Canada during the greater part of the seventeenth century, we must bear in mind that a two-fold object was constantly kept in view by the French kings: *first*, the establishment and extension of the colony at the expense of the English settlers in America: and *secondly*, the conversion of the Indians to the Roman Catholic faith. The French kings and their ministers wished to profit not only by the fur-trade of America, but to build up on this continent a colony where the religion of the Roman Catholic Church should be held and practised by the whole population, Indian as well as French.

By far the most interesting portion of the history of French Canada is the story of the Jesuit missions among the Indians. Full of holy zeal for the salvation of the Red men, missionary after missionary of the religious society called Jesuits, made his way to the Hurons in the Georgian Bay district, to the Algonquins to the

---

* Canada, is a word of Indian origin, and is supposed to mean "a collection of huts."

north and up the Ottawa, and to the fierce Iroquois in the Mohawk Valley.

Among the Algonquins they suffered want and hardship, dwelling in wretched tents full of smoke and filth and often ill-treated and despised by the people they were trying to benefit. At first their efforts were of little avail; even the Hurons, the most intelligent, kindly, and well-to-do of the Indian tribes thought the missionaries brought them trouble in the shape of drought, sickness, and ill-success in hunting and war. But no amount of failure could discourage these patient and unselfish men. After a while the Indians began to respect them, and then came a general willingness to be baptized and to accept the religion taught by the missionaries. It was not long before nearly all the Hurons became converted to Christianity, and left off their heathen practices and habits. Two names will always be remembered in connection with these Huron missions, those of Father de Brébœuf and Father Lalement; the first strong in frame, brave of heart, and capable of enduring any amount of hardship; the second, delicate, refined, loving, and unselfish. Other missionaries took their lives in their hands and went among the cruel and treacherous Iroquois, hoping to do some good to the fiercest enemies of the colony. But little, however, came of these missions. The Iroquois did not trust the French, and the missionaries after a brief stay were either murdered or compelled to escape for their lives. The name of Father Jogues, who suffered first, mutilation, and later on, death, at the hands of the Iroquois, is one that shines bright on the roll of Martyr missionaries.

2. **Indian Wars.**—The story of Indian missions is also a part of the story of Indian Wars. The Algonquins and the Hurons were the friends of the French, while the Iroquois were bent on the destruction of the feeble colony and its allies. The Hurons lived in populous villages between the Georgian Bay and Lake Simcoe, and were said to number thirty thousand people, most of whom accepted Christianity through the labors of Jesuit missionaries. St. Ignace, St. Louis, St. Joseph, and St. Marie, were among the most important of these missions. In 1648, St. Joseph was suprised by the Iroquois, while most of the Huron hunters and warriors were absent. Seven persons were captured and killed, the

missionary, Father Daniel, meeting his fate while ministering to the dying. The next place to fall was St. Ignace ; then St. Louis was attacked. Here Fathers Jean de Brébœuf and Gabriel Lalement, refusing to leave their helpless flocks, were made prisoners and put to the most cruel tortures. Brébœuf's nails were torn from his fingers, his body hacked with knives, red hot hatchets hung round his neck, his gums seared, and finally his heart cut out, no word or token of pain escaping from his lips. His tortures lasted four hours. Lalement, so delicate, sensitive, and frail, was tortured for seventeen hours before his sufferings were ended in death. St. Marie was the next object of attack. It was manfully defended by a few Frenchmen and Hurons, and after a fierce conflict the Iroquois retreated.

The Huron missions were destroyed, and the people were scattered. An effort to transfer the missions to Isle St. Joseph or Christian Island, near Collingwood, and gather the terror-stricken Hurons together again, ended the following spring in another dreadful massacre on the mainland, by the Iroquois, where the Hurons had come in search of food for their starving families. Ten thousand Hurons had perished, a few came to Quebec with the missionaries, the rest were scattered far and wide among other tribes in the north, east and west. The once powerful, brave and intelligent Hurons, as a nation, ceased to exist ; and with them perished the principal fruits of the Jesuit Missions.

3. **Growth of New France.**—Let us now return to what was going on in the colony, during this period of Indian strife and bloodshed. The Company of One Hundred Associates did not carry out what it had promised to do ; very few settlers were brought out by it, and its attention was almost entirely taken up with the trade in furs. It sent out scarcely one thousand colonists, much less the six thousand it had promised. The population grew very slowly, so slowly that in 1662, it had less then two thousand souls. But a great interest was taken in the spiritual welfare of the colony, and out of this interest came the founding of Montreal as a mission, in 1642, by a number of devoted men and women, who came from France for that purpose. Here, the little band prayed and fought, for the Iroquois lay in wait, night and day, right under the guns of the rude fort to kill and scalp the unwary.

Many a sad and heroic tale comes down to us of this troublous time. The story of Dulac des Ormeaux and his sixteen companions recalls the bravest deeds of the best days of the ancient Greeks and Romans. In the year 1660, hearing that a large number of Iroquois were coming down the lakes and rivers to attack the feeble garrison on the St. Lawrence, these young men determined to sacrifice their lives and save the colony. They made their wills, confessed their sins, received the sacrament, and took a sad farewell of their friends in Montreal. Then, with a few Christian Hurons and Algonquins they took possession of an old fort near the Long Sault Rapids, on the Ottawa. Here they awaited the descent of the Iroquois, prepared to sell their lives dearly. Soon two hundred came down in their boats, and landing, attacked the little band in their hastily constructed breastwork of logs. For days the unequal struggle lasted. The Hurons deserted to the Iroquois in dismay. Dulac and his companions fought on until worn out with want of sleep and nourishment, the four that were left alive fell into the hands of the enraged savages. Three were mortally wounded and were burnt alive, the fourth was saved for Indian tortures. The Hurons who so basely deserted to the enemy found no mercy at the hands of the Iroquois, and were put to death. Thus perished Dulac and his companions, but not without saving the colony. The Iroquois were checked and disheartened and for a time the settlement had peace.

The colony, as already stated, made slow progress. Governor after Governor was appointed to no purpose ; the Company of One Hundred Associates was doing nothing to further its interests, and Indian raids threatened the very existence of the settlement. In 1659, the Abbé Laval came to Canada. His arrival marks a new era in the life of the colony. Zealous, devoted, able and enthusiastic, for many years he laboured in the interest of the Church, and his influence did much to mould the future of Canada. His first stay was a brief one ; he was anxious to prevent the sale of brandy or "fire water" to the Indians, but the traders found it too profitable to be given up, although its effects on the Indians were frightful. Finally, Laval sailed to France to get the French King to stop the wretched traffic, and to have the Governor who refused to put the law in force against the offenders recalled.

4. Royal Government.—Up to this time *fur companies* aided by the leading clergy, had governed the colony. Now a change was decided upon. The ONE HUNDRED ASSOCIATES lost their charter, and Canada was placed under the government of the French King. This change was due largely to the influence of Laval at the French Court, and took place in 1663. A Governor, Intendant, and Bishop were appointed, and these aided by a Supreme Council, acted under the instructions of the King. The Governor was at the head of military affairs; the Bishop, of Church affairs; and the Intendant, of legal and money affairs. The Governor and the Bishop appointed the members of the Council, at first four, but afterwards increased to twelve, in number. The Intendant made laws for the people, and published them at the church doors or from the pulpit. Even such small matters as pew rents, stray hogs, fast driving, family quarrels, were dealt with by him. The Bishop, too, took an active part in the affairs of the colony, and because the duties of the Governor, Bishop, and Intendant, were not very clearly stated, frequent quarrels took place between these, the chief officers of the King. The law in force was very different from the law of England, and is known as the CUSTOM OF PARIS, the same law that prevailed at that time in France. It is still in force in Quebec Province and suits the French people better than our English laws. The colonists had nothing to say in making their own laws, they had no Parliaments or Municipal Councils, everything was managed for them by the King, through the Governor, Bishop, Intendant, and Supreme Council. To hear complaints and settle disputes, courts were established at Quebec, Three Rivers and Montreal; these courts being under the control of the Supreme Council, and presided over by the "seigneurs" or holders of large tracts of land from the King by *Feudal* or *Military tenure*. These seigneurs were gentlemen who came out to Canada from France, enticed by the offer of large grants of land for which they paid by bringing out settlers and giving their services in time of war, in defence of the colony. They generally settled near Quebec, Three Rivers, and Montreal, along the banks of the St. Lawrence, so as to have the river always near at hand to bring in and take out what they bought and sold. Besides, when attacked by the Iroquois, they could more easily escape to one of the forts by water than by land.

5. **Talon.**—M. de Mezy, was the first Governor, Laval the first

Bishop, and Talon the first Intendant. Talon was a very able man and used his power and talents in the interests of the colony. But, unfortunately Laval and the Governor could not agree, and De Mezy was recalled. A new Governor, De Courcelles, took his place; and about the same time the Marquis de Tracy was sent out with the famous Carignan regiment to help the colony in its struggles against the Iroquois. A number of settlers also came, bringing sheep, cattle, farm implements, and a few horses, so that the population was increased by two thousand persons. This new strength enabled the settlers to attack their enemies, the Iroquois, and two expeditions, the one in the winter, and the other the following summer, invaded the Mohawk territory, fired the villages of the Indians, and destroyed the stores of grain kept by them for a winter supply of food.

These attacks annoyed the Governor of New York, who thought it an invasion of English territory—but they had the effect of giving the colony peace for eighteen years. The Iroquois allowed missionaries to go to them, and some of them accepted their teachings, and became less barbarous. Canada now made better progress. Talon did his utmost to utilize the natural resources of the country and to promote trade with the West Indies. He also sent out exploring expeditions to Hudson's Bay, the Great Lakes, and the Mississippi of which he had heard from the Indians. He induced many of the soldiers to settle in the colony, and gave grants of land to the officers and men. As women were few in number, the French Government sent out a large number of young women to become wives for the soldiers and settlers. As soon as these ship-loads of women arrived, the men who wanted wives came down to the vessels, and chose their partners. These curious marriages generally turned out well—the couples thus brought together living fairly happy and contented lives. Some serious drawbacks to the success of the colony must be noted. One was the sale of "fire-water" to the Indians and settlers, although Laval did his best to have it stopped. Another was the tendency of young men to take to the woods, to live and trade with the Indians. These "*Coureurs du Bois*," as they were called, often became more savage than the Indians themselves, dressed in Indian fashion, and took Indian wives. Once used to this mode of life, it was found impossible to bring them to settle down and till the soil. The trade in furs was too profitable to be abandoned for civilized life. Then again, the colony suffered by its trade being placed in the hands of a few men, who enriched themselves at the expense of the people. So it happened that Canada did not grow as fast as the English colonies to the south of it, simply because the government did not allow the settlers sufficient freedom in managing their own affairs.

6. Discoveries in the Great West.—The Jesuit missionaries were the first explorers of the far West. They united the work of discovery with their mission labors, just as Livingstone and Moffat in recent years have done in Africa. Talon was anxious to prevent the English from extending their trade westward, and with this in view, he established trading-posts and missions at Sault Ste. Marie and other points. Before, however, his great plans could be carried out, he returned to France, and left to his successors the task of discovering and exploring the Mississippi.

Talon returned to France in 1672, and about the same time Courcelles the Governor also asked to be recalled. The new Governor, Louis de Buade Count de Frontenac, is the most striking figure in the history of New France. No Governor was so successful in his dealings with the Iroquois; they feared and respected him, at the same time giving him their regard and confidence. He treated them as children, threatening them with punishment if unruly, and rewarding and encouraging them if they behaved well. He made a great display of force when treating with them, and managed to impress them with the greatness and power of the French King, the "Great Father," across the Big Waters. He was not so successful with his COUNCIL, for his hasty temper and haughty bearing, together with his attempts to control everything and everybody, led to many a scene in the Council Chamber, and caused bitter quarrels in the colony. His rule however, will be always remembered with gratitude for, as long as he was Governor, Canada was safe from Indian attacks. More important still were the discoveries in the west in his time by Joliet, a merchant, Marquette, a missionary, and Robert Cavelier, Sieur de la Salle. Father Marquette, who lived and labored among the Indians on the shores of Lake Superior and Michigan, was joined by Joliet, and these two brave men, in 1673, in bark canoes, with five men, went down the mighty Mississippi, until they reached the Arkansas river. Fearing to fall into the hands of the

Spaniards, they returned and Joliet brought the news of his discoveries to Quebec. The story of his exploit filled La Salle, who had obtained a grant of land at Lachine (so-called it is said because La Salle thought the St. Lawrence led to China), with the desire to explore the West. Before Joliet made his great discovery, La Salle had found his way to the Ohio, although his doings at this time are not very well known. Courcelles had planned building a fort at the foot of Lake Ontario, where Kingston now stands, and his successor in office carried out his plan and founded Fort Frontenac. This fort served as a trading-post, and also as a check on the Iroquois in time of war. At first the fort was of wood—afterwards La Salle, in 1674, built it of stone and promised to keep it up, if he were granted the privilege of engaging in the fur trade. It was from this point that he set out to find his way to the Mississippi. After years spent in braving the dangers of the wilderness, and overcoming obstacles which would have daunted most men, he succeeded in 1682 in launching his canoes on the Father of Waters—the broad Mississippi. In the month of April he reached the Gulf of Mexico, and took possession of the Great South and West in the name of Louis XIV. under the title of Louisiana.

Five years after, La Salle was basely murdered by some treacherous followers, while engaged in a venture to found a colony at the mouth of the Mississippi.

7. **Frontenac.**—Let us now turn to what was going on in Canada under Frontenac's rule. The colony was at peace with the Indians; but Frontenac quarrelled with his Intendant, with the Governor of Montreal, with Laval and the Jesuits, in fact with everybody that would not do as he wished. His conduct was so violent and unjust, that many complaints were made to the King. Laval and the missionaries were anxious to stop the sale of liquor to the Indians, but Frontenac was too greedy of gain to forbid it. At last, after ten years of disputing and wrangling, the King grew wearied and Frontenac was recalled (1682).

But not for long. The Iroquois were soon on the war-path again, incited by the Governor of New York, Colonel Dongan. The English colonists were anxious to take away from the French the trade with the Indians, and they generally succeeded in keeping on good terms with the Iroquois, who saw that the English colonies were growing much more rapidly than the French settlement. It needed but the treachery of Denonville, one of Frontenac's successors, to bring on the colony a terrible calamity. To gratify a whim of the King, he seized at Fort Frontenac fifty Iroquois chiefs, who had come to a friendly meeting, and sent them in chains to France to work at the galleys. He followed up this outrage by leading two thousand men into the country of the Senecas, one of the five nations of the Iroquois. For several days he pillaged and burned their villages, destroying their food supplies, and putting many to death.

The Five Nations soon united to punish the French. Fort Niagara at the mouth of the Niagara River, and but recently built, was levelled to the ground. Fort Frontenac had to be abandoned and burnt, with all its stores and trading vessels. The Island of Montreal was surprised and more than a thousand of its inhabitants were killed or carried off prisoners for further torture. This is the *Massacre of Lachine*, 1689. The colony was in despair, and its people had to take shelter in the forts of Quebec, Three Rivers, and Montreal.

To save the colony from perishing Frontenac was again despatched to Canada as Governor. He brought with him the chiefs seized by Denonville, and sent them back to their tribes to act as peacemakers. At this time a war arising out of the English Revolution of 1688 was raging on in Europe between England and France. Frontenac determined to punish the English colonists for the part they had taken in stirring up the Iroquois to attack the French settlements. Bands of French and their Indian allies made frequent raids into New York, New Hampshire, and other border colonies, scalping and murdering the defenceless people. Schenectady in New York, and Salmon Falls in New Hampshire were burned to the ground, and their inhabitants butchered. For years this cruel border warfare lasted, leaving a dark stain on the early history of the American settlements.

In 1690 an effort was made by the British colonists to drive the French out of Canada. Sir Wm. Phips was sent by Massachusetts to capture Port Royal in Acadia (Nova Scotia). This he accomplished, and then sailed up the St. Lawrence to take Quebec. Before this, however, an expedition under the command of Colonel Winthrop had been sent to take Montreal. Sickness and a lack of supplies led to its failure and it returned to Albany. But Phips

reached Quebec and demanded its surrender. The demand met with
a haughty and indignant refusal from Frontenac, who had prepared
for a spirited defence. In vain Phips opened a furious fire on the
town and landed his raw soldiers on the Beauport shore. He was
driven back with heavy loss by the French and their Indian allies,
and compelled to beat a retreat to Boston. Thus ended the second
attempt by the English to capture Quebec. Meanwhile the savage
border warfare went on unchecked. The Abenaquis Indians aided
the French in the work of murder—the Iroquois, the English. A
single incident will give us a glimpse of the savage nature of this
warfare. Hannah Dustin of Haverhill, taken prisoner in one of
these border raids, avenged the murder of her week-old child by
slaying ten out of twelve of her sleeping Indian captors, and then
succeeded in escaping to the British settlements. These were the
days when both French and English offered prizes to the Indians
for human scalps. Little wonder that the border settlements did
not prosper. The Treaty of Ryswick (1697) put an end for a short
time to the war between England and France, and each country
restored to the other its conquests. The next year saw the death of
Frontenac in his 78th year. His memory was cherished as the one
man whose energy saved Canada when on the verge of ruin.

8. State of the Colony.—The war of the Spanish Succession in
Europe, which broke out in 1702, was the signal for a renewal of
the horrors of warfare between Canada and the English colonies in
America. Not until the Treaty of Utrecht in 1713, did the settlers
along the frontier again breathe freely. This treaty gave Acadia,
Newfoundland, and Hudson's Bay Territory to England, while
France kept Canada, Cape Breton, and Louisiana. For over thirty
years the colony had rest, and a chance to grow and prosper. The
principal Governor of this time was Vaudreuil, whose term of office
began in 1703. He foresaw that a fierce struggle must take place
between the French and the English for control of the North
American continent, and he laid his plans accordingly. The fortress
of Louisburg in Cape Breton was begun ; Quebec, Montreal and Fort
Frontenac were strengthened, and a new stone fort was built at
Niagara. Trade, ship-building, and manufactures were encouraged,
and we find even woollen and linen goods among the home produc-
tions. Canada, at this time, exported largely to France and the

West Indies such products as staves, tar, tobacco, flour, pease, and pork. She brought in rum, sugar, molasses, and most of the manufactured goods she needed. Roads were opened up between the parishes, and a letter-post established. Law was better administered than in the earlier days of the colony. With all these improvements it made but slow progress. The feudal system of land tenure, while good for military purposes, did not encourage the peasants who held the land from their seigneurs, to make many improvements. The people had no say in making their own laws, and the general want of education kept the colony in a dull and lifeless state. Young men tired of the quiet home-life of the farm took to the woods, and lived and traded with the Indians. In 1702-22, Quebec had a population of seven thousand, and an agreeable society, whose principal element was the military class. Montreal had about two thousand inhabitants, and the whole of Canada about twenty-five thousand. The whole country to the west was a forest with a few trading posts and forts at Kingston, Niagara, and Detroit.

9. Braddock's Expedition.—Vaudreuil died in 1725, and was succeeded by the Marquis de Beauharnois. In his time Fort Frederic, at Crown Point, on Lake Champlain was built, and soon became an important post in the wars between the rival colonies. No new stirring events took place until the outbreak of the War of the Austrian Succession, which brought England and France once more into conflict. It was not long before their colonies were engaged in a deadly struggle, a struggle that lasted, with a brief intermission, until the flag of England floated over the walls of Quebec. In 1745, Louisburg was taken after a brave defence, by an army of New England farmers and fishermen under Sir William Pepperell. The French tried to retake this the second strongest fortress of the New World, but without success. Peace was for a short time restored in 1748, and Louisburg, to the great annoyance of the people of New England, was given back to France. In these days, it often happened that while the mother countries, France and England, were at peace, their children in India and America carried on a bitter strife. Not until 1756 was war once more declared in Europe; yet, in 1754, hostilities broke out in the valley of the Ohio. The French claimed the Great West, and sought to shut in the English to the strip of territory between the Atlantic and the Alleghany Mountains. To carry out this plan, a fort was constructed at a point where two branches of the Ohio River meet, the Monongahela and the Alleghany. This fort got the name, Du Quesne, from the French Governor of Canada at that time. The English colonists of Virginia sent George Washington, a young officer and surveyor, to build another fort near at hand. Unfortunately

LAKE COUNTRY AND WESTERN FORTS.

Washington fired upon a party of French and Indians who came to warn him that he was encroaching on French territory. This act was the beginning of the final struggle for the mastery of the New World. General Braddock was sent out from England with two regiments of regular troops and was placed in command of the militia of the colonies. He thought he knew more about bush warfare than such men as Washington, and would take no advice. He was so stubborn and arrogant that many of the best militia officers would not serve under him. The French too, made preparations for the conflict. Baron Dieskau brought to Canada a strong military force, and was accompanied by the last French Governor of Canada, De Vaudreuil, a son of the former Governor of that name.

In the spring of 1755, Braddock began his march from Virginia to Fort Du Quesne. He had a force of two thousand men, regulars and colonial militia, but his movements were hampered by taking a train of baggage-waggons and artillery. One hundred men with axes went before to cut down trees and make a road for these to pass over. The journey was a slow and weary one, and the French garrison at Fort Du Quesne was well aware of Braddock's movements. As he neared the fort, an ambuscade of French and Indians was formed, with the hope of checking his march. In spite of repeated warnings from Washington and others, Braddock neglected to take the most ordinary precautions against surprise. Passing through a thickly wooded defile, a sudden hail of bullets was poured into the astonished and dismayed ranks of the British regulars. On all sides was heard the terrible war-whoop of the Indians, and the work of destruction began. The British soldiers huddled together and fired their muskets into the air or into their own ranks. They were mown down by the bullets of the concealed French and Indians— without being able to offer any defence. Braddock had five horses shot under him, and was mortally wounded. Fotunately for the regulars, the colonial forces, used to Indian modes of fighting, took shelter behind the trees and fought the enemy in their own fashion, and kept them at bay. This enabled the terror-stricken soldiers who survived, to escape from the defile. More than one-half had fallen —the remainder, panic-stricken, fled, and paused not till they had put forty miles between them and the dreaded enemy. Braddock was carried in a dying condition on a litter from the field, and that night with his life paid the penalty of his folly.

Fort Niagara, the forts on Lake Champlain, and Beauséjour in Acadia, were also marked out for attack by the English. The expedition against Niagara never reached its destination; Beauséjour was not able to make any defence and was easily taken; and Baron Dieskau was defeated and made prisoner near Lake George by Colonel William Johnson, at the head of a body of colonial militia and Mohawk Indians. This Colonel Johnson was a remarkable man in many respects. He had acquired a wonderful influence over the Mohawks, and was made one of their great chiefs. He built two great strongly fortified houses in the Mohawk valley, and made them headquarters for the surrounding Indians—one of whose daughters, the famous Molly Brant, sister of Joseph Brant, he married in Indian fashion. Johnson was made a knight for his victory over Dieskau, and received a large grant of money from the Crown.

10. **Capture of Quebec.**—The next year (1756) war was formally declared between England and France, and the struggle went on with increasing bitterness in America. This war is known as the *Seven Years' War*, and was carried on in Asia, America, and Europe simultaneously. The French sent out as Commander-in-Chief, the famous Marquis de Montcalm, an officer of great skill, courage and energy. The English had by far the greater number of men, and the greater wealth and resources, but for a time they were badly officered and led. Their first Commander-in-Chief was the Earl of Loudon, who proved a wretched failure. Another general, almost equally unfit, was Abercrombie, who allowed Oswego to fall into the hands of Montcalm. A still greater disaster befell the English at Fort William Henry, on Lake George, in August 1757. After a spirited defence the garrison was allowed to go out with the honors of war, engaging not to serve against the French for eighteen months. Montcalm promised them protection against attacks by his Indian allies, who sought victims to scalp and torture. The Indians crazed by liquor, fell upon the retreating garrison with their women and children, and in spite of the efforts of Montcalm and his officers, murdered or carried off prisoners the most of them. Almost equally disastrous was the attempt made by Loudon, aided by a large fleet and force, to take Louisburg.

These repeated failures, added to a general want of success in other parts of the world where the war was carried on, led to a change in the British government, and William Pitt, was placed in charge of England's foreign affairs. Very soon a change was noted. Pitt had determined he would drive the French out of Canada, and he made his preparations accordingly. He chose good men to command, and gave them an energetic support. Amherst was made the Commander-in-chief, and Boscawen was put at the head of the fleet in America. Under Amherst were placed Wolfe, Lawrence, and Whitmore, officers young in years, but full of energy and courage. One mistake Pitt did make : he left Abercrombie in charge of the army intended to operate along Lake George and Lake Champlain.

The first fruits of Pitt's policy was the capture of Louisburg.

Against this strong fortress was sent a fleet of over one hundred and fifty vessels, and an army of twelve thousand men, under the command of Amherst and Wolfe. After a siege of seven weeks, in which Wolfe greatly distinguished himself, the garrison of five thousand men surrendered, and were sent prisoners to England.

But victories were not all on the side of the English. A large force under General Abercrombie was repulsed with heavy loss in 1758, while trying to take Ticonderoga, or Carillon, on Lake Champlain. The defeat was due to the death in the early part of the fight of young Lord Howe, and to the utter folly and rashness of Abercrombie, in ordering his brave troops to attack the French, protected as they were by felled trees and a breastwork of timber, with sharpened stakes pointing outward. In this battle Montcalm proved his skill as a general, and the English lost two thousand men, many of them Highlanders, who for the first time in their history, served in the foreign wars of Britain. The campaign of 1758 closed with the easy capture of Fort Du Quesne, by a force sent against it under General Forbes. Forbes, falling sick, was borne on a litter across the Alleghanies with his army. Finding winter approaching, he sent Washington ahead with a smaller force, to take the fort before it could get help. On the 25th of November, without a blow being struck, Du Quesne was taken possession of by Washington, and named Fort Pitt, in honor of England's greatest War Minister.

The year 1759 opened with great efforts put forth by Montcalm to save Canada to the French. The prospects of the colony were gloomy enough. The mother country gave but little assistance; in fact, she was not able to give much. So many men in Canada were drawn into the army, that the farms were only half-tilled, and the crops were scanty and poor. To add to the miseries of the people, the internal affairs of Canada were under the control of the worst official of French Rule. This was the Intendant Bigot, whose whole career was one of extortion, fraud and lewdness. Monopolists plundered the poverty-stricken people; grain, cattle, and horses were seized and sold abroad, and the money put into the pockets of Bigot and his tools. Every man between the age of sixteen and sixty was drafted into the army to defend the colony. Montcalm labored ceaselessly to put Quebec and the other fortresses in the best possible condition for defence, but he was hampered by the Governor and the Intendant. Meanwhile a plan of campaign had been arranged by the British, which was to bring the war to a close by one great and united effort. Amherst was to proceed along the line of Lakes George and Champlain, and take Ticonderoga and Crown Point. General Prideaux, aided by Sir William Johnson and his Indians, was to attack Niagara, while to Wolfe was given the heavy task of assaulting Quebec. Amherst and Prideaux having performed their allotted tasks were to join Wolfe at Quebec. Prideaux was killed while besieging Niagara, and the honor of taking the fort fell to Sir William Johnson. Amherst found little opposition at Ticonderoga and Crown Point, the French falling back on Quebec for the final defence. Amherst, however, lingered at these points, building and strengthening forts to secure the line of Lakes George and Champlain.

Early in 1759, Wolfe sailed from Louisburg to Quebec with his army of less than nine thousand men. Saunders and Holmes commanded the fleet, while Wolfe was assisted by an able staff of officers, Townshend, Monckton and Murray. Landing at the Island of Orleans, Wolfe anxiously viewed for the first time the rock fortress, Quebec, the greatest stronghold of France in the New World. For miles on both the east and west of Quebec, Montcalm had fortified the banks of the St. Lawrence. Between the St. Charles and the Montmorency were more than thirteen thousand men of all ages, and the walls of Quebec itself bristled with guns. Who could hope to capture this Gibraltar of America, with such a small force as Wolfe had at his command? Yet, Wolfe, weakened as he was by a fatal disease, did not shrink from the effort. Soon he seized a strong position opposite Quebec, Point Levi, and their Monckton fixed his batteries. The French made fruitless efforts to dislodge the British fleet, by sending fire-ships down the river, but these were taken in tow by the sailors and did little harm. The batteries from Point Levi began to play upon the doomed fortress, and soon a great part of Quebec was in ruins. Nevertheless, Montcalm strong in his position on the north shore, with entrenchments from Quebec to the river Montmorency, defied every effort of Wolfe to land his troops. On the 31st of July, a desperate attempt was made to gain a footing and storm the heights near the Montmorency; but to no purpose, Wolfe was compelled to retire with heavy loss, and his chagrin and grief brought on a fever.

It looked as if Quebec could not be taken, and winter was

approaching which would bring relief to the garrison. Then it was that one of Wolfe's staff, Townshend, proposed to climb the steep banks of the St. Lawrence, at a point some three miles above Quebec. The plan was adopted, and steps were at once taken to carry it into effect. Early in September, Wolfe managed, under cover of a pretended attack on the opposite (Beauport) shore, to have the main part of his army and fleet moved above Quebec. Taking advantage of a dark night, and knowing that a small body of French soldiers were coming down to Quebec from Montreal

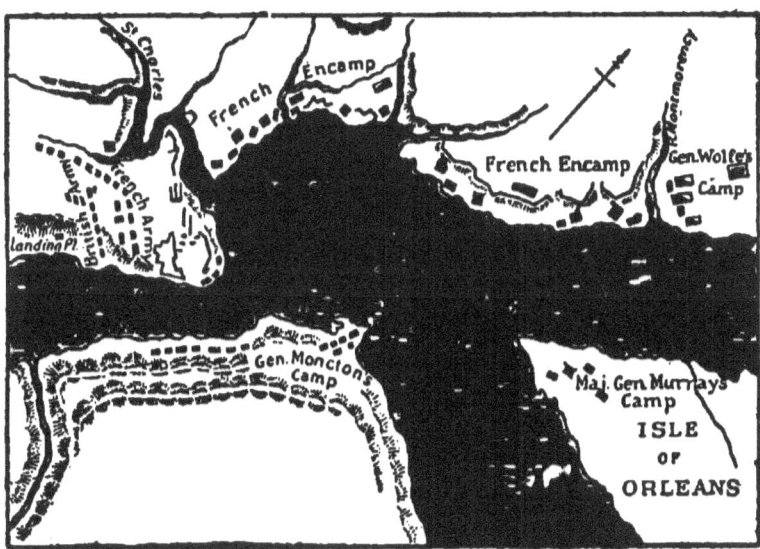

SIEGE OF QUEBEC.

with a supply of provisions, Wolfe's fleet dropped silently down the river, escorting thirty barges laden with sixteen hundred men. With muffled oars they glided down the stream, hugging the north shore. The sentries along the bank were deceived, their challenges being correctly answered (a French deserter having given the English the proper countersign), and they thought it was the convoy expected from Montreal. As the boats glided on, Wolfe, weak with his recent illness, and filled with hope and anxiety, softly repeated several stanzas of Gray's "Elegy" written but a year before. Pausing on the words

"The paths of glory lead but to the grave,"

he exclaimed! "I would rather be the author of that poem than take Quebec." In the early morning, of the 13th September, he landed at what is now known as Wolfe's Cove. His active Highlanders were soon at the top of the path leading up the cliff. The French guard was quickly overpowered, and at daybreak Wolfe and his little army stood ready for battle on the Plains of Abraham. Montcalm, who had been expecting an attack below the city on his lines at Beauport, as soon as the news was brought him broke up his camp, and without waiting for reinforcements hurried to meet Wolfe. Had he remained in the city it is doubtful if Wolfe could have taken it before the coming winter. But his impetuous temper led him astray, and marching through Quebec he flung himself on Wolfe's veterans, who stood calmly awaiting their gallant leader's orders. Not until the French were within forty paces did Wolfe give the command to fire; then, at the given signal, a well-directed volley of musketry, followed by a fierce charge of bayonets, caused the Frencch to give way, and the victory of the Plains of Abraham was won. .It was a dear victory to both English and French, for their brave leaders both fell in the conflict. Wolfe, wounded first in the wrist, then in the chest, lived long enough to know that the victory was won, and his heroic task done. "They run, they run," said an officer holding in his arms the dying general. "Who run?" asked Wolfe ; and when he heard, "Now God be praised" said he, "I die happy." Montcalm was carried fatally wounded into Quebec, and when told his fate murmured sadly, "So much the better, I shall not live to see the surrender of Quebec." He died before midnight, and was buried in a grave made by the bursting of a shell, a fitting close to the career of a brave soldier and a true patriot. Five days after, on the 18th September, Quebec surrendered, and Canada practically ceased to be a French possession.

CHAPTER III.

LAYING THE FOUNDATIONS OF THE CANADIAN CONSTITUTION.

1. **Peace of Paris, 1763.**—General Murray took the command of the British army after the death of Wolfe, and De Lévis succeeded Montcalm. Though Quebec had fallen, the Governor, Vaudreuil, and De Lévis, were not willing to surrender Canada to the English without a struggle. The walls of Quebec had been partly beaten down, and a great portion of the city had become a mass of ruins by the cannonading of the British, and Murray, fully expecting an assault from the French, at once began to put the fortress into as good a condition as possible. His army, especially the Highlanders, suffered much from the cold, which was very severe that winter. The French in Quebec and the British army were on very friendly terms, and much kindness was shown to the suffering soldiers by the inhabitants, the nuns knitting long hose to protect the unfortunate Highlanders from the effects of the frost and cold. Towards spring De Lévis advanced with an army of seven thousand men to re-take Quebec, and Murray was foolhardy enough to march out of the city against him. The British numbered but three thousand men, (so much had they suffered during the winter) and in the second battle of Plains of Abraham, they were defeated and compelled to retreat, in haste, within the walls of Quebec. The siege lasted some time longer, until the St. Lawrence becoming free of ice, a British fleet sailed up the river, and De Lévis, in despair, returned to Montreal. In September, Murray and Amherst united their forces before Montreal, and Vaudreuil and Lévis feeling the impossibility of defending the city with the few weary and disheartened men at their disposal, surrendered all Canada to England, on the 8th of September, 1760.

Three years later the Seven Years' War was brought to a close, and Canada was formally given to England ; France ceding all her possessions in America east of the Mississippi except New Orleans, and the island of St. Pierre and Miquelon near Newfoundland. Besides these great territories England gained largely in India and other parts of the world. The treaty that closed this war is known as the Peace of Paris.

2. **Conspiracy of Pontiac.**—About the time this treaty was made, a very strange and remarkable plot took place. Its object was the seizure of all the British forts along the Upper Lakes and in the Great West, and the holding them for the French. A famous Indian chief, Pontiac, who did not want the British to rule in Canada, and who did not know that the French had given up all hope of recovering it, stirred up the Indian warriors in the valley of the Ohio, and along the line of the Great Lakes, to seize the rude forts in the West recently handed over by the French to the British. A short time after the Peace of Paris was signed, a sudden and almost simultaneous attack was made on these forts, and in nearly every instance they fell into the hands of the Indians, their garrisons being murdered or made prisoners. Detroit was besieged for over a year by thousands of Indians, who managed to prevent supplies and assistance coming to the garrison. At last a strong force came to the relief of the brave defenders of the fort, and the Indians sullenly withdrew. Fort Pitt and Niagara also were able to hold their own against the dusky warriors, and the Indians finding that French power was at an end in America, ceased hostilities. Pontiac, a few years later, while drunk, fell by the hands of a treacherous Illinois Indian.

Two things make this conspiracy remarkable in Indian history. One is the vastness of the scheme planned and carried out by Pontiac with so much skill and success; the other is the determination shown by the Indians in the siege of Detroit, their usual mode of warfare being to capture forts, if at all, by surprise, and not by a long siege.

3. **Military Rule.**—There was an interval of more than two years between the surrender of Canada by the last French Governor and the Peace of Paris, and during that period the colony was governed by *Military Rule.* General Murray ruled over the district of Quebec; General Gage, that of Montreal; and Colonel Burton, that of Three Rivers. A Council of officers met twice a week, and settled all disputes. The people were allowed the free use of their religion, and were treated justly and kindly. The French militia, who had been called from their homes to defend the colony against the British were allowed to go back to their farms and occupations, and the regular soldiers were sent to France. Canada was in a sad

condition at this time. The people had been taken from their usual occupations to defend the country, and their farms had gone untilled, except by the women and the feeble men and boys who were unfit to carry a musket. Bigot, the last Intendant, and a host of greedy followers had plundered the people of the little they had, and the colony was flooded with a worthless paper money. Not many more than sixty thousand inhabitants were scattered along the line of the St. Lawrence between Montreal and Quebec. Peace brought Canada a measure of prosperity. Farms could now be tilled without fear of interruption from enemies, English or Indian. Many of the principal inhabitants returned to France, some of them like Bigot, to answer for their misdeeds to the French King, and to receive merited punishment. Gradually the colony settled down to steady industry, and the mild rule of Murray and his brother officers lessened any feeling of soreness arising from passing under the government of their old-time enemies.

4. The Quebec Act.—After the Peace of Paris, King George III. proclaimed Canada a British province, and promised the French inhabitants the right of free worship, and the "free exercise" of their religion. They were also left in undisturbed possession of their property, and were given in every way the same rights and privileges as the King's subjects of British birth, except that they were excluded from holding public office, because the laws of Great Britain at that time did not allow a Roman Catholic to hold offices in the gift of the State. An effort was made to induce British people to settle in Canada by offering them land grants, and the protection of British laws. A promise, also, made was of British parliamentary institutions as soon as the circumstances of the country would permit ; that is, the people of Canada would be allowed to have their own Parliaments, and make most of their own laws. In the meantime the country was governed by a Governor and Council the latter composed entirely of men of British birth, many of them military officers. The British settlers for many years were few in number, yet they had all the power, and the French had no voice in managing the affairs of the colony. Again, English law was introduced into the courts, and the English language used. Trial by jury was unknown to the French, and they did not like the system. They preferred to be tried directly by a Judge, in a language they understood. On the other hand the English settlers wanted British law in both criminal and civil cases. They did not like the French way of buying and selling land, and settling disputes about property. General Murray the first Governor after 1763, and his successor, Sir Guy Carleton, both, tried to befriend the French, and in so doing displeased the English settlers. To please the former they allowed French civil law—that is the law relating to property and inheritance—to prevail; while the demands of British settlers were met by giving them English criminal law, which includes trial by jury. The consequence was both English and French were dissatisfied, and after considerable delay and many complaints, the British parliament tried to remedy the evil by passing in 1774 what is known as the Quebec Act. This Act extended the boundaries of Canada from Labrador to the Mississippi, and from the Ohio river to the watershed of Hudson's Bay. It gav the French the same political rights as the British, regardless of their religion. It gave the Roman Catholic clergy the right to collect tithes (the tenth part of the produce) and their "accustomed dues" from their own people. The French law or Custom of Paris was made the law in civil cases,—and English law, the law in criminal cases. The Government was to consist of a Governor and Council appointed by the Crown. The Council was to consist of not less than seventeen and not more than twenty-three members, the majority being of British birth.

5. **Canada invaded by the Americans.**—Another reason for passing this law must now be mentioned. The English colonies in America had for many years felt it a grievance that Britain should endeavor to force them to trade exclusively with her. Nearly everything they sold had to go first to England, and they had also to buy the most of their manufactures from the people of the mother country. At that time all European nations thought that their colonies existed for the good of the mother countries, and so they tried to keep the colonial markets for their own trade. So long as the French held Canada the English colonies had to depend upon Britain for aid against the French and their Indian allies; but when Canada became a British possession their fear of attack from the north and west was removed, and the colonies felt more inde-

pendent of England, and more inclined to resent any interference with their freedom. Not long after the conquest of Canada, England tried to tax the American colonies, claiming that as the war in America was for their special benefit they should bear a portion of the expense. The colonies thought the tax unjust, because they were not represented in the British Parliament. After several efforts had been made to settle the difficulty the colonies revolted, and declared themselves independent of Great Britain. Sir Guy Carleton saw what was coming, and he also knew the American colonies would try to get Canada to join in the revolt against England. There was a fear lest the new French subjects of the King should take sides with the discontented English colonies. To prevent this, the Quebec Act was passed, giving the French so many rights and privileges. A few months after this Act was passed the people of Canada were invited by the American colonists to send representatives to a Congress at Philadelphia, to protest against the invasion of their liberties. The Canadians of British birth were known to be discontented with the Quebec Act, because it gave them the French civil law, and did not secure them the protection of the Habeas Corpus Act, which all British subjects highly valued. Nevertheless, very few of the English in Canada were willing to aid in the revolt against Britain, so the invitation to the Congress was refused, and Canada remained loyal to the British Crown.

War began between the colonies and the mother country in 1775, and the Americans sent troops into Canada, with the hope that the Canadians would rise in arms and aid them in throwing off the yoke of England. But they were disappointed, for while the French would do nothing to defend Canada, they would do but little to help the Americans. Two expeditions were sent against Canada—one, by way of Lake Champlain, to take Montreal; the other, under General Benedict Arnold, by way of Maine, to capture Quebec. Governor Carleton could not defend Montreal, and escaped to Quebec, there to make a final stand. The Americans united their forces under Generals Montgomery and Arnold, and advanced against the famous old fortress; but Carleton had taken wise precautions to defend the city. On the last day of the year, at four o'clock in the morning, in a blinding snowstorm, an attack was made on the Lower Town. But it was of no avail; Montgomery was killed, and four hundred of the Americans were hemmed in and taken prisoners. Arnold remained near Quebec throughout the winter, and then, with his forces terribly reduced by sickness and disease, retreated. Thus ended the fifth and last siege of Quebec. Soon after, the arrival of a strong body of British troops, under General Burgoyne, forced the Americans to leave Canada, which was troubled no more by invaders during the Revolutionary war. This war came to an end in 1783, by England acknowledging the Independence of the United States (as they were now called) in the Treaty of Versailles. By this treaty the boundaries of Canada as far west as the Lake of the Woods were fixed. Canada lost the fertile territory lying between the Ohio and the Mississippi, and received as her southern boundary the middle of the Great Lakes, the St. Lawrence, the forty-fifth parallel of north latitude, and the St. Croix River in New Brunswick. The boundary between the present State of Maine and New Brunswick was left very vague, and this gave rise to serious trouble at a later date.

6. **United Empire Loyalists.**—The close of the Revolutionary War brought a large increase of population to Canada. Many of the American colonists remained loyal to England during the struggle for independence, and when the war was over, these people found themselves looked upon with dislike and suspicion by their republican neighbors. So harsh was the treatment they received that the British Parliament took pity upon them, and voted them a large sum of money (over £3,000,000) in consideration of the losses they had borne by remaining loyal to the British Crown. Besides this grant of money they were given large and valuable tracts of land in Nova Scotia, New Brunswick, and in Western Canada, (now Ontario). It is said that over twenty-five thousand left the United States in 1784, and settled in the British colonies, and of these ten thousand came to Upper Canada, settling chiefly around the Bay of Quinté, along the Niagara River, and the St. Clair. Each U. E. Loyalist received two hundred acres of land free; so did each of his sons on coming of age, and each daughter when she married. They were given provisions for three years, in addition to clothing, tools, and farming implements. Disabled soldiers and half-pay officers also came to Canada, and received grants of land and aid for a time from the Government.

7. **The Constitutional Act of 1791.**—All these years the people

of Canada had been without a Parliament, although George III., in 1763, had promised them that as soon as possible they would be given the same rights of self-government as enjoyed by other British subjects. The French portion of the population had never known any other form of government than that of a Governor and Council, and therefore did not feel the need of a change. But the British population were discontented with the Quebec Act, and its French law of buying, selling and holding property, especially land. This discontent rapidly grew greater when British settlers began to take up land in Western Canada. These wanted the British law of "freehold," that is, the right of every man holding land to have it as his own. According to the French system, the farmers held the land as tenants from their "seigneurs," and had to give for its use, money and work, besides being subject to a great many petty exactions and services. They could not freely sell the land without paying the "seigneur" or getting his consent. On the other hand, they could not be turned out of their holdings by being unable or unwilling to pay their debts. Again, the British settlers wanted the protection of the Habeas Corpus Act, Trial by Jury, and other British laws; and the need of these was felt during the harsh and tyrannical rule of Governor Haldimand, who succeeded Carleton in 1778. The complaints from Canada became so pressing and frequent, that William Pitt (a son of the great war minister of that name), who was the Prime Minister of England at that time, brought in a Bill to give Canada representative institutions. The Bill also aimed at settling the difficulties that had arisen out of the difference of the language, laws, religion and customs of the two races in Canada. It proposed to divide Canada into two Provinces, Lower Canada and Upper Canada. The former was French Canada, while the latter was settled mainly by a British population. The boundary line between the two Provinces began at Point-au-Baudet, on Lake St. Francis, extended north to Point Fortune on the Ottawa, and then continued along that river to its head waters and Hudson's Bay Territory. Roughly speaking, it made the Ottawa River the dividing line. Each Province was to have a Governor, an Executive Council, a Legislative Council and a Legislative Assembly. The Governor and the two Councils were appointed by the Crown, but the Legislative Assembly was elected for four years by the people.

In Lower Canada the Legislative Assembly was to have not less than fifty members, and the Legislative Council fifteen. In Upper Canada the former was to have not less than sixteen members, and the latter seven. The Executive Council was chosen to advise the Governor, and the Legislative Council corresponded in a measure to our Dominion Senate, or the British House of Lords. Both Councils were independent of the people, and could not be removed, if they did wrong, by the people's representatives, the members of the Legislative Assembly. The British parliament kept the right to impose taxes or duties for the regulation of commerce; but the Canadian parliaments had the right to collect them. They could also impose taxes for public purposes, such as building roads, bridges, public buildings, and providing education for the people, Unfortunately, the money arising from the sale of wild lands, from timber and mining dues, and from taxes on goods coming in the country was under the control of the Governor and his Executive Council, and this left the people of Canada with very little power to get rid of a bad Government. The Quebec Act was to remain law until repealed by the Provinces; but in Upper Canada all land was to be held by "freehold tenure," and English criminal law was to be the law for both Upper and Lower Canada. Provision was made for founding a Canadian nobility and an Established Church. One-seventh of the Crown lands were set aside for the support of a "Protestant clergy" in both Provinces; but the Roman Catholic clergy in Lower Canada were left with the power given them by the Quebec Act, to collect tithes "and their accustomed dues" from their own people in support of the Roman Catholic Church.

The Bill did not become law without strong objections being made by leading men of British birth in Lower Canada. It was also strongly opposed by Charles James Fox, Pitt's great political rival, who foresaw very clearly the result of attempting to govern Canada by Councils not responsible to the people. He also objected to the clauses relating to titles of nobility and granting Crown lands for the support of a Protestant clergy; and he pointed out what would be the effect of dividing Canada into separate Provinces, one French and the other British. Nevertheless, in spite of these and other objections, the Bill was passed by large majorities in the British Parliament, and became law in 1791. The new Constitution went into force in Canada the following year.

CHAPTER IV.

THE WAR OF 1812.

1. The Beginning of Parliamentary Government.—When the Constitutional Act was passed Canada had a population of one hundred and fifty thousand, of which about twenty thousand belonged to the Western Province. There were few villages or towns then in Upper Canada, the more important being Kingston and Newark (now Niagara). Newark was chosen as the place of meeting for the first Parliament of Upper Canada; but a few years after, in 1797, Parliament was moved to the village of York, or Toronto, because Newark being situated at the mouth of the Niagara river, and just opposite an American fort, it was not considered safe for the seat of Government to be so near the guns of a possible enemy. On the 17th September 1792, twenty-three men came, mostly from farm and store, to Newark to form a Legislative Council and Assembly; seven belonging to the Council and sixteen to the Assembly. They were busy men, and time was precious, so they set to work in earnest. The Governor Sir John Graves Simcoe was equally sturdy and energetic, and equally anxious to build up the Western Province. The first session saw English Civil Law and Trial by Jury introduced, and bills passed to collect small debts, to regulate tolls for millers, and to erect jails and court-houses in the four districts in which the Province was divided. These districts were the Eastern or Johnstown; the Midland or Kingston; the Home or Niagara; and the Western or Detroit. The session lasted less than two months. Parliament met the next year in May, and passed bills offering rewards for wolves' and bears' heads; and what was more important, provided for the doing away with slavery in Upper Canada. There were not many slaves in the province, but the Act passed in 1793, forbade the bringing of any more slaves into the country, and made all children, who were slaves, free at the age of twenty-five. During the time Parliament met at Newark, a government newspaper, the *Gazette*, was started—the first newspaper in Upper Canada.

The Parliament in Lower Canada met in December, 1792, at Quebec, and was composed of fifteen members of the Legislative Council and fifty of the Legislative Assembly. Of the latter, fifteen were of British origin, the rest were French. It was soon found that there were two languages used by the members, so it was decided that a member could speak in either language; but all notices, bills, laws and other papers must be printed in both English and French, and thus the law has remained ever since. Too soon, jealousies and ill-feeling arose bewteen the two races, and the newspapers on both sides helped to increase the mutual dislike. The Lower Canadian Parliament did not pass any law against slavery, but in 1803, Chief Justice Osgoode gave a decision to the effect that slavery was against the laws of England, and this led to the few slaves (about three hundred) in the Province being set free.

2. **Founding of Upper Canada.**—As already stated, there were only twenty thousand people in Upper Canada in 1791, and this small population was scattered along the St. Lawrence, around the Bay of Quinté and along the Niagara and St. Clair rivers. Settlers preferred to take up farms near the rivers and lakes, because it was very difficult to get in or out of the settlements except by water. The land was covered with forests, and every farm was a bush farm. The settler had to chop down the trees before he could plant or sow a crop of any kind. The fallen trees had to be burnt, and among the blackened stumps, with a rude "drag," drawn generally by oxen, he covered up the "seed." Sometimes his crop was planted and tended with the spade and hoe. His dwelling place was a log-hut or "shanty," often built in a small "clearing" in the heart of the forest, and covered with bark or "troughs." There, sheltered by the trees from the rude winter, his family lived, every member able to work doing something to lighten the settler's toil, and improve the common lot. Fortunately, the soil was fertile, and for the amount of seed sown the crop was plentiful. Mills for grinding grain of any kind were very scarce, and often the settler had to make his own flour or meal

by pounding the grain in the hollow of a hard-wood stump, or by using a steel hand-mill, provided in these days by the Government. Instances were not rare of a man trudging forty miles to get a bushel of wheat ground by a grist-mill, and then trudging home again with his load lightened by the miller's toll. Roads were few and rough, made, as they were, through the woods. Frequently there was nothing more than a "blazed" path for the foot-traveller or the solitary horseman. In other places swampy and low ground was bridged over by logs laid side by side, forming the famous "corduroy roads" our fathers and grandfathers tell about, and the remains of which are to be found in many localities to-day. The daily life of these hardy people (for they usually had good health and strong frames) was very simple and free from luxury of any kind, unless the abundance of game and fish may be called such. They wore home-made clothing, had very rude furniture, often, also, home-made, and rode in carts and sleds drawn by oxen. Yet, notwithstanding these hardships, they lived happy, contented lives. They were very sociable with their few neighbours, helped each other in their "logging bees," and their house and barn "raisings," which gatherings were sometimes marred by the rather free use of distilled liquors. Once in a long time, they were visited by a travelling preacher, who, by almost incredible toil, made his way to the "sheep" scattered in the "wilderness." Then, in some rude log-cabin, the few settlers gathered together to listen to a sermon, have their children baptized, and perchance, other solemn religious rites performed. Of education, there was little or none. Not that the settlers despised it, but the inhabitants were too few, too busy, and too poor to employ competent teachers and send their children to school after they could help on the farm. Later on, as we shall find, the Government tried to help the people in this respect, but the aid they got for many years was of little value. Old and worn-out pensioners took to teaching to get a scanty livelihood, and paid for their "board" and small salary by giving the youths of the school district a very imperfect knowledge of reading, writing and arithmetic. The salary of the teacher was too small to enable him to pay for his board, so it was arranged that he should "board around" among the different families sending their children to the school. The prudent teacher usually managed to spend the most of his time in the homes where the most comfort prevailed.

3. **Political Discontent.**—The early settlers cared little for politics, aside from the aid the Government could give in the way of building roads, bridges, and opening up the country for settlement. Nevertheless the defects of the Constitutional Act were soon so apparent and hurtful, that the people of both Upper and Lower Canada began to complain. In both provinces, the Executive Council and the Legislative Council did not consider they were responsible to the people, and used their power to further the interests of themselves and their friends. Judges and other salaried officials were often members of these councils, and the union of law-making and law-interpreting did not work well. The Governors, as a rule, took the advice of their Executive Councils and paid no attention to the remonstrances of the Legislative Assembly. There was no way of getting rid of these men who abused their trust by putting their needy friends into government offices and by granting wild lands to speculators, who hoped by holding the lands until the neighbouring settlers made improvements, to be able to sell at a good profit. They were also accused of spending corruptly the money intended for the U. E. Loyalists and other settlers, and for the Indian tribes. In our day, the people's representatives would refuse to vote any money for the public expenditure, until their wrongs were righted; but, at that time, such a course was impossible, for nearly all the revenue was under the control of the Governor and his Executive Council. In Lower Canada, besides these abuses, they had to contend against race jealousies and religious animosities. The British in that province usually were on the side of the Governor and the Councils—while the French supported the Legislative Assembly, the majority of which was French. The Assembly demanded that judges should not sit in Parliament, and after a struggle the Governor and the Legislative Council yielded. Another demand was that the revenue of the Province should be expended by the Assembly. This, however, was not granted for many years. But the quarrels between the Assemblies and the Governors were, in 1812, dropped to meet a pressing common danger.

4. **Cause of the War of 1812.**—To explain this danger we must refer to what had been going on in Europe for nearly twenty years. In 1793 England was drawn into a war with France, and, except

for a brief period in 1802-3, there had been a continuous struggle against the power of the French General and Emperor, Napoleon Bonaparte. In 1806, when Napoleon had conquered the most of Europe, he issued a "decree" from Berlin in Prussia to the effect that English goods were not to be bought or sold on the Continent of Europe, and that other nations should not trade with England. England, who had been for many years the mistress of the sea, retaliated by forbidding all neutral nations to trade with France, and threatening their vessels with seizure if they did not call at English ports. These "Orders-in-Council," as they were called, pressed very hard on American vessel owners as they could not trade with either England or France without their vessels being liable to seizure. Besides, England, anxious to secure men for her navy, stopped American vessels on the seas, and searched them for runaway sailors and British subjects. It was said that this was often a mere pretext to take American sailors to man British war-ships. The American Congress complained loudly against England's abuse of power, but got no redress. At last the United States, which just then was governed by the Democratic party—a party, from the time of the Revolution, always hostile to England and friendly to France—declared war, although the hateful "Orders-in-Council" were repealed within a few days of the declaration.

5. **The Campaign of 1812.**—The declaration of war was made on the 18th of June, and was very much against the wishes of a considerable portion of the American people. The New England States were anxious for peace, for war to them meant loss of trade and injury to their commerce. Consequently they refused to give any active aid, and thus, although the population of the United States was eight millions, and that of Canada only about one quarter of a million, the difference in numbers did not really show the difference in military strength of the two countries. The United States hoped to take Canada with very little effort ; for it was known that only 4,500 regular soldiers were in the colony, and a few militia scattered along a frontier of fifteen hundred miles. It was also known that England was too busy fighting Napoleon in Spain to be able to give Canada any immediate help. When the war broke out, Sir George Prevost was the Governor-General of Canada, and General Sir Isaac Brock the acting Lieutenant-Governor of Upper Canada, in the absence of Mr. Francis Gore then in England.

The American plan of campaign was to invade Canada with three armies. One was to cross at Detroit, a second at the Niagara frontier, and the third by the way of Lake Champlain. These were the armies of the West, the Centre, and the North respectively, General Dearborn being the Commander-in-Chief.

The first blow was struck at Fort Michillimackinac at the entrance of Lake Michigan. This post was held by the Americans, and was important on account of its trade with the western Indians. Acting under orders from General Brock, Captain Roberts with a small body of men from St. Joseph, took the fort by surprise, and by so doing secured the support and confidence of the Indian tribes of the West and North-west. On the 12th of July, the American general, Hull, crossed over from Detroit, and by a proclamation invited the Canadians to throw off the yoke of England ; but the invitation met with no response. General Brock immediately sent Colonel Proctor with a few regulars to Fort Malden, near Amherstburg. Here Proctor was joined by the famous Indian chief, Tecumseh, who brought a number of warriors to help the English in the struggle against the Americans. Tecumseh was a Shawnee, and for years had sought to unite the various Indian tribes against the Americans, for he saw very clearly that the Indians were being pushed back, farther and farther, by the steady encroachments of the white people. At this time, Tecumseh was in the prime of his noble manhood, and wielded a great influence over the Indian tribes, who believed him to be of supernatural birth.

.For a short time, Hull remained in Canada, and then getting afraid of Indian attacks, returned to Detroit and shut himself up in that strong fort. On the 5th of August, Brock set out for Detroit with a small force of regulars and York militia. A week later he reached Amherstburg, and there met Tecumseh with seven hundred warriors. Tecumseh sketched for Brock, on a piece of birch bark, the plan of Detroit, and it was resolved to attempt its capture, although Brock had only fourteen hundred men, half of them Indians, while Detroit was defended by over two thousand. Brock demanded the surrender of the fort, and the demand being refused, crossed the river and made preparations for an attack. Greatly to the surprise of the English and the Indians, and to the garrison itself,

Hull surrendered the fort and the territory of Michigan without a
shot being fired, he and all his men being made prisoners. Brock
sent the regulars of Hull's army to Montreal as prisoners of war;
the militia were allowed to return home. A large quantity of
military supplies, ammunition and cannon, fell into the hands of
the English, which proved a very timely aid to Brock in carrying on
the war. Brock then returned to Toronto, and found that General
Prevost had agreed to an armistice, by which the war was stopped
for a time on Lake Champlain and the Niagara frontier. This gave
the Americans an opportunity to collect their armies and carry
supplies along Lake Ontario to Niagara. Before the month of
August ended, war was renewed, and the Americans gathered six
thousand men under General Van Rensselaer at Lewiston, opposite
Queenston, on the Niagara river, with the intention of invading
Canada. To oppose this force, Brock had only fifteen hundred
men, mostly militia and Indians. Brock's troops were scattered all
along the Niagara river from Fort George, at its mouth, to Queenston,
seven miles up the stream. His men were kept on a constant
watch against attempts of the Americans to cross.

On the 13th of October, in the early morning, the American army
began crossing the river at a point below Queenston Heights. The
few regulars and militia stationed there poured a destructive fire
into the boats of the Americans as they approached the shore, many
of which were sunk, and their occupants killed or taken prisoners.
The Canadians thought they had driven back the invaders, when it
was discovered that a large force of Americans had, under cover of
the night, made their way to the top of Queenston Heights. Hearing
the sound of firing, Brock, who was at Fort George, galloped in
hot haste for the scene of conflict, leaving his *aides* to follow him,
and hurrying forward the troops as he sped past them. When he
reached Queenston and saw that the Americans had succeeded
in getting a footing on the Heights, he put himself at the head
of a small body of men and rushed up the mountain side eager
to dislodge the enemy. While cheering his followers on, he was
struck in the breast by a musket ball and fell, mortally wounded.
His tall figure and bright uniform had made him a mark, all too
good, for the American riflemen. His brave soldiers, though few
in number, were anxious to avenge his death, and again made an
attempt to dislodge the foe—but only to be driven back with heavy

loss. Among those who fell in this second attempt was Brock's *aide-de-camp*, Colonel MacDonnell of Glengarry, a noble young man only twenty-five years of age, whose life was full of promise. Soon after General Sheaffe arrived from Fort George with three hundred men and some artillery. All the men that could be mustered were now marched through the fields back of Queenston, and unperceived they ascended the Heights, and concealed themselves among the trees. The Americans in the meantime were landing fresh troops, and carrying off their dead and wounded. About three o'clock in the afternoon, the British moved rapidly through the woods against the unsuspecting Americans. A number of Indians who were in the Canadian army, as soon as they saw the enemy raised the terrible war-whoop, and rushed on their prey. The rest of the troops joined in the shout and the onslaught. The Americans gave one volley and then fled. But there was no escape, save by the brow of the mountain overhanging the river. In their terror many of the enemy threw themselves over the precipice, only to be dashed on the rocks, or drowned in the river. The American shore was lined with their fellow-countrymen, but no help was given. Soon two American officers ascended the mountain side bearing a white flag, and with difficulty the slaughter was brought to an end. One thousand Americans were made prisoners and a hundred slain. Thus dearly was the death of Brock avenged. In one of the batteries of Fort George, amid the booming of minute guns from friend and foe, Brock and MacDonnell side by side found a resting place. A month's armistice was unwisely agreed to by General Sheaffe, which enabled the Americans to gather troops for another attack on the Niagara frontier. Towards the end of November, General Smythe, who succeeded Van Rensselaer, attempted a landing near Fort Erie, but his men were driven back by a small force of Canadians. This ended the attempts, in 1813, of the army of the Centre to gain a footing on Canadian soil.

Nor was the army of the North under General Dearborn more successful. In November, Dearborn advanced with an army of ten thousand men by way of Lake Champlain to take Montreal. The French Canadian militia under Major de Salaberry, felled trees, guarded the passes, and used every possible means to check his advance. At Lacolle, near Rouse's Point, a British outpost was attacked by Dearborn's troops, but in the darkness of the early morning, his ███ became confused and fired into each other's ranks. When they discovered their mistake, disheartened and cowed, they returned to Lake Champlain, and Dearborn finding the Canadian militia on the alert, gave up his attempt on Montreal and retired to Plattsburg.

To sum up :—The results of the land campaign of 1812 were the capture of Detroit, the surrender of Michigan, the great victory at Queenston Heights, and the repulse of Dearborn at Lacolle by a small body of Canadian militia. On the sea, however, the Americans were more successful, gaining several victories over British men-of-war, and controlling the great lakes.

6. Campaign of 1813.—General Sheaffe succeeded General Brock as Lieut.-Governor of Upper Canada, and the Parliaments of both Provinces met to vote money for the defence of the country. They issued Army Bills, or promises to pay, instead of gold and silver, and this paper money was not to be exchanged for coin until the war was over. The Americans made great preparations this year to conquer Canada, and, as in 1812, placed three large armies on the frontier. That in the west was led by General Harrison ; that on the Niagara frontier by General Dearborn ; and that in the east by General Hampton. A regiment of British soldiers arrived in the depth of winter from New Brunswick to help the Canadians. The war was continued throughout the winter ; Major Macdonald capturing Ogdensburg, with a large quantity of arms and supplies, and Colonel Proctor in the west, defeating General Winchester in a battle at Frenchtown, a place about twenty miles south of Detroit. Vessels were built on the lakes by both sides, but the Americans were the sooner equipped, and sailing out of Sackett's Harbor General Dearborn and Commodore Chauncey with two thousand men attacked and captured York; which was defended by only six hundred men, regulars, militia, and Indians. General Sheaffe retired from the old French fort at York, to Kingston, taking the regulars with him, and was replaced in Upper Canada by General de Rottenburg, Sheaffe's conduct at York being blamed. Having taken York the American fleet and army sailed across Lake Ontario to the mouth of the Niagara river to take Fort George. General Vincent with fourteen hundred men held the fort for some time against Dearborn, and then, his ammunition failing, retreated to a strong position on Burlington Heights, having first spiked his guns and blown up his magazine. Fort George was now taken possession of by the Americans. While Chauncey was at Fort George, Sir George Prevost and Sir James Yeo, a naval officer just arrived from England, crossed the lake from Kingston with a large force and attacked Sackett's Harbor, hoping to destroy the naval stores there. When on the point of success, Prevost withdrew his men, imagining the Americans were trying to entrap him. These disasters were more than balanced by two brilliant exploits, one at Stony Creek, near Hamilton, the other at Beaver Dams. At the former place, on the 4th of June, Colonel Harvey, of General Vincent's army, with seven hundred men, made a night attack on four thousand Americans who had advanced from Fort George to drive Vincent from his post on Burlington Heights. The attack was completely successful, the Americans taken by surprise, after a brief resistance, retreating hastily with the loss of four cannon, and one hundred and twenty prisoners, including two generals. At Beaver Dams (near the present town of Thorold), Lieutenant Fitzgibbon with a small force was stationed. General Dearborn hoped to surprise this post, and for that purpose sent six hundred men from Fort George, under Major Boerstler. A Canadian heroine, Mrs. Laura Secord, became aware of the plan, and set out on foot to warn the British of the intended attack. To avoid the American sentries she had to walk twenty miles, a journey that took all day, from early morning till sunset. Fitzgibbon, warned, made such a skilful arrangement of his few men in the woods, that the Americans thought they were surrounded by a large force, and, after a brief resistance, surrendered to only one half of their own number of men. The Americans were now, in turn, besieged in Fort George by Vincent and his small army.

Two serious disasters now befell the Canadians. Captain Barclay, with six British vessels, was defeated on Lake Erie by Commodore Perry, with nine American vessels; and this loss compelled Colonel Proctor and Tecumseh to abandon Detroit and retreat into Canada, as their supplies could no longer come to them by the lakes. Proctor was closely followed by General Harrison with a large force drawn from the west, many of them Kentucky riflemen accustomed to border warfare. Tecumseh urged Proctor to make a stand against the Americans, but Proctor continued his retreat until he reached Moraviantown, on the Thames river. There, at last, on the 5th Oct., Tecumseh persuaded him to prepare for battle on a favourable ground. Soon Harrison and his men appeared, and a fierce struggle began. Almost at the beginning of the fight, Proctor fled and left Tecumseh and his Indians to uphold the honour of British arms. Tecumseh and his warriors fought with desperate courage and great skill, but they were soon overpowered and Tecumseh was killed. Had Proctor stood his ground, the battle of Moraviantown might have ranked in our history with that of Queenston Heights, and other brave deeds. The few of Proctor's men, that escaped, fled and joined General Vincent.

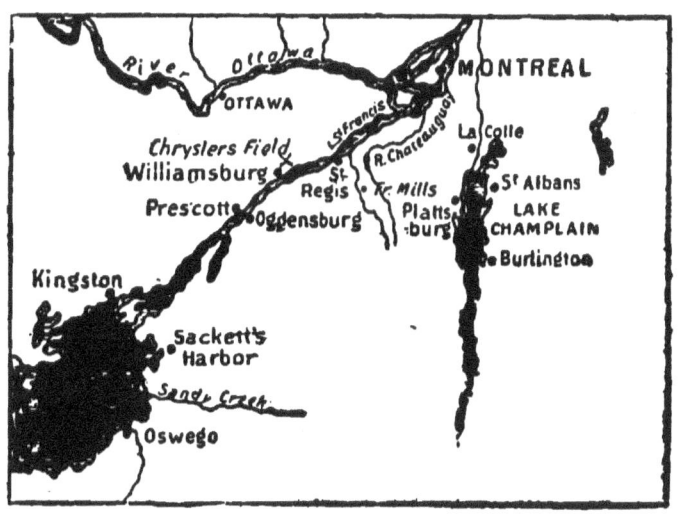

CHATEAUGUAY AND CHRYSLER'S FARM.

The Americans had now possession of the western part of Canada, and hoped soon by two large expeditions to take Montreal. The first of these, nine thousand strong, under General Wilkinson set out from Sackett's Harbour, in boats, expecting to take Kingston and Prescott, and then float down the St. Lawrence and make a junction with General Hampton, who was to approach Montreal by Lake Champlain. Kingston was not molested, and Wilkinson was so annoyed by the Canadians along the bank of the St. Lawrence, that he landed below Prescott with four thousand men, to beat back his enemies. Here, in an open field, called Chrysler's Farm, with only eight hundred men Colonel Morrison and Colonel Harvey, the hero of Stony Creek, on the 11th Nov., inflicted so heavy a defeat on the forces of Wilkinson, that they were glad to return to their own side of the river. The other expedition under General Hampton, with three thousand men, had been defeated by Colonel de Salaberry, with four hundred Canadian militia, at the battle of Chateauguay, Oct. 26th. These two victories put an end for a time to the attempts to take Montreal.

In Upper Canada, General Vincent had been compelled by the defeat of Proctor, to retreat again to Burlington Heights, and the Americans had the control of the Niagara peninsula. But the bad news from the east led the American general, McClure, to abandon Fort George; not, however, before he had committed the inhuman act of burning the village of Niagara, turning the people out of their homes in the depth of a very severe winter. After the retreat of the Americans to their own side of the river, the British under General Drummond, arrived on the frontier, and determined to avenge the burning of Niagara. Fort Niagara on the American side was surprised, and three hundred prisoners taken. Lewiston, Black Rock, Buffalo, and other American villages were burned, the destruction of Buffalo closing the campaign of 1813.

7. **1814 and the Close of the War.**—The winter of 1814 was used by the Canadians to carry, on sleds, supplies from Montreal to Kingston and Toronto for the troops in the west.

The Americans had gained a footing in the western peninsula by their success at Moraviantown, but General Harrison returned to Detroit and took no further part in the war. Lower Canada was the first to be attacked this year. In March, General Wilkinson with five thousand men tried in vain to take a strong stone mill at Lacolle defended by five hundred Canadians. He was repulsed with heavy loss, and retreated to Plattsburg. In May, General Drummond and Sir James Yeo made a successful raid on Oswego, and carried off a large quantity of supplies. The Niagara frontier was the scene of two bloody battles. The Americans, four thousand strong, crossed at Buffalo, took Fort Erie and then pushed on to Chippewa. General Riall, with two thousand men, tried to check their progress, but was defeated at the battle of Chippewa, July 5th. He then retreated to Lundy's Lane, now a street in the village of Niagara Falls South. The American soldiers began plundering and burning the buildings of the farmers, and destroyed the pretty village of St. David's. They then advanced against Riall at Lundy's Lane. General Drummond heard of the invasion, and the battle at Chippewa, and hurried from Kingston to aid General Riall. He reached Fort Niagara on the morning of July 25th, and with eight hundred men pushed forward to Lundy's Lane. At five o'clock in the afternoon he met General Riall retreating before a strong body of American troops under Generals Brown, Ripley, and Scott. Drummond at once stopped the retreat, and faced the foe. The Americans were four thousand strong, the Canadians had three thousand. From five o'clock till midnight the battle raged. The utmost stubbornness and courage were shown by both armies in the fierce struggle for the British guns. General Riall was taken prisoner and three American generals, Scott, Brown, and Porter, were wounded. At last, worn out in the vain effort to force the British position, the Americans retreated, leaving their dead to be burned by the victors, for the number of slain was so great that burial was impossible. The loss to the enemy was nearly nine hundred; to the British, about the same. The scene of this battle, the best contested and bloodiest of the whole war, is marked to-day by a little church and graveyard in which many a Canadian hero sleeps.

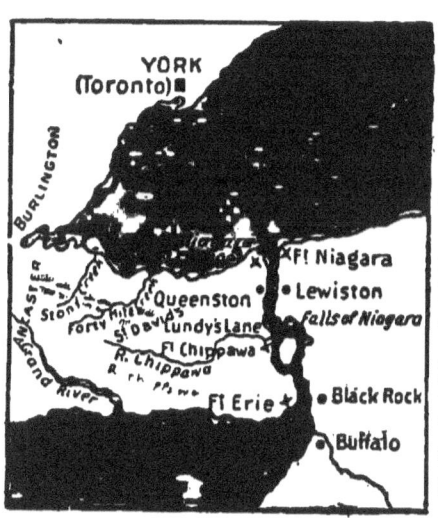

THE NIAGARA FRONTIER.

The war was drawing to a close. The Americans after the battle retired to Fort Erie, which they held for some time in spite of the attacks of General Drummond, and then withdrew across the river. In the meantime the war in Europe had been brought to an end by Napoleon's defeat and his retirement to the island of Elba. England could now assist Canada, and in August sixteen thousand men arrived. A great expedition was planned against Plattsburg, in which eleven thousand men, and the fleet on Lake Champlain were to take part. Sir George Prevost led the land army, and Captain Downie commanded the British flag-ship. Prevost waited for the British vessels to attack the American fleet before proceeding against Plattsburg which was defended by a small force. Unfortunately the British ships were defeated and many of them destroyed in the engagement that followed, and Prevost, without any good reason, retreated without striking a blow. His officers were so chagrined that they broke their swords, vowing they would serve no longer. Meanwhile, in August, the British entered Chesapeake Bay, captured Washington, the capital of the United States, and burned the public buildings, including a valuable library. This was in revenge for the burning of Niagara by General McClure. At last, on the 24th of December, 1814, the Treaty of Ghent was signed, which restored to the United States and to Canada their losses, but did not settle the points in dispute which led to the war. Two weeks after the peace was made in Europe, a bloody battle was fought at New Orleans, where the British general, Pakenham, endeavored to carry by assault a strong line of entrenchments defended by General Jackson. The English general did not know that the war was over, and many of Wellington's veterans fell in a worse than useless contest.

CHAPTER V.

THE STRUGGLE FOR RESPONSIBLE GOVERNMENT AND THE REBELLION OF 1837-38.

1. **Growth of the Colony.**—The war of 1812 brought no territory or glory to the Americans, save the victories they won on the lakes and the high seas. They had been defeated in most of the battles on land; their trade and commerce had been greatly injured by British vessels, the New England States had threatened to leave the Union, and a very heavy public debt had been contracted.

Canada, too, suffered by the farmers being taken away from their farms to serve in the militia, many of them never returning to their homes, and many others returning wounded and crippled. To the latter the Government gave small pensions for life; and the widows and orphans of the killed received small grants of money. The country was too poor to pay heavy pensions, or to recompense families for the loss of their bread-winners. During the war the British Government had spent large sums in the colony, and this for a time seemed to make it prosperous. But when the struggle was over, and the expenditure ceased, the effects of the cruel conflict began to be felt. For a few years there were hard times, and these were made worse by the failure of the wheat crop in Lower Canada. So great was this failure that the Governor, on his own authority, took the public money to help the farmers to buy seed, and the Lower Canadian Parliament, the next year, voted a still larger sum. But the colony soon recovered its prosperity, for the soil was fertile and the people were hardy and industrious. Efforts were made to bring in settlers by offering free passages across the ocean and one hundred acres of land to each man, besides giving him help the first year of his settlement on a farm. Very unwisely Americans were not allowed to become citizens of Canada, the Government fearing and disliking them. This was one of the bad effects of the recent war. The years from 1815 to 1820 saw a great many people settle in Canada from Great Britain and Ireland. The county of Lanark was settled about this time by immigrants from Scotland, and the failure of the crops in Ireland brought in 1820 many Irish to Canada.

There was a growth not only in population but also in trade, commerce, and manufactures. In the absence of good roads, grain and other products of Upper Canada had to be taken down to Montreal and Quebec by water. The rapids of the St. Lawrence prevented vessels from coming up, so large flat-bottomed or "Durham" boats floated down the river from Kingston to Montreal, laden with goods. These boats were then sold as it did not pay to bring them up the rapids. After a while, as the trade grew larger, canals were built between Kingston and Ottawa, and along the St. Lawrence below Prescott. These we know as the Rideau and Lachine Canals. Further west a more important work was begun in 1819. This was the building of a canal between Lakes Erie and

Ontario to overcome the obstacle to navigation caused by the Falls of Niagara. Hon. W. H. Merritt, of St. Catharines, had the honor of proposing and carrying out the project, which was finished in 1829. Very early in the century steamboats came into use on the lakes and rivers, the credit of which must be given largely to the Hon. John Molson of Montreal. Quebec became noted for shipbuilding, and a brisk trade in timber with the Old World sprang up at this port. The manufacture of potash and pearlash was a profitable industry; but grain crops, in the absence of good roads, could not find a ready market. Then, as now, there was a good deal of smuggling along the frontier between Canada and the United States, and in consequence the revenue suffered considerably.

To meet the demand for money to carry on the growing trade of the country, Banks were founded, among the earliest being the Banks of Montreal, Kingston, and Quebec; and a little later the Bank of Upper Canada. The population, and therefore the trade, of Upper Canada grew more rapidly than that of Lower Canada, and this led to disputes between the Provinces. After the Constitutional Act of 1791, it was arranged that Upper Canada was to have as her share one-eighth of the customs duties collected at the chief ports of Lower Canada. Thirteen years later the proportion was changed to one-fifth, and then, in 1822, there still being dissatisfaction, the British Parliament passed the Canada Trade Act, which gave Upper Canada £30,000 of arrears due by Lower Canada, and arranged for a more just division of the revenue in the future.

Education was improving very slowly. Governor Simcoe had planned the founding of a college in his time, and for that purpose brought from Scotland John Strachan, a young but clever school teacher, to be its head. When Strachan arrived he found Simcoe had left the colony, and he started a grammar school at Cornwall, where many of the most noted men of Upper Canada were educated. In 1807, the Parliament of Upper Canada voted £500 for the support of eight *grammar* schools; and in 1816, *common* schools were granted £6,000 to help in paying teachers and buying books. In 1823, McGill University in Montreal was organized for teaching, and four years later we have the beginning of King's College at York. In 1829 Upper Canada College was founded to prepare pupils for the coming University. Few people, at that time, could afford to give their sons a college education, so these young universities for many years had but little to do.

2. **Political Abuses and Troubles.**—Canada had no more wars with foreign nations, and her history, save for political troubles, since 1814 has been the history of growth in wealth, in population, and in enterprises for opening up the country for settlement, and for utilizing her natural resources. But, of political struggles, from the day she became a British colony until the present, she has had her full share. The war of 1812 had hardly ceased when a political struggle began which ended in rebellion and bloodshed; also, fortunately, in better and freer government. We have now to tell very briefly the causes of this strife, and how it resulted.

In Lower Canada, as already stated, great discontent was aroused by the action of the Governors and the Councils in refusing to allow the Legislative Assembly to control the expenditure of the revenue arising from timber and mining dues, the sale of Crown lands, and the taxes collected at the Custom-houses. The Assembly offered, if it were given the control of all the revenue, to provide for the necessary expenses of the Province, including the payment of the salaries of judges and other civil officers. This offer, however, the Governors and their advisers would not accept, and the Assembly then tried to stop the supplies. But the Governor took the money from the treasury, without asking permission, to pay the necessary salaries and expenses. The British Parliament was petitioned to redress these grievances, and to pass an Act giving the Legislative Assemblies the control of the expenditure of all public money. Little heed was given in England for some time to these complaints, as the Governors and their Councils generally succeeded in keeping their side of the case well before the British Government. Besides this trouble about the control of public money, there was the more serious difficulty due to the difference of race, religion, and language in the population. The British element disliked the French, and sided with the Governors and their Councils; while the French elected the most of the members of the Assembly. The Councils were mainly British, and the Legislative Assembly, French. In 1828, an effort was made by the Home Government, by a half-measure, to settle the difficulty arising from the control of the revenue. This measure proposed to give the Assembly the control of the duties on goods, in return for a permanent support of the judges and other officials. It did not grant the control of the other revenues, nor did it make the Legislative Council elective, and therefore subject to the control of the people. So this effort to conciliate the people failed, and the discontent was increased by a harsh measure passed by Lord John Russell in 1837, which refused the just demands of the people.

Turning to Upper Canada, we find much the same troubles and abuses as in Lower Canada. There was, however, for some time, an important difference in the political situation. In Lower Canada the Assembly was bitterly opposed to the Government; but, in Upper Canada the Assembly contained so many Government officials, such as postmasters, sheriffs and registrars, that the majority of the members supported the Governors and their advisers. A small but increasing number of the members complained of the abuses of the time, and were treated by the ruling body as malcontents and traitors. It was not safe to say anything in the press or on the floor of Parliament against the Government and their management of affairs. The men who for many years really controlled the province were known as the Family Compact, on account of the closeness of the alliance they had formed to get and retain the offices of the Government. Many of them were U. E. Loyalists, who prided themselves on their loyalty to British institutions. Others were emigrants from the mother country, who, unwilling to make a living by hard work on bush farms, managed through the influence of friends in the Old Land to get office in or under the Government. Very soon this Compact of office-holders came to believe that it had a right to manage the affairs of the Province, fill all the offices, and make profit out of the wild lands for themselves and their friends. The management of these lands was one of the great grievances of the settlers. Not only were large grants given to the friends of the Compact for purposes of speculation, but a company of British capitalists, called the Canada Land Company, bought up large tracts which it held without making any improvements. The County of Huron suffered more than most places from this bad policy, as for many years this fine, fertile district was left uncleared and unsettled. Then, land had been set aside in each township as Clergy Reserves and for the support of common schools. So much uncleared land coming between the farms of settlers made it difficult to construct roads and fences, and separated the farmers so much that they could not form school districts without a great deal of trouble and inconvenience.

Then again, there was great discontent because the English Church clergy claimed that they alone were entitled to share in the Clergy Reserves grant. The Church of Scotland also claimed a share, as it was the Established Church of Scotland, and after some dispute its claim was recognized. This left out the Methodists, Baptists, Roman Catholics and other denominations, and, therefore, did not mend matters much. In 1836, Sir John Colborne the Governor, and his Executive Council, endowed fifty-seven rectories of the Church of England with a part of these church lands. This was done because the Reform party (the party opposed to the Family Compact) was in the majority in the House of Assembly, and it was feared something might be done to prevent the Church of England from getting the benefit of the endowment.

As already stated, for a time the Family Compact controlled the Legislative Assembly. This did not last long, for the abuses of power were so great that the people began to elect as members men who tried to remove the evils from which they were suffering. In 1824 this Reform party elected a majority of the members, and chose one of their own number as Speaker, or Chairman of the Assembly. The most prominent members of this party at this time were Dr. Rolph, Peter Perry, and Marshall Bidwell. At this time also the noted William Lyon Mackenzie began to make his influence felt. Mackenzie was a Scotchman who had emigrated to Canada a few years before—had been a storekeeper in different places—and then had come to Toronto to start a newspaper. His paper, "The Colonial Advocate," attacked the abuses of the Family Compact so fiercely that a gang of ruffians seized his press and threw it into Lake Ontario. This made Mackenzie and his paper more popular than ever, and he was elected member of the Assembly for the County of York, the most populous county in the Province. On the floor of the Assembly he made himself very troublesome to the Executive Council, and was continually unearthing frauds and scandals in connection with the public accounts, and the management of such works as the Welland Canal. Another man of a higher character and better judgment was elected, a little later, in the town of York. This was the fair-minded and moderate patriot, Robert Baldwin. In 1830 the elections resulted in favor of the Family Compact, and it used its majority in the Assembly to have Mackenzie expelled from the House for a breach of parliamentary privilege. Mackenzie was re-elected, and again expelled, and once more elected. He was then sent to England with petitions to the King for a redress of grievances. In 1835 the election gave a majority to the Reform party, and next year the Governor, Sir John Colborne, resigned his position and left the Province.

3. **The Rebellion in Lower Canada, 1837-38.**—Meanwhile matters were hastening to a crisis in Lower Canada. The French were much under the influence of M. Papineau, an eloquent speaker and writer, who had the power to stir the feelings and passions of the *habitants*. There had been a deadlock in Parliament, as the Assembly had refused to vote money for the payment of judges and other officials, and the Governor had taken what was needed out of the treasury without the consent of the Assembly. As soon as it was known that Lord John Russell had carried through the British Parliament resolutions opposed to granting the Canadian people their rights, the excitement in Lower Canada was very great, and broke out in a revolt, under the leadership of Papineau and Dr. Wolfred Nelson. The rebels were poorly prepared for a rising, and the revolt was soon suppressed by Sir John Colborne and his regulars. Engagements took place at St. Denis on the Richelieu, where Lieutenant Weir was shot by the rebels while attempting to escape from his captors; at St. Charles, where the rebels were defeated; and at St. Eustache, on the Ottawa, where many of the rebels were burned in a church.

The constitution of Lower Canada was now suspended, and a Special Council, half of the members of which were English and half French, was created to govern for the time being. Lord Durham, a nobleman of great intelligence and fair-mindedness, was sent out from England to examine into the cause of the rebellion, and to report to the Home Government. On his arrival, he at once began to inquire into the true state of affairs in both Provinces, and corrected several abuses in the management of the Crown lands. He found a great many political prisoners in the jails, and not thinking it wise to try them before the ordinary courts, or by courts-martial, he released the most of them, and banished Nelson and eight others to Bermuda. He forbade Papineau, who had fled to the United States, to return to Canada, under pain of death. In doing these things, Durham acted without authority, and he was blamed by the British Parliament, which annulled his sentences. Durham was so chagrined at this seeming insult that he resigned his position and returned to England in broken health. His important work was, however, the drafting of a Report on the state of Canada, containing a great many valuable suggestions about the best way of governing colonies. He advised that Canada should be given *Responsible Government*, that is, the Governor should choose for his advisers the men having the confidence of the people's representatives. Besides, he recommended that Canada should have only one Parliament instead of two, and suggested the Union of all the British provinces in North America under one Parliament. Later on, it will be seen that this Report had a very great influence. After Durham had left Canada, Sir John Colborne became Administrator. The people of Lower Canada despairing of justice once more broke out in revolt, and a few slight engagements took place. Once more the rebellion was crushed—this time with considerable loss of life and property. Twelve of the leaders were tried by court-martial, and executed at Montreal. This ended the rebellion in Lower Canada.

4. **Rebellion in Upper Canada, 1837.**—After Sir John Colborne's retirement in 1836, from the Governorship of Upper Canada, the British Government, by a curious mistake, sent out as his successor, Sir Francis Bond Head, a man who had never taken any interest in politics, and who was quite ignorant of the state of affairs in the Province. At first the Reformers thought Sir Francis would be friendly to their cause, but, like all preceding governors, he soon came under the influence of the Family Compact. He invited leading Reformers to join the Executive Council and the invitation was accepted. But he would not listen to the proposal that the Council should be responsible to the Assembly, and, in consequence, the Reform members of the Council resigned. Soon after this there was a general election, and Sir Francis threw himself into the contest with great zeal and effect. He made the people believe that their

loyalty was at stake, and succeeded in having Mackenzie and other Reform leaders defeated at the polls. Mackenzie and some of his associates now despaired of having the grievances of the people removed by peaceable means, and unwisely listened to the suggestions of Papineau to join in a revolt. As if to encourage them, Sir Francis Head sent all the regular troops from Upper to Lower Canada to aid in suppressing the rebellion there, leaving York and its armory wholly unprotected. Mackenzie began to stir the passions of the people by articles in his paper, and by violent speeches. Soon the disaffected began arming and drilling throughout the western part of the province, and, although warned of what was going on, Sir Francis refused to take any steps to stop these dangerous proceedings. In fact the Governor acted as if he wished to hasten a revolt. Finally it was arranged that a rising should take place on the 7th December, that York should be surprised, the government buildings and armory seized, the Governor and Council taken prisoners, and then a republican form of Government established. It so happened that the leaders of the revolt in York, Dr. Rolph being the chief, changed the time for attack from the 7th to the 4th, without informing all the leaders outside of the change.

On the day appointed, about four hundred men gathered at Montgomery's Tavern, four miles from Toronto. They were badly armed, worn with travel, and disappointed at the mistake in their plans. Still, had they marched at once to York, it could easily have been surprised and captured; but Rolph, either through fear or treachery, counselled delay until more men arrived. Before this could happen the rebels were discovered, and steps taken to defend the town, the armory and the government buildings. It was now too late to attempt a surprise. The next day Mackenzie wished to attack at once; but Rolph still counselled delay, promising support from friends in the town if the attack were delayed until after dark. The night attack was a failure, and the following day Colonel McNab having arrived from Hamilton with a number of loyalists, a force of nine hundred men was sent against Mackenzie, who with four hundred men stood his ground near Montgomery's Tavern. The conflict was brief and decisive—the few rebels, without proper arms or support, being easily defeated and scattered. Mackenzie, with a reward of £1,000 on his head, escaped with great difficulty; and after many exciting adventures in travelling from

York round the head of Lake Ontario to the Niagara frontier, crossed the Niagara river, and found refuge on American soil.

5. The "Patriot" War, 1837-38.—Besides Mackenzie, Rolph and some other leaders thought it prudent to leave Canada. Still others were taken prisoners, and during the administration of Sir George Arthur, who succeeded Sir Francis Bond Head, Lount and Matthews were hanged at Toronto, an act of severity for which there was but slight excuse.

Mackenzie, unfortunately, did not rest content with the failure of his schemes. He now gathered together, at Buffalo, a number of ruffians and sympathizers from the slums of American cities, promising them land and bounties after they had liberated Canada. These men took possession of Navy Island, about two miles above Niagara Falls, fortified it, and made preparations to invade Canada. Colonel McNab defended the Canadian shore with a number of militia and Indians. A little steamer, the "Caroline," was used by the "Patriots" to carry supplies from Buffalo to Navy Island, and McNab determined to capture and destroy it. This he did by sending a party of men under Lieutenant Drew across the river at night, who cut the vessel from her moorings, set her on fire, and allowed her to drift over the Falls. This act of violence greatly incensed the United States Government, but an apology by the British Government smoothed over the difficulty. A little later, Navy Island was abandoned, and the frontier at Detroit and on the St. Lawrence, became the points of attack. A number of Americans crossed at the former place, took possession of Windsor, and marched on Sandwich. Colonel Prince met them with a body of militia, defeated them, and shot four prisoners without a trial. On the St. Lawrence the most important event was the landing of a number of Americans at Windmill Point, a little below the town of Prescott. They took possession of a strong stone windmill, from which they were driven with some difficulty. The garrison, about one hundred and thirty in number, surrendered; about fifty were killed—the Canadians losing thirteen killed and a number wounded. The leaders of this raid, Von Schultz and nine of his companions, were tried and executed. The "Patriot War" was over, and Mackenzie was an exile. After many years of hardship and suffering, he was pardoned and allowed to return to Canada, and once more entered political life.

CHAPTER VI.

THE GROWTH OF RESPONSIBLE GOVERNMENT.

1. **The Act of Union—1840.**—The rebellion had failed because the Canadian people were loyal; nevertheless, it called the attention of the Home Government to the need of a change in the government of the Colony. The influence of Lord Durham's report now began to be felt, and it was decided by the British Government to unite the two Provinces of Upper and Lower Canada under one Parliament. To bring this about, Charles Poulett Thompson was sent out as the Governor of Canada. No great difficulty was met with in Lower Canada, because the Lower Canadian Parliament had been suspended on account of the rebellion, and the Special Council that was acting in its place was quite willing to aid in bringing about the desired union. But the French were not quite so willing, for they feared the loss of their influence as a race. Their petitions against the union were not heeded, and the Council passed a strong resolution in favor of uniting the Provinces.

In Upper Canada the Assembly was prepared to support the project, but the Family Compact which controlled the Legislative and Executive Councils did not like the idea of losing its power, and bitterly opposed the proposed measure. Mr. Thompson, with great tact and skill, made the Compact feel that the British Government was anxious for the change, and by appeals to their loyalty induced the members of the Legislative Council to pass a resolution in favor of Union. A Bill stating the terms of the Union was now drawn up, approved of by the Parliament of Upper Canada and the Council of Lower Canada, and sent to the Imperial Parliament to be made into a law. The Bill passed the British Parliament in 1840; but the Union did not take place till February, 1841.

By the terms of the Union, Upper and Lower Canada were to have but one Parliament, composed of a Legislative Council with not less than twenty members appointed by the Crown for life, and a Legislative Assembly of eighty-four members—forty-two from each Province. The Executive Council was to consist of eight members, who were to be *responsible* to Parliament; that is, the Governor was instructed by the Home Government to choose his advisers from the political party having a majority in the Assembly. The Assembly was given the control of all the revenue; but had to make a permanent provision for the payment of judges and for other necessary expenses of government. The judges now became independent, like the judges in England, and could not be dismissed without good cause. Thus most of the demands of the people were conceded, although some years had to pass before Canada got a full measure of responsible government.

2. **The Municipal Act of 1841.**—For his services in bringing about the Union Mr. Thompson was made a peer, with the title of Lord Sydenham. The first united Parliament met at Kingston in 1841, and it was found that the election, which followed the Union, had resulted in the two political parties being of nearly equal strength. Lord Sydenham tried to govern by means of an Executive Council composed of members of both parties; but the Reform element, finding it difficult to work harmoniously with their political opponents, resigned office, and the Government became a Conservative Government. Nevertheless, in spite of the difficulty experienced in working the new machinery, many important measures were passed the first session.

Of these the most important was the Municipal Act, which gave local self-government to the villages, towns, townships and counties of Upper Canada. The people of each municipality could now manage such matters as building roads, bridges, jails and court-houses, through men elected for that purpose, and who were called councillors in villages, towns and townships, and aldermen in cities. Other measures were the taking over of the Welland Canal as a government work, the placing of public works under the control of one of the members of the Executive Council or Ministry, and the encouragement of numerous enterprises for the development of the country. Unfortunately for Canada, Sydenham died from the effects of a fall from his horse, and one of the best and safest guides in political affairs Canada has ever had was removed, Sept. 19, 1841.

3. **Sir Charles Metcalfe.**—The British Government that appointed Sydenham was a Liberal Government, but it had lost

power, and a Conservative Government appointed his successor. This was Sir Charles Bagot. He was a Conservative, but he pursued the same policy as Sydenham, and during his short term of office, he tried to carry out the principle of Responsible Government. He formed a new ministry, the principal members of which were Mr. Baldwin, Mr. Lafontaine and Mr. Francis Hincks. This was the first Reform Ministry of Canada. Bagot died in 1843, and was succeeded by Sir Charles Metcalfe, whose political experience had been gained in India and Jamaica. He was an able and upright man, but utterly unfit by his previous training for governing a colony where the people wished to manage their own affairs. He soon got into trouble with his Ministry and the Assembly. He claimed the right to make appointments to government offices, such as registrarships and shrievalties; but his advisers objected on the ground that they were responsible for all such appointments, and therefore, should recommend the persons to be appointed. As the Governor would not yield, Messrs. Baldwin and Lafontaine and all the members of the Executive Council, except one, resigned. For some time Metcalfe tried to govern without a ministry, as the Conservatives were not strong enough in the Assembly to form a Government. At length he succeeded in getting Mr. Draper to take office and form a Ministry, and then dissolved the Assembly and had a new election. In this election Sir Charles Metcalfe took an active part, and managed to get a small majority in favor of his Ministers and his policy. Soon after this, he asked to be recalled, on account of ill-health, and Earl Cathcart acted as Governor until Lord Elgin arrived in 1847.

· 4. Ashburton Treaty.—While Canada was thus slowly working out a free system of government some important events of another character had taken place. In 1842, England and the United States settled the boundary line between Maine and New Brunswick and between Canada and the United States as far west as the Lake of the Woods. The map that showed the boundary decided upon in 1783 had been lost, and disputes had arisen about the line between the State of Maine and New Brunswick. After various fruitless efforts to get a satisfactory decision Lord Ashburton and Daniel Webster were appointed by the British and United States governments respectively to decide what was the right boundary line. The result of the negotiation was that Webster succeeded in getting for the United States the lion's share of the disputed territory. The treaty gave seven thousand square miles to the United States and five thousand to New Brunswick. It fixed the forty-fifth parallel of latitude as the dividing line as far as the St. Lawrence, and then traced the line up that river, and through the great Lakes as far west as the Lake of the Woods. From that point west the forty-ninth parrallel of latitude was to be the boundary to the Rocky Mountains. The treaty also had a clause providing for the sending back to their own country of escaped criminals accused of arson, forgery, piracy, robbery and murder. This is known as the first "Extradition Treaty."

5. **Educational Progress in Upper Canada.**—More important than the Ashburton Treaty was the great change made in our Public School system by Dr. Egerton Ryerson. In 1839 the Parliament of Upper Canada had set aside two hundred and fifty thousand acres of land for the endowment of *grammar* schools; but little provision had been made for the *common* or, as we now call them, the public schools. In 1841 Parliament granted two hundred thousand dollars a year for educational purposes; but three years later it repealed the Act. In 1844 Rev. Egerton Ryerson, a Methodist clergyman, who had taken an active part in journalism and politics, was appointed Chief Superintendent of Education for Upper Canada. He at once began to lay broad and deep the foundations of our Public School system. He crossed the Atlantic many times to examine the schools of Scotland, England, Prussia, and other European nations, and wisely selected from each system what was best adapted to a new country. His scheme was submitted to Parliament in 1846, and its main features adopted. Later on, in 1850, it was improved; and from that time to the present our Public School system has undergone many changes, all of which were intended to make it as perfect as possible. The system now provides for the free education of every child at the expense of the public; and gives each locality or district a large measure of control over its own schools, subject to the inspection and oversight of the Government.

In the meantime some progress had been made in higher education. In 1841 Victoria University, at Cobourg, got its charter, and the same year Queen's College, Kingston, was founded. Both these colleges were denominational—Victoria being connected with the Methodist body, and Queen's with the Church of Scotland. King's College, Toronto, had been founded as a Church of England institution, and put under the charge of Dr. Strachan. But the growing strength of other religious denominations soon compelled the adoption of a more liberal policy, and, in 1849, the University of Toronto (as it was now called) became a non-denominational institution and was opened to all classes of the people on the same terms. Dr Strachan was not satified with the change, and at once took steps to establish a college under the control of the Anglican Church. The result of his efforts was the founding of Trinity University, Toronto, in 1853.

6. **Lord Elgin's Administration.**—When Lord Elgin reached Canada he found a bitter party conflict going on. The Draper Administration was weak and tottering to its fall. Its opponents were led by Messrs. Baldwin and Lafontaine, and the country was disquieted by an agitation over the "Rebellion Losses Bill," and by a demand from the more extreme Reformers for a different policy with regard to the Clergy Reserves. In 1840 a partial settlement had been made of the latter question by giving one half of the proceeds of the Reserves to the Church of England and the Church of Scotland, and the remaining half to the other religious denominations. This did not satisfy a large portion of the people, who thought the land should be sold, and the money received used for educational and other purposes. The other cause of disquiet, the Rebellion Losses Bill, was a measure intended to make good to the loyalists of Upper Canada the losses they had sustained by the rebellion of 1837-38. The Draper Government proposed to take the money received from certain taxes and pay the losses with it; but the members from Lower Canada demanded that the losses in Lower Canada should also be paid. An attempt was made in 1847 to satisfy the people of Lower Canada by voting a sum of money to the loyalists; but the amount was so small that it had no effect in quieting the agitation. In 1849 the Draper Government was defeated at the polls, and the famous Baldwin-Lafontaine Administration came into office.

The Rebellion Losses Bill was once more brought into Parliament—this time by a Reform Government. It was a more sweeping measure than that of the previous administration, and proposed to pay a large sum to the injured loyalists of Lower Canada. At once a great outcry was raised that rebels were to be paid as well as loyalists, and the country was wild with excitement. Nevertheless the Bill passed both Houses, and was assented to by Lord Elgin, who felt it his duty to act on the advice of the Government, supported as it was by a large majority of the members of Parliament. This course did not please the opponents of the bill, a number of whom were foolish enough, in their excitement, to cause riots in Montreal and Toronto. In the former city Parliament was in session, when an infuriated mob broke in, drove out the members and ended by setting the Parliament buildings on fire. The mob prevented all attempts at saving the contents, and a very valuable library containing documents of great importance was burned. Lord Elgin was pelted with stones and rotten eggs when driving through the city, and some of the leaders of the agitation, in their excitement, went so far as to talk openly of annexation to the United States. Lord Elgin asked to be recalled ; but the Imperial Government commended his actions, and refused his request. As a consequence of this riot, Parliament met no more in Montreal, its sessions being held alternately every four years in Quebec and Toronto.

Soon after his arrival, 1847, Lord Elgin announced at the opening of Parliament that the duties in favour of British goods had been removed by the British Parliament, and that henceforth Canada would be free to place on goods coming into the country such duties as she wished. At the same time the Governor advised the building of a railroad from Halifax to Quebec. We shall find that it took many years to carry this proposal into effect. The same year saw a great immigration of people from Ireland, due to the terrible failure of the potato crop in that unhappy land. Thousands of ill-fed and ill-clad people were crowded into the vessels crossing the Atlantic, and, in consequence, fever and pestilence broke out in the ships. When they reached Canada this pestilence spread along the frontier and many people besides the poor immigrants died.

7. **Commercial Progress.**—Let us now see what the people of Canada had been doing since the Union in opening up the country and in acquiring wealth. We have already pointed out that for a

long time Canada had few means of taking her products to distant markets, and was dependent on the boats that navigated her lakes and rivers. This state of things now began to change rapidly. The need of better means of carrying goods and the products of farm and shop to market led to the building of railroads through the more thickly settled parts of the country. The first line built was one between La Prairie and St. John's in Lower Canada, which was opened for traffic in 1836. The first road begun in Upper Canada was the Northern Railway, the first sod of which was turned in 1851. Then came in rapid succession the Great Western and the Grand Trunk, the latter receiving from the Government important aid. These roads helped very much in opening up for settlement the north, west, and east of Canada, and made the farms of the settlers much more valuable. In 1852 the Municipal Loan Fund Act was passed, which gave the Government power to lend money to towns, villages, and other municipalities for local improvements, such as roads, bridges, and public buildings. The terms were very easy, and many municipalities got so heavily in debt that they were unable to pay back to the Government either principal or interest. There are many municipalities in Canada that yet feel the burden of a foolish extravagance at this time. Besides, there was in Canada, as elsewhere, a kind of railway craze, and a great deal of money was spent on roads that did not pay for their construction. Parliament was too free in making grants to railroads and other public works, and the result was that Canada began to have a heavy public debt, which has ever since been steadily growing. In 1851, another event of importance took place: the Canadian Government was given control of the Post-office, and immediately established a uniform rate of postage— threepence on every half-ounce—and, besides, introduced the use of postage stamps. Before this, when a letter was sent or received, postage had to be paid in money. In 1846 England adopted Free Trade as her policy, and a few years after threw open her markets to all countries on the same terms. For a time this injured Canadian farmers and producers, who had not as good means of carrying their products to English markets as the Americans. But with the building of railroads and the establishment of better lines of steamships the evil was lessened, and Canada prospered greatly, increasing rapidly in both wealth and population. This prosperity was partly due to a very important treaty made in 1854, through the tact and wisdom of Lord Elgin. In that year Canada and the United States agreed upon a Reciprocity Treaty, by which the products of the sea, the farm, the mine, and the forest could be freely exchanged. The United States obtained the right to fish in many of Canada's waters, and the use of the St. Lawrence and Canadian canals; while Canada, in return, was given the right to navigate Lake Michigan. The treaty was to continue ten years from March, 1855, and after that could be ended by twelve months' notice from either party.

8. The Clergy Reserves and Seignorial Tenure.—Meanwhile, political agitation was going on over two burning questions. One was the old grievance of the Clergy Reserves, which the Baldwin-Lafontaine Administration hoped had been settled in 1840. But a strong and growing body of the more radical Reformers, led by George Brown, the editor and manager of the *Globe*, a powerful political newspaper, wished to take the reserves away from the denominations and use them for the general good of the Province. The other question, that of Seignorial Tenure, was one of great interest to the people of Lower Canada. It was seen that holding land under the old French system of feudal tenure was a great hindrance to the prosperity of the farmers of that Province; the services and payments by the peasants to the "seigneurs" having become a grievous burden as the Province became better settled and the land more valuable. It was found impossible to dispose of one question without dealing with the other; so in 1854, the Reform Government of Mr. Hincks having been defeated by the temporary union of the extreme wing of the Reformers with the Conservatives, the new Conservative Ministry of Sir Allan McNab, brought in two bills; the one to divide the Clergy Reserves among the different municipalities of Upper Canada according to population, the proceeds to be used by them for local improvements or for educational purposes; the other, to abolish Seignorial Tenure, and to allow the land in Lower Canada to be held by the people as *freeholds*. In both cases compensation was made by Parliament for the losses the clergy and the seigneurs suffered by the change. In this way two grievances of long standing were happily removed, and the last link uniting Church and State in Upper Canada was broken. Two other political changes must be noted. In 1853, the population having increased greatly since the Union, the number of members of the Legislative Assembly was increased from eighty-four to one hundred and thirty, each Province still having an equal number of members. Three years later, the Legislative Council became an elective body, the existing members retaining their positions for life. The population of Upper Canada was now fully one million and a quarter, and that of Lower Canada about three hundred thousand less.

9. **A Political Dead-Lock.**—A curious state of affairs now arose in Canada. The old political parties became shattered, and new alliances were formed. In Upper Canada the more advanced Reformers gained great influence, and began agitating for a change in the basis of representation in Parliament. They claimed that as Upper Canada was more populous and wealthy than Lower Canada, and paid more taxes, it should send more members to Parliament. Against this it was urged that at the time of the Union Lower Canada had a larger population, greater wealth, and a smaller public debt than Upper Canada—yet, it was given the same number of representatives. It was, therefore, contended that Lower Canada should continue to have as many members of Parliament as Upper Canada. The agitation was continued for many years, and parties became nearly equally divided on the question of "Representation by Population," as it was called. On the one side was a majority of the members from Upper Canada, and a minority from Lower Canada; while opposed to the new policy was a minority from Upper Canada, and a majority from Lower Canada. John A. Macdonald and George Etienne Cartier were prominent leaders of the Conservative party; George Brown, William McDougall and A. A. Dorion the principal advocates of "Representation by Population" and the Reform policy. Several administrations were defeated in the years between 1858 and 1864, and finally it became evident some change in the constitution must take place if good government was to continue.

10. **Steps towards Confederation.**—In 1864 a dead-lock of political parties was reached, and the leaders of both sides recognizing the danger, dropped their feuds, and united to form a Coalition Government, which had for its object the Confederation of the Provinces of Upper and Lower Canada, and, if possible, also those of the Maritime Provinces. The principle of this Confederation

was suggested by the form of Government in the adjoining Republic; the object aimed at being to give the several Provinces the control of their own local affairs, matters of general interest to be managed by a common parliament in which all the provinces would be represented. Several things helped along the movement. In 1860 George Brown had proposed in Parliament the principle of such a scheme, but his resolution was lost by a large majority. The country was not then ready for its adoption. But when, in 1864, circumstances forced the policy on both parties, it was found that not only Canada but the Maritime Provinces were discussing Confederation. A Conference or gathering of delegates from these provinces was called to meet in September at Charlottetown, in Prince Edward Island, to arrange for a union, and the Canadian Government asked and received permission to send delegates. At this gathering the Confederation of all the Provinces was seriously discussed. It was decided to call another Conference at Quebec in November, and to invite all the provinces to be present through their delegates. The Conference met, and after much deliberation, the outlines of a scheme of Confederation were approved of by Upper Canada, Lower Canada, Nova Scotia, and New Brunswick. Prince Edward Island and Newfoundland had withdrawn from the Conference, the terms proposed not being agreeable to them. The delegates separated to report to their respective Parliaments, which soon after, in 1865, agreed to the scheme and made the necessary arrangements to get the consent of the British Parliament. In 1866, delegates from the different provinces met in London to draft a Bill for submission to the Imperial Parliament. This Bill was finally passed on the 28th February 1867, and under the name of the British North America Act, is the law which defines our present constitution. It came into force on the 1st of July, 1867. But its passage was not satisfactory to all the provinces. Nova Scotia was brought into Confederation against its will—its Government having accepted the terms without asking the consent of the people. Remonstrances and petitions were sent to the British Parliament: but they were of no avail. The British Government thought that the discontent would soon die away, and that the British pessessions in America would be safer and stronger under Confederation, against possible attacks from the United States, than existing as colonies independent of each other.

11. Minor Events of Importance.—Before giving the terms of this Confederation Act, we must notice some things of less importance, which had taken place while Canada was working out her future form of government. In 1854 our Volunteer system was introduced. Before this the Militia had very little drill, and when danger threatened the country, its defence for a time, depended upon the few regular troops stationed in Canada. Now the young men were encouraged to volunteer and form companies and regiments under their own officers, so that, should an invasion be attempted, there would always be thousands of active men, with some knowledge of drill, ready to resist. In 1858 Bytown or Ottawa, on the Ottawa river, became the fixed place for Parliament to meet. This site was chosen by the Queen, and its choice gave rise to much dissatisfaction on the part of the larger cities. More important to the welfare of the country was the introduction in 1858 of *decimal* currency, whereby we began to reckon in dollars and cents instead of in pounds, shillings and pence; and the completion of a long bridge across the St. Lawrence at Montreal, which was opened by the Prince of Wales in the summer of 1860, under the name of the Victoria Bridge.

In 1861, a civil war began in the United States between the Northern and Southern States, and lasted for four years. It affected Canada in many ways. For a time it made good prices for nearly all the Canadian farmer had to sell, raised the wages of mechanics, and gave good profits to the merchants. On the other hand, there was a serious danger of a war between England and the North, arising out of the sympathy and secret help the people of England gave the South. Many Canadians crossed the frontier to fight in the armies of the North, and many Southerners took refuge in Canada, some of whom made raids across the border into the villages and towns of the North. These raids created a bad feeling towards Canada, so that when the war was over and the Reciprocity Treaty expired in 1866, the United States Government refused to renew it. Canada also suffered from the ill-will of the American Gevernment in another way. On the 1st of June, a body of ruffians called Fenians, and belonging to a secret society having for its object the separation of Ireland from Great Britain, crossed the frontier at Black Rock, took possession of the ruins of old Fort Erie, and threatened the Niagara peninsula. A number of Volunteers from

Toronto and Hamilton were at once sent to join some regular troops, under Colonel Peacock, at Chippewa, but before they could accomplish this they met the raiders at Ridgeway, and, in a badly managed skirmish, were driven back with several killed and wounded. Soon after, Colonel Peacock with the regulars arrived, and the Fenians recrossed to the American side, leaving a few stragglers behind, some of whom were captured, tried, and condemned to death. Their sentences, through the clemency of the Crown, were changed to imprisonment in the Penitentiary. Attacks were also threatened at Prescott, St. Albans and other points on the border, but the watchfulness of the Canadian volunteers prevented any serious attempts being made to invade the country. After a long delay the American authorities put a stop to these raids, which, had the feeling of the United States towards Canada been more friendly, might never have taken place. In one way these attacks did good. They made the British Provinces feel the need of a closer union, and this, doubtless, hastened the formation of Confederation.

CHAPTER VII.

NOVA SCOTIA AND NEW BRUNSWICK.

1. Nova Scotia.—We have now to trace the history of a new and larger Canada. Henceforth it is the Dominion of Canada about which we must speak. We must, also, drop the old names Upper Canada and Lower Canada, and use instead for these provinces—the new names, Ontario and Quebec. For when Nova Scotia and New Brunswick joined in the Confederation, it was decided, to prevent confusion, to change the names of the provinces of Old Canada. In many respects the history of Nova Scotia and New Brunswick is very similar to that of Upper and Lower Canada. As in Lower Canada, the first settlers of Nova Scotia were French, the first settlement being made by De Monts, in 1605, at Port Royal (now Annapolis), a little earlier than that at Quebec by Champlain. The Cabots, it is said, first discovered the country, and on that ground

Nova Scotia was claimed as an English possession. The little colony of Port Royal did not prosper, and in 1614 an English expedition from Virginia took the fort, destroyed it, and then sailed away. At that time the province was called Acadia, and included the present provinces of Nova Scotia and New Brunswick, but in 1624 it was given by England to Sir William Alexander, and he named it Nova Scotia. Between 1624 and 1713 Port Royal changed ownership many times, belonging alternately to the English and the French until the treaty of Utrecht, when it passed finally into the possession of the English.

At this time its name was changed to Annapolis, in honor of the English Queen Anne. Not only Port Royal, but all Acadia was by this treaty given to the English. English settlers slowly found their way to the Province, and the city of Halifax was founded in 1749. But the French inhabitants and the Micmac Indians were not satisfied with the change of ownership, and plots against British rule were entered into between the French inside and the French outside the Province. All efforts to get the Acadians to take the oath of allegiance to the British king failed, and as the English settlements in the Province were in constant danger of attacks from the neighboring French and their Indian allies, it was decided to remove the Acadians from their homes and carry them to a French colony at the mouth of the Mississippi. This severe sentence was carried out in 1755. The sad story of the Expulsion of the Acadians is told in the beautiful and pathetic poem "Evangeline," by Longfellow. The constant fear of attacks from the French was removed when, in 1758, the strong fortress of Louisburg, in Cape Breton, was captured by Wolfe. The conquest of Canada and the Peace of Paris followed, and Nova Scotia, Cape Breton, and Prince Edward Island were surrendered to the British. Until 1784, Nova Scotia, New Brunswick, Prince Edward Island, and Cape Breton formed one Province. Then New Brunswick, Prince Edward Island, and Cape Breton became separate Provinces, but the last named was again joined to Nova Scotia in 1819. A Constitution was given to Nova Scotia in 1758, so that it had representative institutions many years before Lower Canada. It was to be governed by a joint Executive and Legislative Council, appointed by the Crown, and by an Assembly elected by the people. This form of Government did not succeed much better than the similar form in the two Canadas, and for the same reason.

The Revolutionary war of the United States caused some discontent and excitement in the province, and efforts were made to turn the people over to the side of the revolting colonies; but without success. After the war many U. E. Loyalists settled in Nova Scotia; and soon the new settlers began to agitate for a more just and liberal form of government. The agitation was carried on in much the same fashion as in Upper Canada, but it did not lead to rebellion. The same abuses existed as in Upper and Lower Canada, and after a severe political struggle, in which Joseph Howe played an important part, Responsible Government was granted in 1848. Nova Scotia had made considerable progress by this time; her fisheries, forests, mines, and fertile lands being sources of wealth. Her inhabitants were remarkably strong, vigorous and intelligent people, many of them being of U. E. Loyalist and Scotch descent. Her schools and colleges were generously supported by the Government, and education, before Confederation, had become practically free to all her people. Of her colleges, King's, Windsor, was founded in 1788, and Dalhousie, Halifax, in 1820.

Railways were gradually introduced, but not to the same extent as in Upper Canada; and an Intercolonial Railway between the different British Provinces of North America had often been suggested. This, in brief, was the state of affairs when Nova Scotia through her delegates at the Quebec Conference consented to become part of the Dominion of Canada. These delegates, however, did not represent the opinions of the people of Nova Scotia, and a bitter agitation against Confederation began under the old Reform leader, Joseph Howe. In vain the Province, through its Assembly, petitioned against the Union, and sent Howe to England to oppose the passage of the British North America Act. The British Government would not listen to the appeal, and Nova Scotia entered Confederation in much the same fashion as old Scotia entered the Union with England over one hundred and fifty years before. Let us hope that our Confederation may have the same happy results as the Union of 1707.

2. **New Brunswick.**—Until 1784 New Brunswick was a part of Nova Scotia, and its history to that time is therefore the history of

Nova Scotia. Its earliest settlements were at the mouth of the St. John River, and, like the settlements at Port Royal, were made by the French. After the American Revolutionary War, thousands of United Empire Loyalists settled in the province; many of them in the neighbourhood of the present city of St. John. These new settlers were dissatisfied because they were not given fair representation in the Legislative Assembly, and petitioned to have a new province formed independent of Nova Scotia. In 1784 the Home Government granted their petition, and the result was the formation of the present province of New Brunswick, with a government similar to that of Nova Scotia. Fredericton became its capital, although its chief town was St. John. The people of this province did not pay the same attention to farming as the settlers of the other provinces, because the very valuable timber and fisheries of the country made it more profitable to engage in lumbering and fishing than in tilling the soil. In 1809, Britain laid a tax on timber brought from the Baltic, and in this way encouraged the timber trade of New Brunswick.

Its ports became noted not only for their timber trade, but also for ship-building. After the war of 1812-14, many disbanded soldiers settled in the province, and, as in Upper Canada, received liberal grants of land. But a serious disaster in 1825, checked the prosperity of the province. The summer of this year was very hot and dry, and bush fires raged fiercely. On the 7th of October, a terrible wave of fire swept over the country, from Miramichi to the Bay of Chaleurs. Five thousand square miles of forest and farm, village and town, were made desolate, and hundreds of lives were lost. The political atmosphere, too, was troubled for many years. The struggle for Responsible Government took place in this province as elsewhere in British America, and New Brunswick had its Family Compact as well as Upper Canada. But, unlike Upper Canada, its rights were won without rebellion and bloodshed. In 1837, the control of the revenue was given to the Assembly, and in 1848, responsible government was fully conceded. In these struggles for freedom to manage its own affairs, Lemuel Allan Wilmot took a prominent part as a champion of the people. The dispute about the boundary line between Maine and New Brunswick kept the province in a state of alarm and uncertainty for years; and at one time it was feared that the quarrels along the border for possession of the disputed territory would lead to war. The Ashburton Treaty, in 1842, resulted, as we have seen, in taking away from New Brunswick a large territory which rightfully belonged to it. In the twenty years before Confederation, by means of railways and steamboats, great progress was made in opening up the country; in extending the trade of the province, although the timber trade was threatened with injury by the removal of the duties from timber exported from the Baltic to England; and in improving the educational system of the province. Good public schools were established; and among other colleges, the University of Fredericton and Mt. Allison College at Sackville, were founded. The former is a state college, the latter is connected with the Methodist denomination.

The story of the Union with the other provinces has already been told. As in Nova Scotia there was strong opposition to Confederation, and in the first election held after the Quebec Conference, the Confederation party was badly beaten at the polls. For a time it seemed as if New Brunswick would refuse to proceed any further with the scheme, but the Home Government was anxious for Confederation, as also were the Governor and the Legislative Council. These influences, aided by the alarm caused by the Fenian invasion, helped to bring about a change in the popular feeling, and another election being held the Confederation party was successful. Union resolutions were now passed, and delegates sent to London to aid in framing the British North America Act.

CHAPTER VIII.

CANADA SINCE CONFEDERATION.

1. The British North America Act.—We must now give the terms on which the four Provinces, Ontario, Quebec, Nova Scotia, and New Brunswick, agreed to share a common lot. The principle of their union was that each Province should manage its own local affairs, and leave to the Dominion the control of matters which were of common benefit and interest. To carry out this principle it was necessary to have local Legislatures or Parliaments, as well as a general or Dominion Parliament. This part of the scheme was suggested by, if not borrowed from, the system of government existing in the United States. But in several very important respects the United States model was not copied. Perhaps the most important difference was the retention of Cabinet or Responsible Government in the management of all our affairs, whether belonging to the Dominion or to the Provinces. Again, in the United States each State is free to make its own laws, so long as it does not go beyond the bounds of the Constitution; but in Canada it was agreed that the Governor-General, on the advice of his Ministers, should have the power to *veto*, or forbid from becoming law, any measure passed by the local Parliaments, if these measures were thought to be hurtful to the general welfare of the Dominion. The Provinces were given the control of many matters such as education; the appointment of courts of justice (but not of the judges); the management of Crown lands within the Province; asylums and jails; the regulation of the sale of intoxicating liquors; and the general power of enforcing the laws. They were permitted to raise a revenue by *direct* but not by *indirect* taxation; that is, they could impose such taxes as were paid only by the people on whom they were placed, but not such taxes as duties on goods coming in or going out of the country, which are called *Customs*, or taxes on articles made in the country, which we call *Excise*. *Custom* and *Excise* duties are supposed to be paid eventually by the people who buy the goods and use them, and not by the seller or manufacturer. One of the important benefits expected to come from Confederation was the removal of the barriers preventing the different Provinces from trading with each other. To make it impossible for one Province to tax the goods coming into it from another Province, the Dominion Parliament was given the sole right of raising a revenue by Customs or Excise duties. This, however, would make it very difficult for the Provinces to collect money enough to defray their expenses; therefore it was arranged that the Dominion should pay the Provinces annually a large sum out of its revenue, in return for the right to collect these duties. Besides this right of *indirect* taxation the Dominion kept the control of the Militia, the Post-office, the currency, the penitentiaries, the appointment of judges, the construction and management of the more important public works, and the control of all Crown lands not belonging to any of the Provinces. To carry out this scheme it was necessary to have a good deal of political machinery; so each Province was given a Lieutenant-Governor, appointed by the Governor-General of the Dominion for a term of years, a Legislature elected by the people for four years, and, if the Province wished it, a Legislative Council or Senate. Of the four Provinces Ontario was the only one that felt content to do without a Legislative Council. In each Province there was to be an Executive Council, or Ministry, responsible to the people through their representatives in the Legislature. The Dominion Parliament was to have, as its head, a Governor-General, appointed by the Crown; a Senate, composed of members from the different Provinces, and appointed by the Governor-General for life, and a House of Commons elected by the people. Each Province was given a certain number of senators, Ontario being given twenty-four, Quebec twenty-four, Nova Scotia and New Brunswick twenty-four; in all, seventy-two. The number of members of the House of Commons, at the outset was to be one hundred and eighty-one, of which Quebec sent sixty-five, Ontario eighty-two, Nova Scotia nineteen, and New Brunswick fifteen. A census was to be taken every ten years, and the number of members given to each Province was to be regulated by the population; Quebec to send sixty-five, and the other Provinces in proportion to their population. In this way the problem of "Representation by Population" was solved. The real government of the Dominion was to be in the hands of an Executive Council, chosen by the Governor-General from the political party having a majority in the House of Commons, and was to consist, at first, of thirteen members. The Governor-General could reserve any law passed by the Dominion Parliament for the sanction of the Home Government; and, on the advice of his Council, could, within a year from the time of its passing, *veto* any bill passed by a local Parliament. This power of *veto* was given because it was feared that the Provinces might pass laws injurious to the Dominion as a whole, or hurtful to the rights of some of the people in them. Having settled the terms of the political partnership, it was thought that there would be a closer union if a railroad were built between the Maritime Provinces and Quebec. It was, therefore, agreed that the long-talked-of Intercolonial Railway should be constructed from Halifax to Quebec, the British Government to give its aid in carrying out the costly scheme.

2. New Provinces.—The principal events of our history since confederation must now be told very briefly, for this part of our history is so recent, that we cannot say, yet, which of its events are the most important, or whether some things that have taken place since confederation are for the good of Canada, or not.

The first Governor-General of the Dominion was Lord Monck, and his Prime Minister was Sir John A. Macdonald, who had taken a leading part along with the Hon. George Brown in carrying through the Confederation scheme. His principal colleagues were Sir George E. Cartier from Quebec, the Hon. Charles Tupper from Nova Scotia, and the Hon. S. L. Tilley from New Brunswick. The first Prime Minister of Ontario was the Hon John Sandfield Macdonald, the Lieutenant-Governor being the Hon. William P. Howland. The majority of the people of the Dominion were content to give the new constitution a fair trial, except the people of Nova Scotia. In the first parliament elected after the union, the members from that province were nearly all opposed to confederation, and had to be quieted by the grant of "better terms."

In 1868, steps were taken to get possession of the vast territory held by the Hudson Bay Company in the North-West. This territory, known as "Prince Rupert's Land," had been given to the Hudson Bay Company in 1670 by King Charles II. of England, and had been used by it, for two hundred years, to carry on a profitable trade in furs. The value of this territory was but little known, and the Company fearful of losing its charter always strove to make the English people believe that it was fit for nothing except grazing buffaloes, and providing trapping grounds for Indians. A very few settlers had made their way into this unknown and lone land—the only settlement of importance being at Red River, where Lord Selkirk had founded a colony in 1811. The whole population numbered but ten thousand souls, and was gathered mainly at the different trading posts.

The charter of the Company was expiring, and the Canadian Government induced the British Parliament to pass an Act by which the North-West or Hudson Bay Territory could be surrendered to

Canada, on payment of the just claims of the Company. Canada offered to give the Company three hundred thousand pounds sterling, one twentieth of the land, and the right to retain their trading privileges. The offer was accepted. Unfortunately, little thought was given to the small settlement of French and half-breeds on the Red River when taking possession of the country and making provision for its future government. Surveyors were set to work near Fort Garry at the junction of the Red and Assiniboine rivers, and the inhabitants became alarmed lest their lots and homes should be taken from them. The necessary steps were not taken to quiet their fears, and when Hon. Wm. McDougall endeavoured to enter the new Province of Manitoba, as its Governor, he found his way barred by an armed force. The chief leaders of the revolt were Louis Riel, a Frenchman, with some Indian blood in his veins, and M. Lepine. A Provisional Government was formed by these men, and they made prisoners of all who were supposed to be in sympathy with the Canadian Government. Among others thus seized was Thomas Scott, a brave, outspoken, loyal subject. For some reason or other Riel had taken a strong personal dislike to Scott, and, after giving him the form of a trial, had him sentenced to be shot. The sentence was carried out under circumstances of great brutality, in March, 1870. When the news reached Ontario there was great excitement, and when, a few months after, volunteers were called for, to go with General Wolseley to crush the rebellion, thousands of young men offered their services. Only the best fitted to endure hardship were chosen, and when, after a long and trying march over what was known as the Dawson Road, they reached Fort Garry, they found the rebels scattered and everything quiet.

Many of these volunteers received grants of land in the new province and became permanent settlers. Soon there began to rise at Fort Garry a prairie city which, to-day, is the fine flourishing capital of the Province of Manitoba—the city of Winnipeg. In 1870 the "Manitoba Act" was passed. It defined the limits of the Province of Manitoba, and stated how it was to be governed. Its form of government is very much the same as that of Ontario; and, like Ontario, it decided to do without a "Second Chamber" or Legislative Council. It was given the right to send four members to the House of Commons, and was allotted two senators. The next year saw the admission of another province to the Confederation. This was British Columbia on the Pacific Coast, which, separated from the rest of the Dominion by the Rocky Mountains, made it a condition of becoming a part of the Dominion that a railway should be constructed across the prairies and through the Rocky Mountains, so as to connect British Columbia with the Eastern provinces. Although the population of this new province was very small, it was given six members in the House of Commons and three in the Senate.

Two years after, still another province was added to the growing Dominion. Prince Edward Island, which in 1866 refused to become a part of the Confederation, was now willing to cast in its lot with the other provinces. This little island, with its hardy and intelligent population, formerly belonged to Nova Scotia; but in 1784 it received a separate government. Its history before 1873 was much the same as that of Nova Scotia and New Brunswick, except that it had trouble in connection with the way its land had been parcelled out to a number of men called "proprietors," who did not live on the island, and yet refused to give up their claims to those who were the actual tillers of the soil. The Legislative Council of Prince Edward Island was elective; in this respect it differed from the other provinces. On entering Confederation it was given six members in the House of Commons and four in the Senate. No new territory has since been added to the Dominion; but the North-West has been divided into districts, and given a form of government, consisting of a Lieutenant-Governor and Council, in which the people have a slight control over their own local affairs. They have also been given representation in the House of Commons—four members at present being returned from the four districts, Assiniboia, Alberta, Saskatchewan and Athabasca.

3. **Political Changes.**—The party struggles that embittered the politics of Canada before Confederation were dropped for a short time after the Union of the provinces, only to be renewed with almost equal intensity at the general election of 1872. The Government of Sir John A. Macdonald had aroused strong opposition by its share in the Washington Treaty, and its mode of dealing with the proposed Pacific railway. Several points were in dispute between England and the United States, and between the United

States and Canada. During the Civil War between the North and South the English authorities had carelessly allowed some vessels, fitted out in British ports, to escape to sea, where they were used by the South to attack and plunder the merchant vessels of the North. The most notorious of these vessels was the "Alabama," which did a great deal of harm to the shipping of the North. After the war was over, the United States claimed damages for injuries caused by this vessel, and the matter was left for peaceable settlement to a "Joint High Commission" of which Sir John A. Macdonald was a member. Canada was greatly interested in this Commission, for she had claims against the United States for injuries inflicted by the Fenians. Besides, the ownership of San Juan, an island on the Pacific coast, and the boundary line between Canada and Alaska were in dispute. The Americans, too, were anxious, now that the Reciprocity Treaty was no longer in force, to get fishing privileges in Canadian waters. The Commission met, in 1871, at Washington, and agreed to submit the Alabama Claims to arbitration, the result being that the United States received $15,500,000 for the supposed injuries inflicted by the Alabama on her commerce. The claims of Canada for damages on account of the Fenian raids were not even considered; but England, as a slight compensation, agreed to guarantee for Canada a loan of £2,500,000.

The dispute about the island of San Juan was left to the Emperor of Germany for his decision, which was given the next year in favor of the United States. The Treaty also gave the United States the use of Canadian fisheries for twelve years, in return for the use of their fisheries, and the right to sell fish and fish-oil in United States markets. As this was not considered enough for the use of the valuable Canadian fisheries, a commission was to meet at Halifax later on and decide what sum of money should be paid the Dominion by the United States as an equivalent. This Halifax Commission met in 1878, during the Mackenzie Administration, and awarded $5,500,000 to Canada; the success of this negotiation being due largely to the fact that it was conducted on behalf of Canada by Canadians; Sir Alexander Galt being the principal Canadian representative.

The other cause of political feeling, the building of the Pacific Railway, arose out of the agreement with British Columbia, when that province entered Confederation, that an all-rail route should be built in ten years from Ontario to the Pacific. Many thought such a bargain could not be carried out, that the time was too short, and the cost too great. The elections of 1872 were fought mainly on this issue, and resulted in a majority for the government. The next year Mr. Huntington, the member of Parliament for Shefford, made a formal charge in Parliament that the government had agreed to give a charter to Sir Hugh Allan to build the Pacific Railway, in return for large sums of money to carry the elections. The charge, and the publication of certain letters bearing upon this alleged corrupt bargain, caused great excitement in the Dominion, and after a fierce struggle in Parliament, the government resigned.

The Governor-General, Lord Dufferin, called on the Hon. Alexander Mackenzie, the leader of the Liberal Party, to form a government. Mr. Mackenzie accepted the trust, and after forming a ministry, of which the principal members were the Hon. Edward Blake from Ontario and the Hon. A. A. Dorion from Quebec, asked for a new election. This took place in January, 1874, and resulted in giving a very large majority to the new government. Mr. Mackenzie continued in office till 1878, when his government was defeated on the question of a trade policy for the country. There was a general commercial depression at this time and Canada, with other countries, felt the pinch of hard times. A great many thought that the industries of the country would be benefited if the tariff was raised and foreign goods competing with Canadian products kept out. This policy of "protection" was opposed by the Mackenzie Government, but, when the elections took place in September, 1878, it was found that the doctrines of the "National Policy" were very popular, and, in consequence, Sir John A. Macdonald, who had advocated them, was once more called to be Prime Minister of Canada. That position he held till his death, which took place June 6th, 1891. He was succeeded in the Premiership by Hon. J. J. C. Abbott, who at the time of writing holds the office.

4. **Important Laws.**—Amid all this strife many measures became law, some, at least, of which will likely remain for years on the Statute-book. In 1874, during the Mackenzie Administration, a Ballot Act was passed, which provided for secret voting by ballot, instead of "open voting." This reform was introduced to prevent

bribery and intimidation, which was very common under the old system of "open voting." It is very doubtful whether the Act has had all the effect on bribery it was expected to have. Another and a later law bearing on elections was the Dominion Franchise Act, which made the right to vote for members of the Dominion Parliament the same throughout the Dominion. Previous to this act the franchises for the Dominion elections were the same as the franchise in the several Provinces. This Act was passed in 1885, and besides making the franchise uniform, it greatly increased the number of voters, so much so, that now nearly every man twenty-one years of age, and over, has a vote. Before this was passed another measure which created a great deal of ill-feeling, became law. This was the Redistribution Bill of 1882, which seriously changed the boundaries of nearly every constituency in Ontario, for the purpose, it was said by the Government, of equalizing the number of electors in the different constituencies. The Liberals complained that the change was made so as to give their Conservative opponents an unfair advantage in the coming elections.

Among other political measures since Confederation we must notice the increase in the number of representatives in Parliament—there being now ninety-two from Ontario, sixty-five from Quebec, sixteen from New Brunswick, twenty-one from Nova Scotia, six from Prince Edward Island, five from Manitoba, six from British Columbia, and four from the North-West Territories. A Supreme Court of Appeal was established in 1875, to avoid the expense of taking appeals from Canada to the British Privy Council; although appeals are yet allowed to the Privy Council, and are frequently taken there. Then again, in 1879, a new tariff was framed, which greatly increased the duties on foreign goods; and although every session changes are made, yet they are generally arranged for the purpose of "protecting native industries."

5. **Provincial Legislation.**—Though many important laws have been passed by the Dominion Parliament, equally important measures have been enacted by the Provincial Legislatures. These laws deal with a great many subjects, such as education; the regulation of the liquor traffic; aid to railways; the establishment of asylums for the deaf, dumb, blind, and insane; the better management of prisons; the sale of timber limits; mining regulations;

and improvements in our municipal laws. In Ontario, under the long administration of Hon. Oliver Mowat which began in 1872, two very important laws have been passed—one dealing satisfactorily with the indebtedness of municipalities to the Municipal Loan Fund, and the other, with the regulation of the liquor traffic. The latter, popularly known as the Crooks' Act (so called from the Hon. Adam Crooks, its framer), has done a great deal to lessen drunkenness, vice, and crime. Then again, the franchise has been greatly extended in the different provinces, and voting by ballot, except for school trustees, has been made compulsory. Unmarried women and widows in Ontario, with the necessary property qualifications, have been given the right to vote in municipal elections, but not in elections for members of either the Provincial or Dominion Parliament. In Prince Edward Island the difficulty with the "proprietors" has been settled in the interests of the people. Quebec has, by the payment of four hundred thousand dollars, disposed of the "Jesuit Estates" question, while Manitoba has secured the right to build railways within her borders. Ontario has had several legal conflicts with the Dominion as to her proper boundaries, her right to regulate the liquor traffic, and her right to control the Crown lands in her territory, all of which questions have been decided by the British Privy Council in favor of the Province. The exercise of the right to *veto* provincial laws has caused some friction between the Provinces and the Dominion ; but the wise decisions of the British Privy Council have led to a strong feeling in the Dominion against interfering with provincial legislation. To avoid any undue influence being exercised by the Dominion over the Provinces, members of the Dominion Parliament are not allowed to be members of Provincial Legislatures.

6. **The North-West Rebellion.**—One painful incident in our history must now be told. In 1885 a number of French Half-breeds, who had settled on the Saskatchewan River, in the North-West, rose in revolt against the Dominion, and induced several Indian tribes to join them. The cause of this rebellion was the fear these people had that their lands were to be taken from them and given to the incoming settlers. Surveyors had been sent among them, and this excited fears, which were not regarded until it was too late to prevent mischief. There were also complaints of ill-

treatment and neglect of duty by Dominion officers in the North-West, and the petitions of the half-breeds and Indians did not receive prompt attention from the proper authorities. The result was that the excited half-breeds sent for Louis Riel, who was living in the United States, to advise and lead them. One false step led to another, until the discontent broke out in an attack, led by Gabriel Dumont, on some armed Police and volunteers at Duck Lake, in March, 1885. Several of the volunteers were killed, and open rebellion spread over a wide district, a number of Indian chiefs with their followers joining in the revolt. A large force of volunteers, under General Middleton, was sent in the depth of winter from Quebec and Ontario to crush the rebellion. Aided by the Mounted Police, and the volunteers of Manitoba and the North-West, the rising was speedily brought to an end, the last important and decisive engagement taking place at Batoche, where Riel was captured. Many lives were lost in the campaign, and great hardships were endured by the volunteers, half-breeds, and settlers, before this needless outbreak was suppressed. Riel and several Indians were tried for treason and murder; some, among whom was Riel, were executed, the remainder being either imprisoned or pardoned. The execution of Riel caused great excitement in Quebec, where considerable sympathy was felt for the people he so sadly led astray. The rebellion had its uses—for an inquiry was made into the grievances of the Indians and half-breeds, and many of the causes of complaint removed.

7. **Material Progress.**—Since Confederation there has been a marked change in the material condition of the country. Railways now reach nearly every part of the older Provinces, whilst the territories in the North-West and British Columbia have been connected with the great world of trade by the Canadian Pacific Railway. This great enterprise was completed in 1886, the first sod being turned in May, 1881. A portion of the road had been partly built by the Mackenzie Government; but after that Government was defeated the contract was given to a strong company of capitalists, the chief members of which are Canadians, the company agreeing to build the road for a subsidy of $25,000,000, and 25,000,000 acres of land in the fertile districts of the North-West. The company has shown great energy and ability, so that the Cana-

dian Pacific Railway, with its numerous branches, its large traffic and its connecting steamships on the lakes and on the Pacific, is now one of the most important lines in the world. Then again, the Grand Trunk has gradually obtained the control of many lines formerly independent, the most important being the Great Western and its connections. These two companies—the Canadian Pacific and the Grand Trunk—now control nearly all the roads in Canada, except the Intercolonial, which was built by the Government, at a great cost, to connect the Western provinces with those down by the sea.

Canals, too, have been deepened, widened, and straightened; the new Welland Canal, constructed by the Mackenzie Government, being a very important public work. Great harbour works have been undertaken and built, and lake and ocean vessels have been wonderfully improved, although Canada has as yet no line of fast steamships crossing the Atlantic. In all our cities and larger towns Street Railways are to be found; while electric lighting, and machinery worked by electricity are among recent industrial changes.

Turning to the farms of Canada, we find that the most fertile portions of Ontario and Quebec have been cleared and tilled, and that thousands of the farmers of the older Provinces are finding their way to the rich prairies of Manitoba and the North-West, where the forests are few and the soil easily brought into cultivation. Large towns and villages now dot the face of Ontario, while the two cities of Montreal and Toronto are rapidly increasing their population, wealth, and trade. The population of Canada has increased until it is now estimated at five millions, and of this Ontario is thought to have two millions. This is a part of the bright side of our material condition. Against it we have to place the tendency of so many of our young men to leave Canada for a home in the United States; the increasing difficulty our farmers experience to make farming pay; and the want of a large foreign market for our manufactures.

8. **Literary and Social Progress.**—Perhaps it is because the energies of the Canadian people have been directed so largely towards overcoming the difficulties met with in settling a new country, that we have so few great writers of prose or verse. Our

Public and High Schools are efficient, and our Universities with their too small endowments, are doing a good work ; yet, of native Canadian authors, there are none who rank with the great writers of the Mother Country. Nevertheless, there are many good writers of verse, some clever journalists and essayists, and not a few historians who have done good and faithful work. Every year the number of those who seek literary and scientific fame is increasing, and with greater wealth and leisure, the growth of higher and nobler ideals, and the development of a stronger national sentiment, Canada may hope yet to have among her sons and daughters, worthy rivals of Shakespeare, Milton, Macaulay, Scott and George Eliot. The love and practice of art in its various forms is also becoming more and more apparent ; Canadian artists already having won fame and distinction in song and painting. With the increase of education, wealth, leisure, and foreign travel, there has been a marked change in the customs and health of the people. Social refinement and luxury have in recent years greatly increased, and a type of character is being gradually developed which is distinctly national. With her magnificent resources of soil, forest and mine ; her strong, hardy, intelligent, and vigorous people ; her relatively pure, simple, and healthy domestic life ; her free systems of education ; and her excellent form of government, Canada certainly possesses the promise and potency of a great nation.

www.ingramcontent.com/pod-product-compliance
Lightning Source LLC
Chambersburg PA
CBHW031958230426
43672CB00010B/2200